EurographicSeminars

Tutorials and Perspectives in Computer Graphics

Edited by W. T. Hewitt, R. Gnatz, and D. A. Duce

EurographicSeminars

Tutorials and Perspectives in Computer Graphics

Eurographics Tutorials '83. Edited by P. J. W. ten Hagen.
XI, 425 pages, 164 figs., 1984

User Interface Management Systems. Edited by. G. E. Pfaff.
XII, 224 pages, 65 figs., 1985

Methodology of Window Management. Edited by F. R. A. Hopgood,
D. A. Duce, E. V. C. Fielding, K. Robinson, A. S. Williams.
XV, 250 pages, 41 figs., 1985

Data Structures for Raster Graphics. Edited by L. R. A. Kessener,
F. J. Peters, M. L. P. van Lierop. VII, 201 pages, 80 figs., 1986

Advances in Computer Graphics I. Edited by G. Enderle, M. Grave,
F. Lillehagen. XII, 512 pages, 168 figs., 1986

Advances in Computer Graphics II. Edited by F. R. A. Hopgood,
R. J. Hubbold, D. A. Duce. X, 186 pages, 96 figs., 1986

Advances in Computer Graphics Hardware I. Edited by W. Straßer.
X, 147 pages, 76 figs., 1987

GKS Theory and Practice. Edited by P. R. Bono, I. Herman.
X, 316 pages, 92 figs., 1987

Intelligent CAD Systems I. Edited by P. J. W. ten Hagen,
T. Tomiyama. XIV, 360 pages, 119 figs., 1987

Advances in Computer Graphics III. Edited by M. M. de Ruiter.
IX, 323 pages, 247 figs., 1988

Advances in Computer Graphics Hardware II. Edited by
A. A. M. Kuijk, W. Straßer. VIII, 258 pages, 99 figs., 1988

CGM in the Real World. Edited by A. M. Mumford, M. W. Skall.
VIII, 288 pages, 23 figs., 1988

Intelligent CAD Systems II. Edited by V. Akman, P. J. W. ten Hagen,
P. J. Veerkamp. X, 324 pages, 114 figs., 1989

Advances in Computer Graphics IV. Edited by M. Grave, M. Roch.
In preparation.

Advances in Computer Graphics V. Edited by W. Purgathofer,
J. Schönhut. VIII, 223 pages, 101 figs., 1989

W. Purgathofer   J. Schönhut (Eds.)

Advances in
Computer Graphics V

With 101 Figures, 12 in Color

Springer-Verlag Berlin Heidelberg GmbH

EurographicSeminars

Edited by W. T. Hewitt, R. Gnatz, and D. A. Duce
for EUROGRAPHICS –
The European Association for Computer Graphics
P.O. Box 16, CH-1288 Aire-la-Ville, Switzerland

Volume Editors

Werner Purgathofer
Technical University Vienna, Karlsplatz 13/180
A-1040 Vienna, Austria

Jürgen Schönhut
Fraunhofer Computer Graphics Research Group (FhG-AGD)
Wilhelminenstraße 7, D-6100 Darmstadt, FRG

ISBN 978-3-642-64798-7   ISBN 978-3-642-61340-1 (eBook)
DOI 10.1007/978-3-642-61340-1

© Springer-Verlag Berlin Heidelberg 1989
Originally published by EUROGRAPHICS The European Association for Computer Graphics,
P.O. Box 16, CH-1288 Aire-la-Ville, Switzerland in 1989.

Softcover reprint of the hardcover 1st edition 1989

2145/3140-543210 – Printed on acid-free paper

Preface

This book collects together several of the tutorials held at EUROGRAPHICS'89 in Hamburg. The conference was held under the motto "Integration, Visualisation, Interaction" and the tutorials reflect the conference theme. The Springer series EurographicSeminars with the volumes "Advances in Computer Graphics" regularly provides a professional update on current mainstream topics in the field. These publications give readers the opportunity to inform themselves thoroughly on the topics covered. The success of the series is mainly based on the expertise of the contributing authors, who are recognized professionals in their field.

Starting out with one of the conference's main topics, the chapter "Visualization of Scientific Data" gives an overview of methods for displaying scientific results in an easily surveyable and comprehensible form. It presents algorithms and methods utilized to achieve visualization results in a form adequate for humans. User interfaces for such systems are also explored, and practical conclusions are drawn.

The chapter "Color in Computer Graphics" describes the problems of manipulating and matching color in the real world. After some fundamental statements about color models and their relationships, the main emphasis is placed on the problem of objective color specification for computer graphics systems. It is very hard to match colors between devices such as scanners, printers and displays. Some suggestions on the effective use of color for graphics are also made.

Solid modeling is more and more becoming the relevant data description structure. Still many research problems exist, and "Advanced Topics in Solid Modeling" explores some research directions currently under consideration. In particular, advanced techniques for CSG visualization and for manipulating boundary models are covered. An outlook on the next generation of solid modelers completes this part.

Many computer graphics tasks have their roots in geometrical problems. "Computational Geometry and its Application to Computer Graphics" relates the two aspects from a practical point of view. Hidden surface removal, windowing, and intersection problems are typical examples. Also such areas as triangulation, convex hull computation, and proximity calculations are handled. A reference to additional research on the topics of grids, combinatorial geometry, partition trees, and random sampling completes the discussion.

Chapter five contains another field with a close relationship to computer graphics. "Object-Oriented Graphics" explains how object-oriented concepts can be utilized in the world of visualization. After an introduction to the underlying concepts of object-orientation with an emphasis on computer graphics, a comparison with classical concepts demonstrates the usefulness and advantages of the object-oriented paradigm. The design of a simple animation system is used as an example.

Integrated documents meet an ever increasing demand for high quality output. "Page Description Languages (PDLs)" provide today's means to achieve these quality requirements. The underlying concepts of PDLs are illustrated with the example of PostScript, and to some extent also Interpress. Applications of PDLs and related problems are discussed. Special attention is paid to performance issues and missing functionality problems. Standardization and conformance form the necessary framework for an outlook on the future of page description languages.

The main aim of "Standards for Computer Graphics and Product Model Data Exchange" is to give an overview of such standards. This should lead to an ability not only to see the value of standardization in the computing environment but also to compare and discuss standards in this field. GKS, CGM, CGI, PHIGS, IGES, VDAFS, SET, and STEP have been discussed very heavily in the last decade and form the core of this area.

This book will be a source of state-of-the-art knowledge in the areas covered for systems designers and application programmers, as well as for researchers.

Vienna, May 1, 1989   Werner Purgathofer, Jürgen Schönhut

Table of Contents

1. Visualization of Scientific Data
Mikael Jern   1

1. Introduction   1
2. Graphics Software Solution   2
3. Practical Implementations of the Visualization Concept   5
4. The Importance of the User Interface 12
5. Computer Graphics Metafile 14
6. Network Access to High Resolution Hardcopy Pictures 15
7. Conclusion 16

2. Color in Computer Graphics: Manipulating and Matching Color
Gerald M. Murch, Joann M. Taylor 19

1. Introduction 19
2. Color Models and the User Interface to Color 19
3. Color Fidelity 37

3. Advanced Topics in Solid Modeling
Martti Mäntylä 49

1. Introduction 49
2. Deficiencies of Solid Modelers 50
3. Advanced Techniques for CSG Visualization 54
4. Advanced Techniques for Boundary Models 62
5. Beyond Solid Models: Features 67
6. Next Generation of Solid Modelers 70

4. Computational Geometry and its Application to Computer Graphics
Mark H. Overmars 75

1. Introduction 75
2. Shape of Objects 76
3. Proximity 81
4. Windowing 85
5. Intersection Problems 93
6. Hidden Surface Removal 97
7. Other Research 100

5. Object-Oriented Graphics
Edwin H. Blake, Peter Wisskirchen 109

1. Introduction to Object-Oriented Concepts 109
2. Object-Oriented and Classical Graphics Systems 119
3. New Concepts in Object-Oriented Programming for Graphics 130
4. A Simple Animation System 142
5. For Further Study - An Annotated Bibliography 147

6. Page Description Languages (PDLs)
Jürgen Schönhut 155

1. Introduction 155
2. Basic Concepts of Page Description Languages 157
3. Applications and Performance Problems 173
4. Standardization of PDLs 175
5. Conformity Testing 175
6. Internal Structures of a PostScript Interpreter 176
7. Conclusions 177

7. Standards for Computer Graphics and Product Model Data Exchange
Michael Mittelstaedt, Anne M. Mumford 181

1. Introduction 181
2. Computer Graphics Standards 182
3. Product Data Exchange Standards 200
4. Abbreviations 217

Addresses of Authors 223

Chapter 1
Visualization of Scientific Data

Mikael Jern

1.   Introduction

"Data visualization" has recently become one of the hottest buzzwords in the computer industry, especially when preceeded by the word 'scientific'. A great deal of interest has been generated in this relatively new field, and most computer vendors have jumped on the bandwagon.

Much of the interest in visualization can be traced back to an influential report written by the National Science Foundation (NSF) in 1987. The report, presented in connection with the ACM SIGGRAPH, defined a new market "Visualization in Scientific Computing" (ViSC), which involved the application of graphics and imaging techniques to computational science.

Scientific Data Visualization uses sophisticated computer graphics techniques to produce pictures of complex physical phenomena. Such pictures enable scientists to simulate the problems they are investigating and allow them to gain insight into the nature of the solutions. Indeed, visualization is often the only means by which scientists can contend with the huge quantities of multi-variables, two and three dimensional data generated by laboratories or gathered by measurement devices in the field. The quantities of data are so vast that understanding them without visualization is almost impossible.

With the advent of the supercomputer, the potential value that visualization holds for science has already begun to emerge. However, despite the fact that supercomputers can crunch algorithms beyond human comprehension, the results are incomprehensible without the tools to visualize them. The NSF report took up the issue, and criticized the computing world, stating that it concentrated too much on processing power and not enough on visualization. It then went on to make a series of recommendations- or necessities - for "ViSC" tools. Visualization is not new, but its awareness by the general scientific community is.

"Visualization" is the collective word for the largely independent but converging fields of computer graphics, image processing, animation and user-interface prototypes. The concept of visualization of scientific data via computer graphics, is based on the fact that the human eye is the most efficient mechanism available to the brain for capturing data. It can also interpret spatial relationships and visual trends far more easily than it can a long list of numbers. The transfer of large data sets into graphically represented models, therefore greatly assists the rapid comprehension of complex data relationships, as well as the decision process which is fed by that comprehension.

Scientific breakthrough depends on insight. Better visualization of a problem leads to a better understanding of the underlying science and often to an appreciation of something new and unexpected. Management has found that visualization tools make companies more productive, more professional and more competitive.

The sheer breadth of use of graphics, together with the wide recognition of its significance, both in presentation and interpretation of scientific data, has led to a new generation of graphics user. Scientists who a few years ago thought that PCs and their inherent menus and icons were mere playthings, now expect a sophisticated but easy-to-use graphics environment.

2.   Graphics software solution

The graphics workstation has become an indispensable problem solving tool in scientific data visualization. However, it is often the case that scientists are spending a great deal of time with low-level graphics programming. Visualization should be seen as a scientific aid, and high-level graphics application software allows the development of visualization software to be carried out more quickly, leaving the scientist with more time to actually analyze his results.

In providing an ideal environment for visualization of scientific data on a graphics workstation, the quality of the graphics application software is clearly an important factor. The graphics software environment should include a high-level application graphics library callable from C, FORTRAN and Pascal or easy-to-use interactive graphics programs. The application graphics should directly and completely exploit the speed and functionality of the graphics workstation hardware.

Use of a high-level application graphics library makes application programming much easier than arduous low-level graphics standards such as GKS or PHIGS. Application graphics utilities such as axes, charts, 2D and 3D contour display, 3D rendering and image display should be invoked using only a single call to a subroutine or a key stroke.

For example, you have just received your new supergraphics workstation together with a GKS or PHIGS graphics software library. You are eager to produce a graphical representation of your discovery. A simple graph of 1000 data points would be suitable. You are searching in the GKS reference documentation for an application routine to plot a logarithmic axis together with a curv chart. After many hours of reading, you realize that you must program more than 1000 lines of code to draw only the logarithmic axes.

The sophisticated demo plots that you have seen at conferences are not included in the graphics workstation and realize there must be a missing link (figure 1) between your data, and the supergraphics workstation you have just purchased. You have the choice of becoming a full time programmer instead of a scientist or you must purchase "solutions" instead of low-level tools.

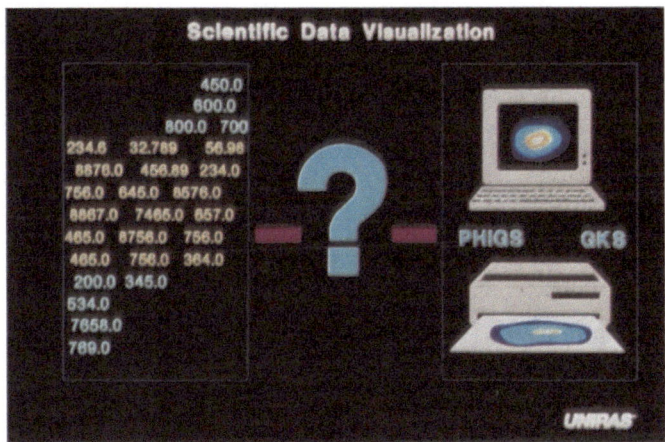

Figure 1: Application Graphics Software is an often underestimated factor within the field of "Visualization" and could represent the missing link to the scientist.

2.1 Graphics software system for visualization of scientific data

A "graphics software system" for visualization of scientific data is defined as a raster graphics system combined with an extensive set of tools for graphics application software development. The effectiveness of such a system is measured by its performance in the integration of four key areas:

o   General purpose computing power

o   Hardware graphics capabilities

o   Graphics application software capabilities

o   Interactive, user friendly development environment

Only systems providing optimal performance on all four accounts can be expected to increase the scientist's productivity by providing highly sophisticated visualization methods combined with faster overall response time.

The NSF report specified a list of advanced graphics software features which it felt would be pre-requisites for ViSC tools:

o   User Interface Management System
o   Low-level raster based graphics kernel
o   Image display capabilities
o   High-level graphics application software utilizing raster technology
o   Interpolation and smoothing methods
o   Graphics editor
o   Computer Graphics Metafile
o   High quality hardcopy
o   Portability

A general graphics software package should offer all these features as integral parts of its software architecture. The applications graphics libraries should provide a powerful and accessible graphics platform for the scientists. An extensive set of facilities should provide both high and low-level capabilities for graphics programming and interaction. The support of advanced color handling, standard output primitives, full support of input for interaction, hidden surface removal, image display, 3D rendering, but also high-level graphics for scientific axes modelling, various types of scientific charts in 2D and 3D, color coded contouring in 2D and 3D and display of 3D volume data are examples of capabilities required of a complete software solution for visualization of scientific data.

A computer independent user interface development system and a fully functional implementations of the Computer Graphics Metafile (CGM) are also important features of the graphics software package.

The combination of the advanced graphics workstation and the high-level graphics application software optimized for the hardware provide a revolution for visualization of scientific data.

2.2 Distributed graphics through X-window technology

The NSF report points out is that there are alternatives to running graphics on a supercomputer, and in some cases the alternatives provide better results. The report also considers distributed graphics, and suggests computing data on a supercomputer, downloading the data, and doing the rendering, or the graphical part on a local workstation. This, the report points out, will eliminate the bottlenecks caused by transferring hugh amount of graphics data over the networks.

The .way computers have been used in graphics has evolved considerably from the era of batch mode graphics processing (1960s-1970s) to interactive graphics on mainframes (1970s-1980s), to the end user computing explosion caused by the PC and workstation (1980s). A new style is emerging, client/server graphics applications based on a network model of computer systems (1990s). In this model, intelligent workstations (clients) have access to a number of systems (servers) via an enterprise network. To the user, the computer system is not a single computer, but any and all computers on the network that the user can access.

X-windows will have an important impact to a recentralization and control of performance, system administration and management under a MIS control. The pendulum swung to the PCs and workstations as a consequence of the non-responsiveness of MIS to end-user needs, but is beginning to swing back as databases and graphics application software become too complex and timeconsuming to maintain for the scientists. A X server strategy allows the scientists to focus on their research, having access to any needed graphics application or database on the network, without having to worry about the support of these products.

The X server strategy also allows MIPS to be allocated to the applications requiring them. For example, many of the pseudo-color images presented in this paper use time consuming, advanced interpolation algorithms before the final image can be displayed. The application will process the heavy interpolation on the supercomputer before sending the graphics primitives through the X server to a workstation or terminal for local graphics rendering. However, a single scientist running a computationally intensive simulation can have a negative impact on the response time of all other scientists on the system. One of the major motivations for the development of the workstations was to guarantee a good response time to the user.

In the client/server model of computing it is possible to better accommodate multiple user sharing the same network. X-windows will make it easier to implement optimized server allocation. Intensive calculations will run on one server while the graphics output is controlled by a different server. The user would not know where the various applications are executed.

The introduction of low-cost "intelligent" dumb terminals utilizing the X-window technology, offers an interesting alternative to the workstations. A "X window terminal" connected to the supercomputer on a network, will bring number crunching capability, high-end graphics applications and modern user interface technology to the scientists at a very low cost. This platform creates an alternative to the scientists who do not want to support unnecessary complexity on a workstation.

This form of distributed graphics is not without problems. I have already mentioned response time in multiple user environment. Further, today's LANs (Ethernet etc) may not provide enough bandwidth to support hundred of scientist connected to a supercomputer, especially if everybody exploit image display capabilities at the same time. However, much faster fiber-optic LANs are on the way with a capacity of 100 Mbits per second or faster.

3.   Practical implementations of the Visualization concept

In order to explore the visualization concepts on a practical level, this paper will explore several examples drawn from a variety of fields. The problems selected utilize real scientific data. The concepts employed here are generic across the whole spectrum of physical science.

3.1 Visualization of spatial data

Engineers from an automotive company are testing new friction material for their disc brakes in the laboratory and want to visualize temperature distribution. At their test site, they place small thermo sensors on the brakes and measure the temperature under different loads. Visualization is used to study the distribution of heat on the brakes and the brakes' ability to conduct or absorb the heat. Figure 2 demonstrates two images generated with modern visualization tools. The 2D and 3D color-coded image techniques will help the scientist to analyze thousands of test data sets and to select the most suitable friction material.

In the 3D relief picture below, the temperature distribution has been superimposed on the 3D representation of the disc brake.

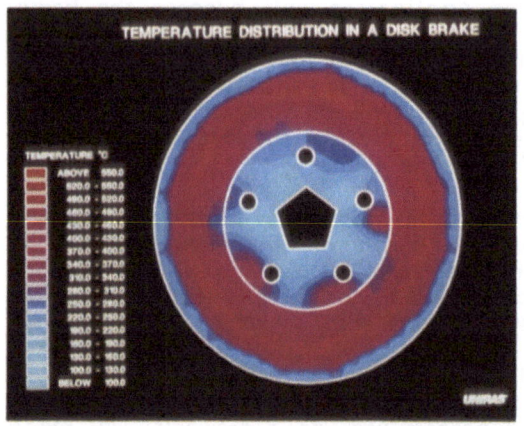 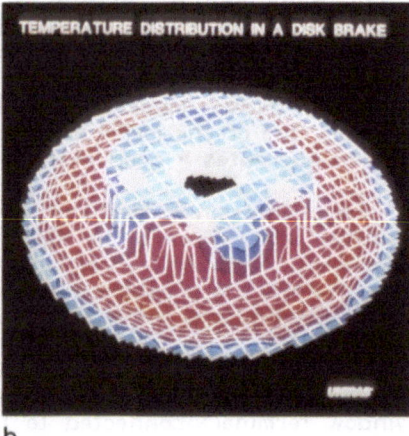

a   b

Figure 2 a and b: A 2D and 3D pseudo-colored image showing the temperature distribution on a disc brake with various friction material.

Many experiments running on a supercomputer will generate hundreds of megabytes of data. Plotting this data with traditional x-y charts, vector contour plots or 3D mesh diagrams is not feasible as it is difficult to interpret large amount of data without using color-coded graphics techniques.

Figure 2 demonstrates the use of a sophisticated color-shaded contouring technique, sometimes referred to as "pseudo-color images", and which is an example of one of the most important graphics tools within the field of scientific data visualization. This display technique offers an effective means of presenting large volumes of scientific information in a form that can be readily assimilated. The amount of information that can be conveyed in a single color image can be considerable. These pseudo-coloring tools also form the basis for animation of complex physical phenomena.

3.2 Data enhancement

Data enhancement is another important task required in most scientific visualization applications. For example, in figure 2, the temperature measured at the thermo sensors must be interpolated into a regular grid before the final color-coded image can be visualized. Each gridded spatial point on the disc brake is represented by an interpolated temperature measurement.

The number of data points used in constructing an interpolated pseudo-color image from scientific data will vary considerably from a small set of a few hundred points to a large one that may contain conceivably 100,000 points for one image. Methods used to interpolate data sets are usually particularly data quantity sensitive. A large data set requires extensive calculations and the interpolation is normally processed on a supercomputer. For small data sets of less than 100 points, however, the interpolation can be performed on a local workstation.

Algorithms for generating pseudo-color images from irregularly distributed data sets are well established in the literature, least squares, multi-quadric, weighted average, local triangular or rectangular patch are examples of frequently used functions to define the calculated surface. The reason why there are so many methods in use is probably because there is no absolute solution to the problem - different cases definitely require different methods of approach.

The interpolation method of the temperature data in this example also takes into consideration the barrier between the two separate areas of the disc brake. Interpolation methods which take into consideration barriers (surface discontinuities) raises servere complications. The interpolation function must not be carried out across any barriers or outside a boundary.

A complete scientific data visualization system should include a selection of sophisticated interpolation methods. Most scientific data is organized in a way that requires preprocessed interpolation techniques before the final pseudo-color image can be produced.

3.3 Visualization of two depenent variables

The example depicted in figure 3 demonstrates how two dependent variables are visualized in one image. The mountain area is plotted in relief while the second variable, TV reception, is displayed using color-coded contours superimposed on the relief. The TV antenna has been placed in a valley at the position (0,0). At various grid nodes in the terrain, both the elevation and a measure of the signal quality has been recorded. One can imagine how a sequence of these images could be used in an animation to show the effect of moving the TV antenna to various locations in the mountain area.

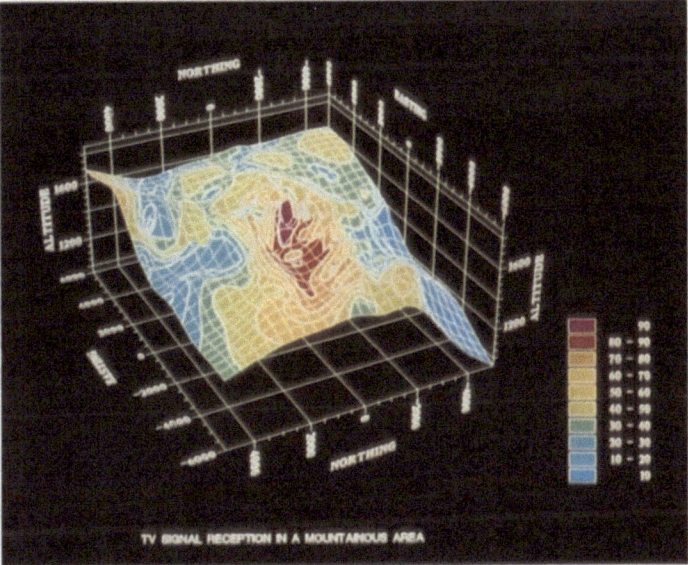

Figure 3: A color-coded 3D contour map visualizing the behavior of two dependent variables, mountain area and TV reception.

8

3.4 Visualization with three or more quantitative variables

Scientific data can exist in any number of dimensions. For example, to visualize engine characteristics showing the advantage of a continuous variable transmission, it is necessary to include the following four variables: engine torque, engine speed, throttle angle, and fuel consumption. The data for those four variables consists of four times 2,500 gridded data points in a "four-dimensional space". How is the scientist to visualize them to understand the complex relationships? How can he peer into this four-dimensional space and see a configuration of points?

The visualization of this "engine characteristics" (figure 4) is an example of a multi-dimensional presentation technique. Using UNIRAS software, a color shaded three-dimensional contour map is created to represent four variables. The fourth variable (fuel consumption) is superimposed on a 3D representation of the other three variables. A traditionally black and white vector based picture representing the same variables is shown for comparison. This graph was actually submitted by the company in question prior to its investment on color graphics.

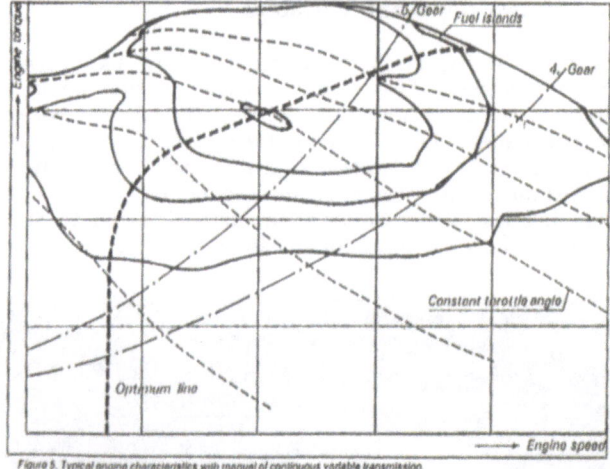

a   Figure 5. Typical engine characteristics with manual of continuous variable transmission.

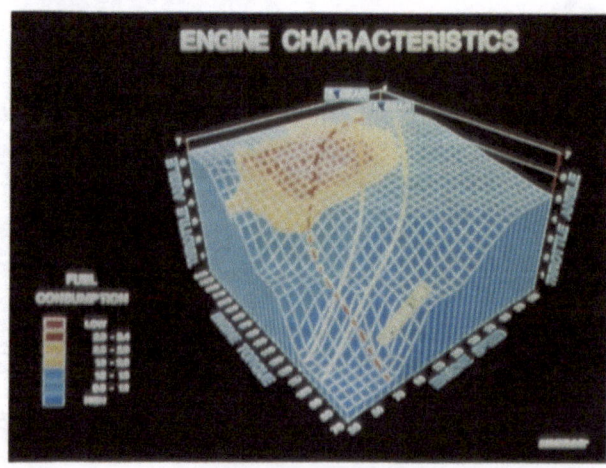

b

Figure 4 a and b: An example of multi-dimensional visualization technique using traditional vector technique and advanced color-coded contouring technique.

The second example (figure 5) is the result of testing asbestos as a replacement material for friction linings for brake systems. The display shows a typical scientific chart of a Fourier analysis of high speed judder. A series a 2D shaded curves (for various velocity) are projected on top of each other to provide an informative multivariable picture.

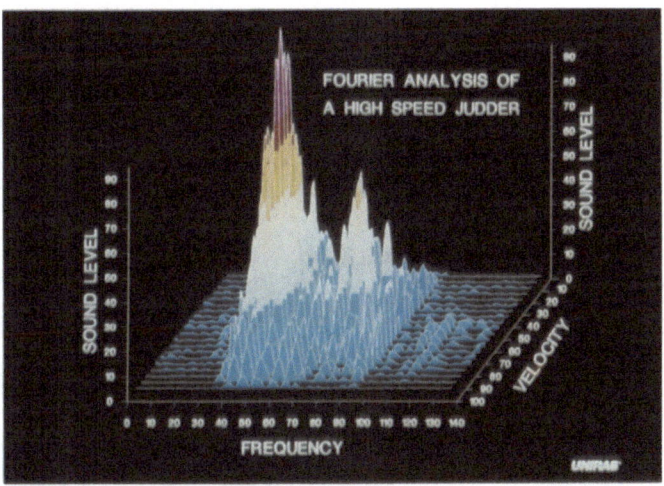

Figure 5: An example of a multidimensional scientific chart

3.5 Visualization of large quantities of data by image display technique

Large quantities of input data can also be processed by image display technology. This relatively simple visualization technique, sometimes referred to as "BitBLK technique", can make the task of data visualization manageable. In these color-coded images the entire plot area can be filled with color, thus representing millions of data values. Color gradation, with different colors corresponding to different values of Z, can highlight subtle physical variations as well as small-scale parameter variations. Moreover, image display graphics can be visualized extremely quickly with an advanced graphics processor and the result can be picked up by the eye and retained by the brain much more effectively than vector plots.

For example, a very accurate display of the mathematical function $Z=F(X,Y)$ is obtained by scanning an imaginary object area, and for each grid point, (i.e. given value of X and Y), computing the function. This technique was used in figure 6 to illustrate molecular properties by calculating the electron density on one of its derivates in a related X-Y plane.

3.6 Animation of data

Color coded image display animations of data from numerical simulations are playing an increased role in data analysis of large, multi-parameter data sets. By employing color animation the researcher may visually inspect large amounts of complex data in a short period of time in order to determine which part should be analyzed more thoroughly. Here, as with most image display application, the emphasis is on productivity through simplicity. The data is frequently calculated on a supercomputer and then visualized on a graphics workstation.

Figure 6 is a time slice from an animation showing the electron density during variation of the molecular geometry. This application visualize the vibration of the molecule. Similarly, the impact of an external magnetic field can easily be demonstrated. These image display capabilities demonstrated in figure 6 can be integrated into application programs for the computation of molecular properties.

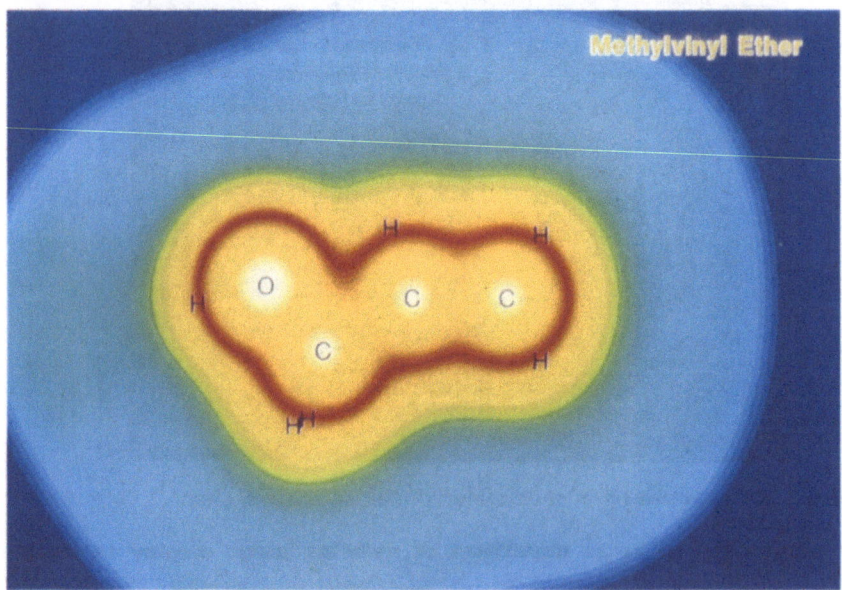

Figure 6: This visualization of the molecular properties highlights the utility of sophisticated graphics techniques in the characterization of complicated mathematical phenomena.

3.7 Display of 3D volumes (3D array of data)

A 3D array of data, where every location in the array contains a measured value, arises in many engineering and medical applications. The value "voxel" at each location in the 3D array corresponds to a physical measurement such as energy or density. The acquired data may be inherently three-dimensional or may be constructed as volume display or as multiple two-dimensional data slices successively placed together to form a 3D array. An essential component in the interpretation of the 3D data array is the ability to manipulate and display the data in a manner such that the size, shape and extent of features in the data can be easily visualized.

Techniques for visualizing 3D array data can be categorized into two major classes: surface oriented and volume oriented. In the first technique, 2D slices of data are displayed along one of the three primary axes. The scientists accesses data from the 3D array of data. 2D arrays of data are extracted and visualized with a projected 2D shaded contouring (pseudo coloring) technique. The second approach is based on a volumetric display technique where the entire 3D array of data is used for visualization. Specialized graphics hardware can be used for real-time display or high-level graphics application software can produce realistic 3D volumes with hidden surfaces removed.

Figures 7-9 show "heat conduction in an insulated plate", a good demonstration on how 3D array data can be visualized. The square plate is bounded by the four lines X=0, X=PI, Y=0 and Y=PI. For a given point (X,Y) on the plate and given time t, let u(x,y,t) denote the temperature at that point at a given time. A 3D array data set V(10,10,10) represents the input model to the graphics system.

In figure 7, we illustrate the 3D data array, where each location is the 3D array, contains a numeric value. The entire array of data represents the input to the 3D volume display routine. An annotated 3D axis system is plotted together with shaded contours of the visible parts of the 3D array. A shaded 2D contour map displaying the initial temperature distribution is also plotted. The color scale legend relates the temperatures and the color shades. In figure 8 the interior of the 3D array data is visualized. The scientist removes pieces of blocks in the 3D array of data to analyze the interior of the data set.

Figure 9 is an example of a surface oriented display technique, successive slices of 3D data are displayed with the use of color encoding. Five time slices, representing five different time values, are accessed from the 3D array of data (used above) and visualized by a projected pseudo coloring method. A 3D axes system relates the selected plates to the X and Y scaling while the Z-axis indicates the chosen time values.

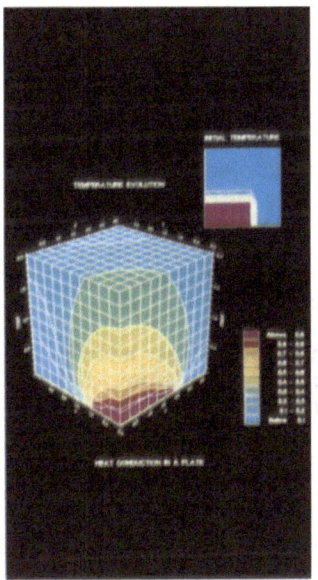
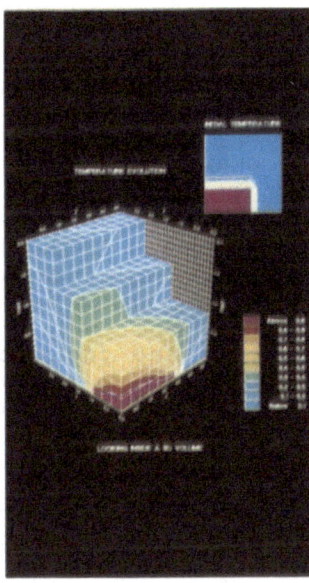
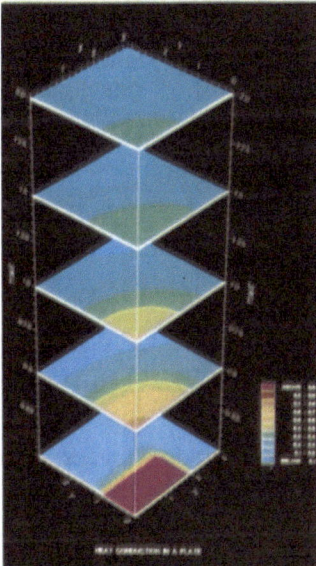

Fig. 7.   Fig. 8.   Fig. 9.

Figure 7-9:   3D array data are visualized by a surface oriented and volume oriented display technique.

4. The importance of the user interface

The quality of the user interface is fast becoming a crucial criterion in determining the success or failure of an interactive data visualization environment. Features such as ease-of-use, speed, user-friendliness and consistency are demanded rather than requested. Software needs to be equipped with enough inherent intelligence to cope with technically sophisticated end users with varying levels of computing experience.

Creating a good user interface for a graphics application is a difficult task, and the software to support the user interface is often large, complex, and difficult to debug and modify. The user interface for an application is usually a significant fraction of the code, between 30% and 70% is not an unrealistic number. Unfortunately, it is generally the case that as user interfaces become easier to use for the scientists, they become more complex and harder to create for the user interface designer.

With this in mind, it is vital that graphics software vendors focus considerable effort on the design and implementation of user interface technology. The number of commercially available fully configurable graphics UIMS is quite small. The rapid growth of the workstation market has brought a new obstacle to light, however. Hardware vendors currently design window management systems and user interface toolkits specifically for their own workstations. As a result software developers, who generally develop applications for a particular window system, are confronted with the gargantuan task of porting their applications among various window managers now available.

What are window managers? Most people know they employ bitmapped graphics to display "multiple windows" that represent one or more "tasks". It is important to understand the various levels of user interfaces:

o Window library (library of callable basic operations such as "draw line", "check mouse button status" etc)

o Window toolkit (library of callable routines for handling more complex operations such as "pop-up and pull-down menus", "get menu selection" etc)

o U I M S (4GL and prototyping tool that allows the developers to quickly build applications that are independent of window toolkits)

These three layers represent levels of increasing granularity in specifying applications. Window libraries give developers the freedom to articulate the exact "look and feel" of applications in fine detail programming thousand lines of C language code. Window toolkits work with the conceptual elements of window applications using fewer lines of code and is the current interface of choice for most programmers. UIMSs enable the non-programmers, e.g. the human engineers, to specify applications using 4GLs and visual object editors.

The key to a UIMS is that it enables the designer to tailor the user interface to the precise level that he or she needs, without requiring complex and time consuming coding and debugging. The UIMS handles interaction with the user and invokes application functionality in response to syntactical valid commands. In other words, the application programmer is protected from the difficulties involved in creating a high quality user interface. The dialogue description defines the interaction with the user and provides a link to consequent application actions.

UIMS provides them with a consistent methodology for developing user friendly front-ends to their visualization programs (figure 10). But perhaps of wider significance, the technology heralds the arrival of the "Mac"-type interface at all levels of computing, incorporating all the widows, menus and icons that are now so familiar in the PC world. In the workstation environment, most UIMSs run under the de-facto windowing standard, X-windows. In the mainframe environment, where the nature of the terminals traditionally does not allow for windowing-type user interfaces, a UIMS must simulate the windowing facilities available on workstations. Effectively, then, the UIMS looks and "feels" the same in all computing environments.

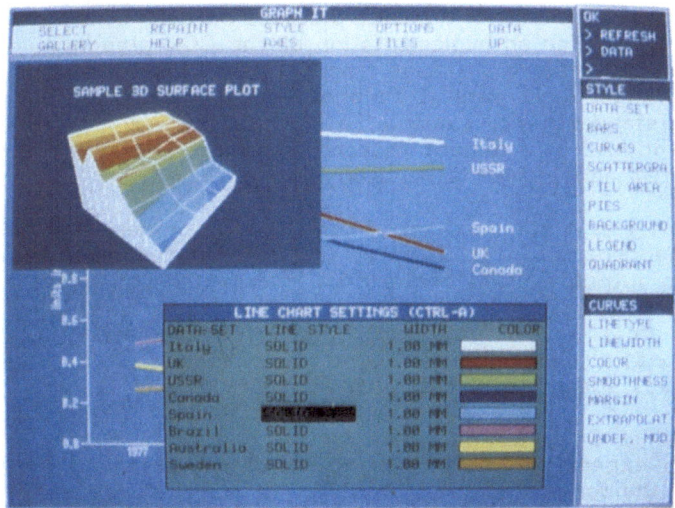

Figure 10: Example of a modern user-interface design, created with UNIRAS' "USEIT" UIMS software package.

The ability to use UIMS technology normally associated with workstations on large mainframes provides a new interesting platform for the scientists. Large companies with mixed computing resources in their R&D labs can offer common user interface across all CPUs.

One of the most obvious barriers to achieving consistent user interfaces is the differences between the modern graphics workstation and the graphics terminals attached to a mainframe or supercomputer. With the X-window server/client strategy it will much easier to create a UIMS which can operate in a mixed CPU network environment.

5. Computer Graphics Metafile

The scientists can not use pictures to communicate ideas and results unless they have access to a common picture metafile language.

The introduction of high quality presentation packages for scientific data such as CA-DISSPLA, UNIRAS graphics, PVI, DPICT, SAS Graph, Harvard, Zenographics etc has resulted in a similar explosion of picture file formats. No two packages store their image files the same way. Millions of graphs are produced with these packages yearly. That means utter chaos when it comes to exchanging image data between scientists or combine pictures generated by different packages.

The need for a standard metafile has been appreciated throughout the development of standards for computer graphics. Most graphics vendors recognize the need for storage of the graphical data created in their application. The immediate advantages are CPU independence, device independence and application independence.

Thanks to the adopted Computer Graphics Metafile (CGM) standard in 1987, it is now possible to transfer pictures between the various graphics packages and maybe even more important to transfer pictures between scientists. Today most graphics vendors offer an implementation of the CGM standard. Software that supports CGM can recieve an image from another CGM-supporting application, modify that image, and pass it to another program or output device that supports the standard. For example, a scientist can recieve an image from a colleague, produced at a distant research laboratory, analyze it with his own graphics system and include a hardcopy in a research report.

The CGM comprises a standard set of conventions for describing an image in a device independent way. To support CGM, a vendor must develop a CGM generator (to output a CGM) and a CGM interpreter (to accept a CGM). The CGM standard specifies 19 graphics primitives including lines (polylines, circular arcs etc.), text (regular text, restricted text, append text, etc.), fill areas (polygons, circles, ellipses, rectangles, etc) and markers. Attributes of these primitives specify qualities such as color, line style, and fill style.

The exchange of CGM files between various graphics vendors could be more difficult than expected. The interpretation of the standard document varies between the vendors. Because the CGM standard does not firmly specify minimum capabilities, most commercial implementations differ in the elements they can place in a CGM and in the elements they can successfully interpret from a CGM.

An example of a weak part of the CGM standard, is the missing support of text attributes like font type and spacing method. Fonts are only represented by numbers. There is a font list where you can name your fonts, but there is no standardization for naming. Kerning is another important attribute which is not included. That means that one package may assign Helvetica to value 1 whereas another may assign Times Roman to value 1. This has more serious implications than you might think. For example, suppose you have drawn an originazation chart, in which text fits snugly into the boxes. You use the company standard Helvetica font, then export the same font to a desktop publishing package. If your graphics package used a font number, you should hope that the recieving program uses the same font for that number, and more to the point, that the font metric tables (which define the widths and kerning points for a font) match.

On the other hand, the graphics package exporting the CGM file may convert the text to polygons, thus eliminating kerning and width problems altogether. The good news is, images containing text in the CGM file will translate perfectly, appearing identically in the recieving grapgics package to the text in the originating package. The bad news is, it's no longer thought of as a text. If you import the image back to your graphics package, you won't be able to select it and change its font because there is no longer any font involved. It's just polygons that look text and the font primitive does not exist.

Nevertheless, it is intended in future extensions to CGM that the font and text definitions being developed for other standards should be included in the metafile standard. So despite the fact that there is still some work to do on CGM, it is a clear step forward in making life easier for the user of scientific data presentation.

6.   Network access to high resolution hardcopy pictures

The real worth of the Scientific Data Visualization is perhaps apparent when scientists are able to present slides at conferences or high quality plots in a journal or magazine. Because one cannot publish interactive systems in a journal, the scientists need access to a high quality hard copy. Aesthetics are nearly as important as the information being displayed. Image quality affects the way the information is received and the way the scientist is perceived by the audience. A multi-dimensional picture on a 35mm slide, can sometimes help the scientist to explain a complex scientific discovery to his audience.

Hard copy also lets you plot different views of the same data together on one sheet (or use successive slides) so relationships can be studied from a variety of angles. In addition, hard copy lets you overlay different types of graphs. For example, a chart of chemical concentrations in selected soil samples can be presented on a map showing where the samples were collected. Combining pictures from various sources, again requires a standard metafile format and a graphics editor which can merge the two images into a new image.

Graphics hardcopy devices such as laser printers, thermal-transfer printers and Digital film recorders with a resolution of 400 dots per inch cost $10,000 or more. Few scientists need or want to spend that amount for a high resolution hardcopy device that attaches to a single workstation serving only one user at a time.

A Scientific Data Visualization system should combine a powerful hardcopy device connected to a network with a Computer Graphics Metafile interface and a device independent graphics package, which can serve 10 or 100 users simultaneously. The cost per hardcopy picture can then be lowered, without affecting the needed high quality of the image.

In many scientific data visualization areas, color can be used to aid clarity and enhance the understanding and impact of the presentation. But in many journals color is not available at a reasonable cost and it is therefore necessary to represent complex pictures in black and white. Figure 11 is an example of a hardcopy produced with the Postscript language.

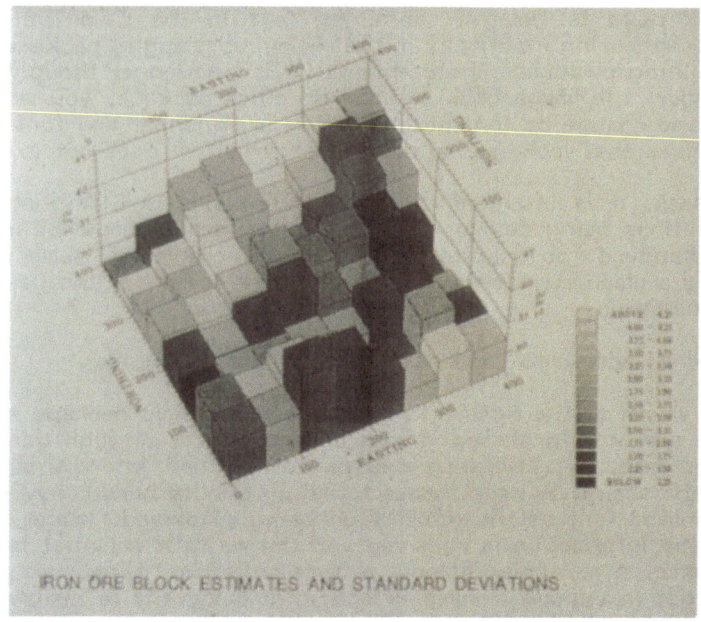

Figure 11:   An example of a grey shaded 3D bar chart, generated with Postscript.

7.   Conclusion

Ten years ago, data visualization was an emerging technology in search of problems to solve. Now, the industrial world is using it widely as a tool for higher productivity, competitive advantage and better communications. The challenge for computer graphics vendors is to provide new sophisticated techniques, via easy-to-use interfaces, to meet these requirements.

Science is becoming a major application for visualization. It is progressing from being unheard of, to something that will be as commonplace as CAD/CAM or business graphics. There is going to be a lot more demand for interactive applications. Scientists are not programmers and will not spend many man-hours attempting to produce useful graphics. They will require easy-to-use programs.

Visualization should not be viewed as the end result of a process of scientific analysis, but rather as the process itself. It is much more than simply the application of techniques for displaying scientific data. Visualization can be used to explore the unknown world of complex physical phenomena.

References

Visualization in scientific computing: Computer Graphics - Volume 21-Number 6 - November 1987 - Bruce H. McCormick, Thomas A. DeFanti, Maine D. Brown - ACM SIGGRAPH.

Visualization techniques in the physical sciences: ACM SIGGRAPH 88-tutorial notes.

Computer graphics in science: ACM SIGGRAPH 88 - tutorial notes.

Creating User Interfaces by Demonstration: Academic Press - Perspectives in computing - Vol 22 - Brad A. Myers.

CGM in the real world: Eurographic Seminars - A.M. Mumford, M.W. Skall - Springer Verlag.

ISO IS 8632 (Parts 1-4) Information processing systems - Computer graphics - Metafile for the storage and transfer of picture description information (CGM), 1987.

Chapter 2
Color in Computer Graphics: Manipulating and Matching Color

Gerald M. Murch, Joann M. Taylor

1. Introduction

Color in graphic workstations has rapidly transitioned from a novelty with great expected potential to a highly useful tool for the communication of complex databases to a human brain. Perhaps the most dominant feature of this transition has been the recognition that color provides a significant mechanism for the communication of such large and complex sources of information. This realization builds a critical cornerstone of the emerging discipline of *interactive visualization*. Although disagreement exists within the graphics industry as to the exact definition of visualization, most experts agree that the concept connotes the ability to render complex databases by visual means in order to capitalize on the sensory processing capability of the visually-oriented human mind.

Earlier uses of color, typified by the pie chart and bar graph types of business graphics, can be termed *qualitative* color applications. Of far greater utility is the *quantitative* color use in which gradations of change can be portrayed as in a topological map or in a thermal analysis of a circuit board. As a tool for visualization, the use of color has changed from a simple means of showing that two or more areas of a graphic display differ from one another to a technology for portraying quantitative color differences. Yet the emergence of the need for qualitative color rendition has underscored a number of problems with graphic systems which place stringent demands on system capability. The resolution of these demands provides the substance of this review. The critical topical areas are as follows:

1. The user interface and underlying color model
2. The fidelity of color rendition between devices such as printer and display

2. Color Models and the User Interface to Color

The accurate control and specification of the parameters of color in CRT displays is of increasing concern to a wide range of users who are utilizing multi-color displays as a means of organizing and conveying comprehensive quantitative information. One fundamental part of the color display system is the user interface which enables the specification, choice, and manipulation of colors on the display screen. The color interface is the essential link between the user and the display system. The number of colors which can be presented on the display screen or how vivid the colors appear is clearly secondary if the interface puts undo limitations on the user or fails to assist him or her in exercising, to the fullest extent, the color capabilities of the display device. The past use of color in displays, with emphasis on qualitative color, has resulted in the development of display-based color systems which are currently employed in user interfaces. However, all of these systems were developed when color, as an integral part of display technology, was a new commodity. These systems addressed the user's need for a large palette of display colors, but little was done to optimize the utility of the interface.

Color display technology has developed significantly over the years and has only been surpassed by the growth of the user market which is continually expanding in terms of people, applications, and task sophistication. Quantitative color-oriented tasks being attempted by today's user would be assisted by an improved color interface. For textile design or advertising layout, color quality is desired in addition to accurate hardcopy rendition of color. In mechanical engineering applications the ability to quickly and accurately render smooth shaded surfaces is essential. In composing simple or complex graphic images efficient color selection is desirable.

Despite the fact that they enjoy widespread use, the color interfaces employed in display systems today are difficult to work with. For most applications, colors adjusted by the operator generally don't conform to the color desired by the operator. Unwanted surprises, difficulties, and unpredictabilities are common. In addition, these systems fail to incorporate the perceptual non-linearities of human color vision. As a result, they are difficult to use because they are inherently perceptually non-uniform and thus unpredictable from the user's point of view.

In order to better understand the requirements for the quantitative use of color in interactive visualization, we need to review briefly the color interface systems currently in use. In all cases, the interface accesses an underlying color model. The model represents both a conceptual set of relationships between color attributes as well as the limits of the specific technology to provide the user with specific color palettes.

2.1 The G Model

Perhaps life in the early days of graphics use was less demanding in the sense that user's choices were severely limited. Monochrome displays of the 60's and 70's came in several shades of green and the user needed to specify whether a specific pixel was to be on or off. Gray level displays emerged soon after the initial one bit units so that the user could specify several intensity levels of green. Beyond this initial green, a number of additional colors were soon available with white and amber being the favorite choices. A rather torrid debate emerged on the issue of which monochrome color was easier on the eyes for long-term viewing with some unique marketing claims made for some of the colors. No research data supported the utility of one color over another for the reduction of visual fatigue. Even at this point, some inherent problems began to emerge which were the result of the hardware driving the monochrome display. Most notable of these was the non-linear relationship between the requested level of green (DAC value) and the amount of light emitted from the screen. The relationship between display DAC and the related light output is shown in Figure 1. This relationship is known as the display *gamma*. As can be seen in the figure, lower DAC values produce very small increases in light output (properly termed *luminance*) while at the upper end of the curve, very large increases occur for small changes in DAC. The DAC to luminance relationship has led to a number of correction algorithms in which the attempt is made to render the relation linear. Here too lies a potential problem as the slope of the resulting gamma correction relation should conform to the human eye's perceived relation. The visual relation is essentially logarithmic which translates into a slope with an exponent of about 0.66.

2.2 The RGB Model

Early color displays utilized an interface that was almost as easy to use as its one-bit monochrome ancestors. Typically, the color palette consisted of eight colors which were formed by switching on one of the three primary electron guns (Red, Green, or

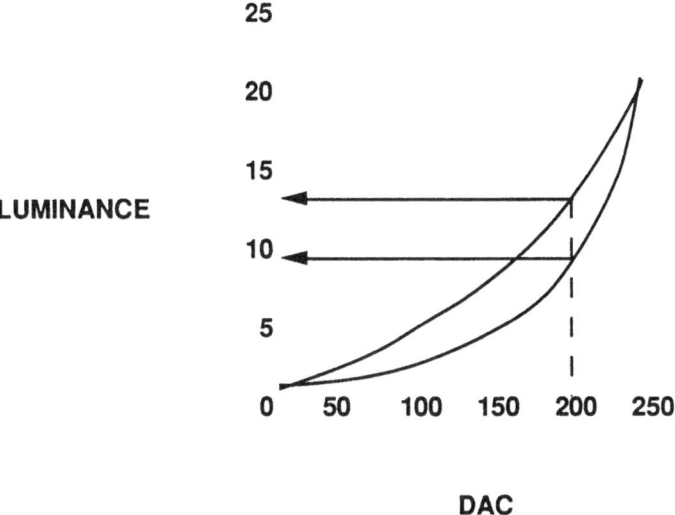

LUMINANCE

DAC

Figure 1. The variation between luminance and Digital to Analog (DAC) gun level for two separate CRT devices.

Blue), the binary combinations of the guns to form Red + Green = Yellow, Green + Blue = Cyan, or Red + Blue = Magenta. Coupled with White, produced by all three guns active, and Black, with all guns off, the user's task was to select Red, Green, Blue, Yellow, Magenta, Cyan, White, or Black (RGBYMCWBk). This interface was touted as direct and simple as the user "talked" directly to the electrons.

The emergence of color displays with more than one bit per gun increased the demands on the user and began to obscure the direct relation between electron gun and color. The resultant system, called RGB, is still in wide use today. In this color system, an entire gamut of colors can be created by conceptually mixing the light emitted from the red, green, and blue phosphors in various proportions and intensities. The RGB system is the most widely available color space for use in display interfaces by virtue of the fact that it is fundamentally tied to the hardware of CRT displays. The RGB system has traditionally been the easiest system for programmers to implement since it requires little mathematical manipulation to obtain the requested colors directly from the electron

The RGB model uses a Cartesian coordinate system that describes a color space represented within the confines of a cube. Figure 2 illustrates the RGB color cube and the locations of the colors achieved by full intensity emissions of the guns either singularly or in combination with one another.

In the RGB system, a user selects color by indicating the intensities and relative proportions of the emissions from the red, green and blue color is specified by three numerical designations, (R, G, B). There are different mathematical embodiments of the RGB system depending upon the number of available intensity levels of each primary. For example, in the 0 - 255 RGB system, each gun may be addressed at 256 levels. This results in over 16 million unique combinations of RGB intensities. Many of the colors in the system are indistinguishable from one another, thus the same perceived color may

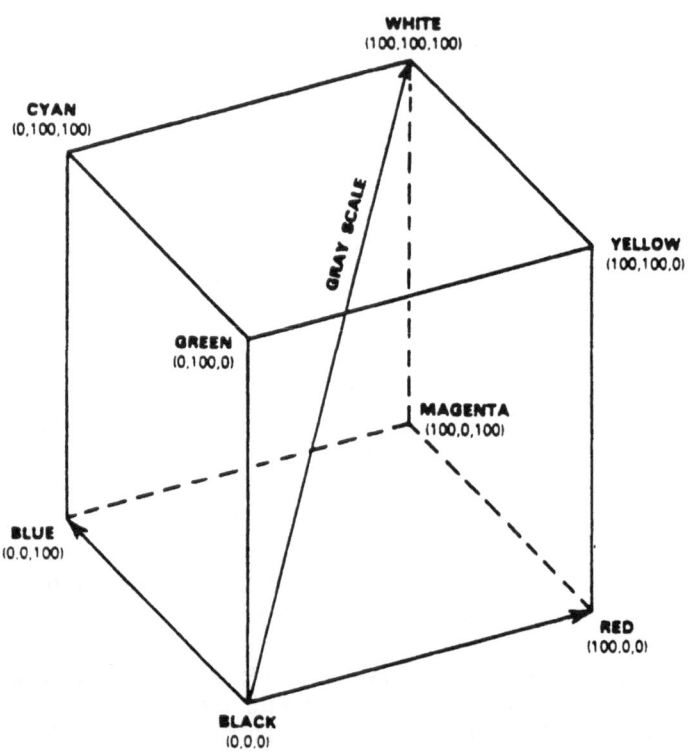

Figure 2. The RGB Color Cube. The entire gamut of video colors is described by the varying intensities of the Red, Green, and Blue phosphor outputs.

result from a number of different RGB designations. This is particularly noticeable in the lower intensities, where there is relatively little response from the electron guns (See Figure 1.). Note that equal step sizes over the available range (i.e. 0 to 255) do not produce equally perceived color changes. Often as many as twenty steps are required to evoke a change in some colors while a single step will result in a perceived change in other colors.

The 0 - 100 RGB system was developed to help alleviate some of the inherent problems with the 0 - 255 version by logarithmically truncating the space, thus eliminating many of the lower response intensities. In the 0 - 100 RGB system, each primary has a range of 101 units so there are over one million possible RGB designations. Despite the attempted improvement, the 0 - 100 RGB system still has many areas in which unique numerical assignments of RGB result in the same perceived display color.

Some of the disadvantages of the RGB system stem from the requirement that the user understand both the nuances of additive color mixture and the idiosyncrasies of the display device. the mental selection of a particular color by entering a triplet of values seldom produces the color envisioned by the user. Additionally, once a color close to the desired one has been selected, editing requires careful increases and decreases in each gun level in non-intuitive ways. For example, the desire to change just the vividness of a selected color requires unequal changes in all three parameters. In using the RGB system, the user finds that the system is difficult to predict in terms of appearance and is non-intuitive since it does not incorporate the perceptual non-linearities of human color vision.

2.3 The HLS Model

In order to address the perceptual inconsistencies associated with RGB, the HLS system was developed by Tektronix in 1978. The overall goal was to create a system which was more visually uniform, more intuitive, and thus user-oriented. Rather than using a model based directly on display hardware, the HLS system utilizes the parameters of Hue, Lightness, and Saturation which are designations that describe color in a more perceptual sense. HLS was designed to be similar to the Ostwald[1] color system, which was developed in 1931 to represent full color, black, white, and the resulting tints, shades, and tones that result from mixing of colors. All color systems used to interface the user to the display's color capability must go through an RGB transformation to address the electron guns in the display. HLS is no exception, however, the transformation is done via firmware and is not apparent to the user.

The HLS model utilizes a three-dimensional polar coordinate system to mathematically describe a color solid that is represented by a double ended cone. This is illustrated in Figure 3. The three parameters of color in the HLS model are designated (H, L, S) and each represents a single perceptual characteristic of color. *Hue*, the property associated with color family, (i.e. red, yellow, purple, etc.) is specified as an angle and ranges from 0° to 359°, with blue at 0°, by convention. The primary colors red, green, and blue as well as the secondaries yellow, cyan, and magenta are distributed uniformly around the color solid. *Lightness,* describes the variation in a color between black and white and is represented as the central vertical axis of the double-ended cone. Lightness ranges from zero (black) to 100 (white) with a series of neutral grays between these two extremes. *Saturation*, is perhaps the most difficult of the parameters to conceptualize, as it describes the vividness of a color, or its variation from neutral gray (zero) to the most vibrant hue (100). As a result of the bounds on the H, L, and S parameters, it is possible to specify over three million unique color designations.

The HLS system has some clear advantages over the RGB system, particularly with regard to ease of use[2]. The main reason for this preference is felt to be the attempt that HLS makes to imitate the more intuitive perceptual quantities commonly used to describe color. There are, however, a number of deficiencies in HLS that limit its effectiveness as a user interface to color.

Despite attempts to the contrary, the HLS system does not take into account perceptual non linearities of human color vision. As a result, there are areas in the color space where multiple designations result in the same perceived color. This is seen particularly well in the green region of color space. Another deficiency is seen in the overall uniformity of the system, in which there are areas of color space where a change of one unit in a single parameter results in a perceptible color difference and other areas in which a 10 unit change is not visually apparent. In addition, the system is normalized in such a way that full saturation, which occurs at a designation of 100, is located at different physical displacements from the neutral (zero), dependent on lightness. This is an artifact of the double-ended cone design coupled with the normalized numbering system employed in HLS. To compound the problem further, the three parameters of hue, lightness, and saturation are not independent of one another. This means that a user is capable of detecting perceptual variation in one parameter, for example, lightness,

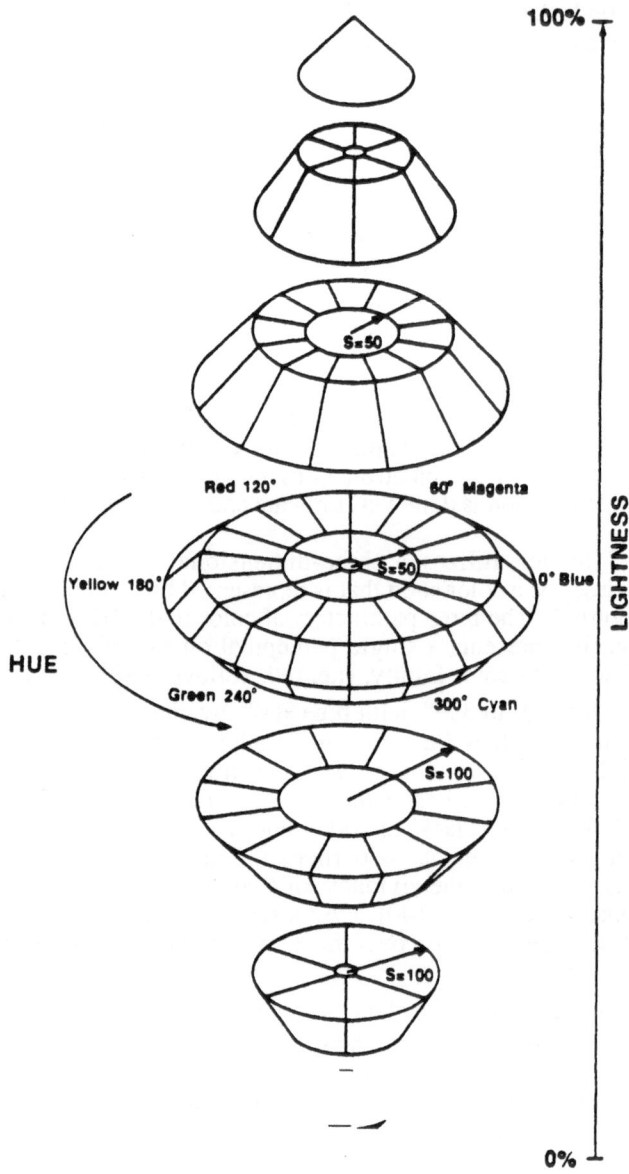

100%

0%

LIGHTNESS

S=50

Red 120°   60° Magenta

Yellow 180°   0° Blue

S=50

HUE

Green 240°   300° Cyan

S=100

S=100

Figure 3. The Tektronix HLS Color Solid. This double-ended cone model incorporates the three descriptive perceptual parameters of Hue, Lightness, and Saturation.

when another parameter, such as hue, is the only one being changed. Figure 4 portrays an example of the non-perceptual nature of the HLS model in which the measured luminance levels for a specified constant Lightness of 50% are shown for selected points around the hue circle. Although one would expect luminance to be constant it is not.

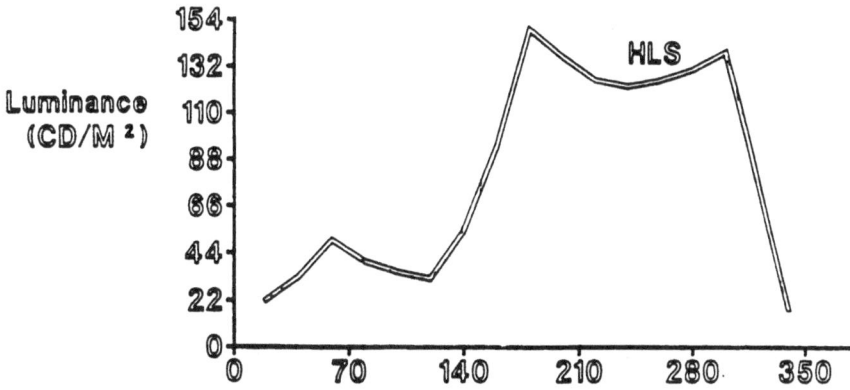

Figure 4. An example of the non-perceptual nature of the HLS model is demonstrated by plotting measured luminance levels for a specified constant lightness of 50%.

A number of variations on the HLS concept have appeared such as HSB (Hue, Saturation, and Brightness), and HSI (Hue, Saturation, and Intensity). Each of these attempts to overcome a specific weakness in the HLS System but each introduces new problems. Common to all of these color models is the underlying non-linear color display which imposes limitations in terms of translating color into human terms.

With the introduction of color displays, the first color printers entered the market. These were similar in capability in that a very limited color palette was available. Little concern was given to the relationship between printer and screen color. This was not particularly important for qualitative color use as the exact color printed did not matter so long as the areas of the display which should appear differently colored were distinguishable on the printed version as well. Unfortunately, the printer industry has been slow to recognize the transition from qualitative to quantitative color. The issue of (fidelity) quality of color rendition between screen and printer has not received adequate attention and the initial solutions have been of limited value.

2.4 The HVC System

The RGB and HLS color models have served users well over the past years. However, numerous applications and the complexity of tasks being addressed by today's users requiring quantitative color demands a new color system that corrects the limitations of current systems as well as providing a link to standard color theory and methods of colorimetry. In addition, neither the RGB nor the HLS system are related to an internationally accepted color standard. As a result, definition and control of color appearance is extremely difficult since there is no way to equate color designations in either system with objective specifications. Also, the specification of colors between two or more devices is meaningless. An RGB or and HLS value on one display will produce a different color on a second display.

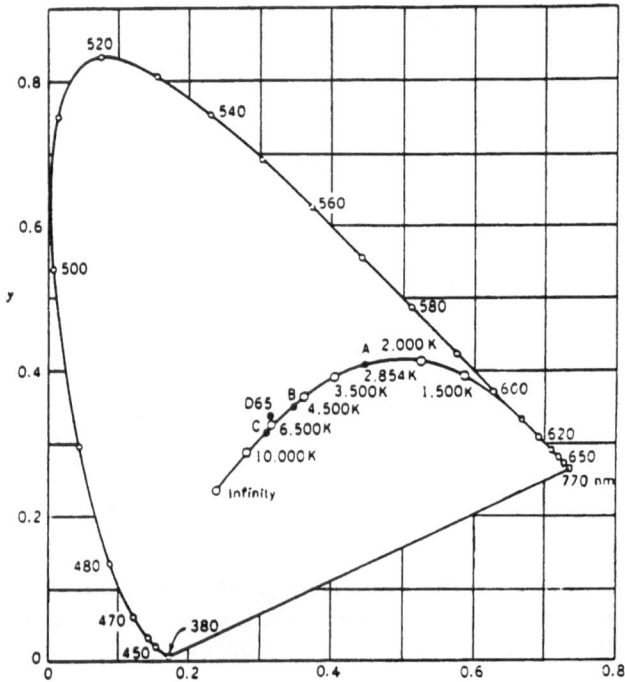

Figure 5. The 1931 CIE Chromaticity Diagram. The x, y chromaticity coordinates for any real color are located within the bounds of the horse-shoe shaped spectrum and the line of purples which joins the spectrum ends.

A new color system, developed by Tektronix Laboratories and known as TekHVC™ (hereafter referred to simply as HVC), incorporates the three truly independent color parameters of Hue, Value, and Chroma. The HVC system is described mathematically by a three-dimensional polar coordinate system which is embodied in an irregularly shaped solid. The HVC system was derived from the 1976 CIE Uniform Chromaticity Scale u′, v′ Diagram and the related CIE L^*, u^*, v^* (CIELUV)[3] color metrics. These systems are both internationally recognized standards for color description and specification. To understand the fundamental concept of HVC it is necessary to review the underlying CIE system.

2.4.1 Elements of the CIE System: The CIE (Commission Internationale de l' Eclairage) or the International Commission on Illumination colorimetric system consists of a series of essential standards, mathematical definitions, and measurement procedures that are necessary to make colorimetry a useful tool for science and industry. This system uses as its basis the premise that a color stimulus results from the proper combination of an illuminant, or light source, an object, and an observer. The CIE system accordingly supports standardization of these three basic components of color experience. It is beyond the scope of this document to provide a rigorous development of the theory and methodology of the CIE system. As a result, the following description of certain features of the CIE system will be simplistic and brief. The reader is encouraged to consult basic color science texts for more formal development of CIE standards, definitions, and practices.[4,5]

The 1931 CIE Chromaticity Diagram, illustrated in Figure 5, was the first diagram accepted internationally for general use.[6] In the diagram, the entire range of the visible spectrum is seen as the horse-shoe shaped spectrum locus. The x and y chromaticity coordinates for any real color are located within the bounds of the spectrum locus and the line of purples which joins the spectrum ends. The x and y coordinates do not completely describe a color, since they contain no information on the inherent lightness of a color. The third dimension of color is denoted by the tristimulus value Y, which represents the luminance factor. Figure 6 illustrates the Y axis position which is perpendicular to and lies on and above the x-y plane. In terms of the 1931 diagram, lighter colors have more restricted ranges of chromaticity, thus there are fewer colors found at higher levels of Y.[7]

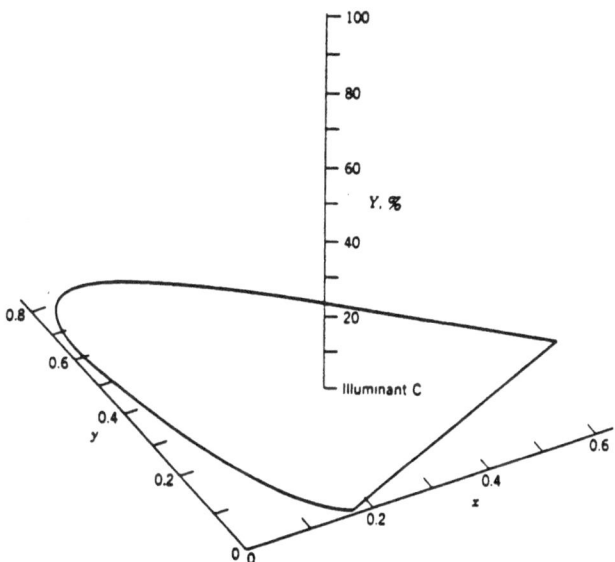

Figure 6. **The orientation of Y (luminance) axis with respect to the CIE 1931 x, y Chromaticity Diagram.**

As mentioned previously, the 1931 diagram was developed primarily for color specification and was not intended to provide information on color appearance. Consequently, the system does not display perceptual uniformity, that is to say, colors do not appear to be equally visually spaced. For example, colors that consist of the same visually perceived hue or color family (i.e. are associated with a specific wavelength) do not follow straight lines within the diagram, but are curved instead. This non-uniformity is similar to how a Mercator projection of a map of the world distorts what is truly represented on a globe. Another problem is that black, or the absence of color, has no unique position in the diagram.

Despite the fact that there is visual non-uniformity, the 1931 Chromaticity Diagram has an important advantage in that it is of value in predicting the additive mixture of two or more colors. This property is one of mathematical additivity in that the tristimulus values (X, Y, and Z) of an additively mixed color are the sums of the tristimulus values of the components or constituent colors. Color generated using a CRT

28

is an example of additive mixing. Over the years, color scientists have worked to develop a chromaticity diagram that more closely represents a perceptually uniform system as well as preserves the additivity inherent in the 1931 diagram.

In 1978, the CIE formally recommended the 1976 CIE u´, v´ Uniform Chromaticity Scales diagram[3], which is the latest implementation of a linear transformation of the 1931 CIE x, y diagram. The goal was to produce a color space in which colors were distributed in a more perceptually uniform manner. This would provide a color space in which distance between colors would indicate the level of color discriminability. An illustration of the 1976 CIE u´, v´ diagram is seen in Figure 7. The u´ and v´ chromaticity coordinates for any real color are located within the bounds of the spectrum locus and the line of purples which joins the spectrum ends. The u´ and v´ coordinates do not completely describe a color, since they contain no information on the inherent lightness of a color. The third dimension of color is denoted by the tristimulus value Y, which represents the luminance factor. The Y axis position, as in the 1931 diagram, is perpendicular to and lies on and above the u´, v´ plane (see Figure 6).[6]

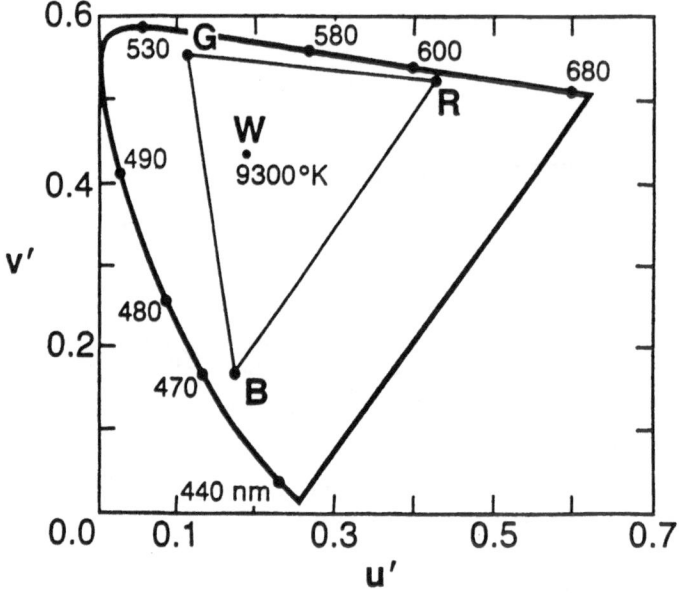

Figure 7. The 1976 CIE UCS Diagram. The u´, v´ chromaticity coordinates for any real color are located within the bounds of the horse-shoe shaped spectrum locus and the line of purples which joins the spectrum ends. The triangle represents the range of chromaticities generally achievable using the additive mixture of typical Red, Green, and Blue CRT phosphors.

In order to develop a color model in which the numerical magnitude of a color difference bears a direct relationship to a color appearance difference, the u´, v´ diagram was combined with the 1976 metric lightness function, L^*, as a basis for developing the CIE 1976 L^*, u^*, v^* (CIELUV) color space. This is an opponent-type color space which means it is based on the opponent-color theory used to describe or model human color vision.[8] The theory behind opponency of colors is based on the assumption that all colors are coded by the eye and brain into light-dark, red-green, and yellow-blue signals. In a system of this type, colors are mutually exclusive in that a color cannot be red *and* green at the same time, or yellow *and* blue at the same time, but a color can be described as red *and* blue as in the case of purple. In the CIELUV color system, there are two opponent coordinate axes, represented by u^* and v^*, that describe the chromatic attributes of color. The u^* axis represents the red-green coordinate, while the v^* axis represents yellow-blue. Positive values of u^* denote red colors while negative values denote green. Similarly, positive values of v^*, represent yellows and negative values signify blues. The L^* axis denotes variations in lightness (darkness) and lies perpendicular to the u^*, v^* plane. The achromatic or neutral colors (black, gray, white) lie on the L^* axis and at the point where u^* and v^* intersect ($u^* = 0$, $v^* = 0$).

The CIELUV color space has a unique location for black by making each of the opponent coordinates a function of metric lightness. As a result, when $L^* =$ zero, the coordinates u^* and v^* are also zero, thus black lies at a single point on the neutral axis.

The CIELUV color space is represented by an irregularly shaped spheroid, illustrated in Figure 8. There are two reasons why the space approaches absolute limits at each end of the L^* scale. At the lower end of the color space, L^* approaches zero. Thus, by definition, so do u^* and v^* since they are functions of L^*. This is what ensures a unique, single point, definition for black. The top portion of the CIELUV space converges for a different reason. Recall that in the standard CIE u', v' chromaticity diagram, as Y increases, the limits on chromaticity become severe and less chromatic variation is possible. As a result, there is a unique white point. The irregularity of the CIELUV color solid as a whole reflects the fact that certain colors are inherently capable of greater dynamic range than others.

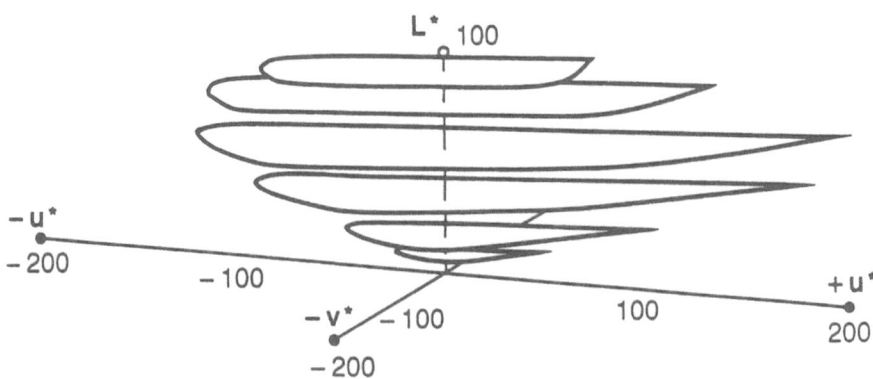

Figure 8. A representation of the CIELUV object-color solid showing constant lightness planes, $L^*=10.0, 20.0, 40.0, 60.0, 80.0,$ and 90.0.

At this point in time, the CIELUV system is currently the best available approximation to a visually uniform color space for additive colors accepted for international use. The deviations from uniformity found in the 1976 CIE u', v' diagram are more obvious in certain regions of color space than in others, particularly towards the limits of the spectrum locus. One advantage to video-based implementations of a color system related to the 1976 CIE u', v' diagram is that the gamut of colors achievable on a CRT lie in the most uniform region of the u', v' diagram.

2.4.2   The HVC Model: The effort in developing the HVC system for a video-based (CRT) implementation, breaks down into two steps consisting of the:

1. Determination of the size and shape of the color space delimited by the display device gamut and relating it to an underlying perceptual scheme.

2. Derivation of the algorithms to describe the color space and descriptive model as well as development of the necessary device transforms.

Determining the size and shape of the video color space requires calculation of the range of achievable colors at all levels of luminous intensity. Determinations are made with respect to the CIE System, so that the ability to describe colors in the related standard terms will be an inherent part of the developed color model. The usual representation of the video gamut, illustrated in Figure 7, can be misleading and it should be remembered that each of the full intensity red, green, and blue phosphor primaries lie at different levels of luminous intensity. A single line of the gamut triangle is actually a projection of the chromaticities of the mixtures of two of the phosphors with no contribution of the third. For example, the line between the red and green phosphors describes all of the colors achievable for all intensities of red combined with all intensities of green, with no blue contribution. Luminance varies as a function of the luminous intensities of the contributing phosphors, but it is not apparent on the diagram.

In order to develop an accurate appearance-based color model, a three dimensional configuration which permits description of both chromatic and luminance attributes is necessary. However, the solid cannot simply consist of the RGB triangle projected through all levels of luminance because the range of achievable colors becomes smaller as luminous intensity approaches the maximum level or the white point. In addition, it is necessary to represent black by a unique point, and as a result, the color solid must taper to this point at zero luminous intensity. As the white to black range describes only luminance variation, this entire series of neutrals should have the same u´, v´ coordinates.

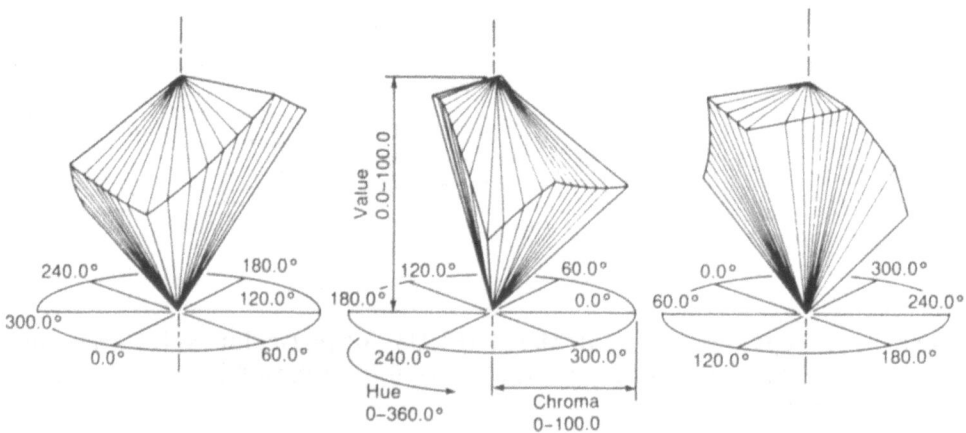

Figure 9.   The HVC Color Solid from three perspectives. All reachable video colors can be specified in terms of the three independent color attributres; Hue, Value, and Chroma. Red is defined at Hue=0.0°. Tektronix 4300 Series phosphor Red is located at 13.0°, phosphor Green at 117.3°, and phosphor Blue at 262.2°.

The lines that connect all maximum chromas and the surface below consist of binary combinations of the display phosphors. The white point is achieved by approaching the maximum luminous intensity of all three phosphors. The colors found within the color space are all achieved by varying the luminous intensity of the three phosphors in discrete quantifiable fashion. For example, starting from the white point, if phosphor outputs are decreased while maintaining the same relative proportions of luminous intensity, the resulting color goes from white, through gray, and approaches black. The functions that maintain consistent progression along chromatic attributes are much more complex.

Achieving a uniform perceptual-based color system requires derivation of functions that describe the colorimetric performance of the display phosphors and permits their specification along perceptual attributes. The HVC Color Solid, illustrated in Figure 9, and the underlying HVC Color System provide such a specification.

In a similarity to the HLS system, *Hue* is the property associated with color family (i.e. red, yellow, etc.). Hue is designated as an angle ranging from 0°.to 360.0°. Unlike the HLS system, Hue = 0.0 represents the best perceived red. This conforms to the layout of conventional color-order systems such as the Munsell System[10] and the Swedish Natural Color System (NCS).[11] In order to assure consistency of HVC color performance between devices with different colorimetric ranges, with respect to the 1976 CIE UCS Diagram, the position of the line between the 9300° K white point and the location of "best red" was determined by experiment and fixed. For the Tektronix 4300 Series Workstations, the full-intensity phosphor red was determined to be somewhat orange in appearance. It should be noted that hues are distributed uniformly around the hue circle on the basis of their appearance and not according to numerical designations. As a result, full Red (at RGB 255, 0, 0) for the 4300 Series displays is located at Hue = 13.0 Full intensity Green falls at Hue = 117.3° and full intensity Blue at 262.2°.

The second parameter of the HVC system is *Value*. Value is the term used to describe variation in lightness. In the neutral center of the system, value has the largest range from black (zero) to white (100.0). Value is a function of luminous intensity.

Chroma is the HVC parameter that describes the saturation or vibrancy of a color, which represents its difference from the neutral center at the same level of lightness. Colors within the HVC System are quantified relative to the Chroma of the most saturated primary, which, in the case of typical CRT's is the red phosphor. For an implementation which utilizes a phosphor or other color primary component that exceeds the colorimetric saturation of the 4300 Series phosphor red, the numerical value of Chroma may exceed 100.0. However, since some colors are perceived as being more saturated than others, the maximum achievable chroma for any hue/lightness designation is often less than 100.0. This is an inherent part of human color perception and as a result must be built into any color interface that is user oriented. The irregular shape of the HVC color solid is not jagged, but consists of triangular shaped leaves of varying sizes. The lines extending between the white point and maximum chroma for all hues demonstrate varying degrees of slight inward curvature.

The HVC system provides a color space that demonstrates enhanced visual uniformity. As a result, equal physical distances along any given dimension of either hue, value, or chroma, are representative of equally perceived color differences. The algorithms that define the HVC system provide an extension of the CIE 1976 Uniform Chromaticity Scales Diagram and the related CIELUV color metrics to the display domain. HVC also attempts to improve on these standard color models by enhancing the overall uniformity of the display color space and allows reversible transformation between RGB, HVC, CIELUV, or any color system relatable to one of these models.

2.4.3 *System Calibration:* The accurate description of the HVC color solid and the underlying attribute model require a series of algorithms which access device colorimetry and calibration data.

In order to ensure the colorimetric accuracy of colors generated using the HVC system, calibration of the display device and determination of display-dependent colorimetric characteristics are the essential first steps. Colorimetric data, in the form of CIE tristimulus values, XYZ, relative to a given illuminant and standard observer, must be obtained for each of the primaries in the display system. A function, f, may then be generated, which describes the display primaries in colorimetric terms, as well as defining the range of available colors for the device. The inverse function, f^{-1}, must then be determined, as it is the path through which the HVC algorithms facilitate all color conversions. In a video-based (CRT) display, this inverse function is a matrix, $[A]^{-1}$ (termed inverse A matrix), which describes the relationship between the primary red, green, and blue phosphor outputs and conventional colorimetric parameters. Secondly, verification of the white point colorimetry should be made to assure that all colors are being described relative to the desired white point and so calculations can be made using the correct white point coordinates.

In addition, it is also necessary to characterize the intensity profile of the display. As an example, for implementation on a video display, gamma data establishes the relationship between display intensity and DAC (digital-to-analog converter) level. Data may be obtained at every DAC for each primary phosphor, or may be taken in discrete intervals and the intermediate values obtained via interpolation. After testing a number of mathematical models, a fifth-order linear regression was determined to provide a good prediction of intensity response when the interpolation approach is desired. No matter how intensity data are determined, the data are stored in look-up tables which are a part of the overall video-based implementation. Storing the equations that characterize the data and calculating the desired intensities, as needed, would also be a plausible

Since each display device has individual characteristics in terms of color, the implementation of the HVC system requires the generation of algorithm constants for each device in order to ensure accurate color rendition. These constants are generally calculated once for each display and then stored. New constants need only be redetermined upon obtaining new calibration data for the display device in question.

Apart from the calibration utility, the calculation of the HVC solid is done via a set of algorithms. These algorithms are capable of generating exactly the same color solid, based on display colorimetry as well as intensity response data and actually function very closely together coupling color conversions in one direction (HVC to RGB) as well as the inverse (RGB to HVC). As a result, calculation of the limits and functions that describe the device color space permit direct addressing of display color. Colorimetric performance is, of course, directly related to the level of calibration obtained.

2.4.4 *Measurement Verification:* Verification of the performance of the HVC algorithms was first made by exhaustive checking of the reversibility of the conversions between HVC and RGB notations as well as those between HVC and CIELUV notations. The algorithms were found to provide repeatable, completely reversible calculation of notations throughout the color space.

Preliminary measurements to verify the performance of the HVC algorithms were carried out on a single Tektronix 4336 Color Monitor. All measurements were taken in a darkened laboratory and data were collected for 47 discrete HVC notations including samples along the neutral Value scale as well as chromatic samples throughout the color solid. The predicted and measured tristimulus values for each of the samples, as well as a calculation of the CIELUV color difference, $\Delta E_{u,v}$, can be found in Table 1. The RMS $\Delta E_{u,v}$ for the 47 colors was 1.98 CIELUV color difference units. A difference of 1.0 represents the perceptual threshold for a just discernable difference[5].

Most color samples exhibited a tendency towards a measured L^* that was slightly less than the predicted Value. After later analysis of the experimental set-up and data, it was felt that the time between successive measurements may have been too short and that short-term CRT stability may be contributing to the error. It is also possible that some other measurement-related factors, such as the currently implemented detector linearity correction, may be at fault. A second trend that was noted were slight systematic shifts in the measured values of u^* and v^*, which was categorized as a potential measurement-related problem but could also stem from less than optimal gamma data obtained for one or two of the phosphor guns. As a result, a new measurement procedure designed to account for these sources of error has been devised and a more comprehensive set of verification measurements planned.

Despite the aforementioned measurement problems, the accuracy of HVC color production lies well within accepted tolerances for color specification. The opportunity is now provided for users to enter specific desired colors, such as Kodak"[†] Yellow or Pepsi"[‡] Red and, provided that they are reachable by the display technology, obtain faithful rendition of that color on the display screen.

Of particular importance for interactive visualization and the quantitative use of color is the facility for automatic smooth gray scaling. Because the underlying model is perceptual in nature and the numeric elements scaled in human visual terms, it is possible to select any two points in the color space and connect them with a smooth gray scale.

2.5 The User Interface to Color

As the complexity of the color capabilities of graphic display systems has increased, so has the demand on the user to manipulate colors in a meaningful manner. Selecting or editing colors 16 million color addresses is a formidable task requiring the application of visualization techniques in itself. The early triplet system in which the user entered in a set of numbers corresponding to electron gun levels in RGB or color positions in HLS were less than intuitive. The problem was confounded by the non-linear relations between the colors and the lack of a correspondence between numerical magnitude of the differences between color addresses and the resulting perceptual color difference[2].

More recently, a number of graphic color interfaces have been introduced which allow the user to manipulate and edit colors visually. These often consist of slider or scroll bars representing the range of available levels of RGB or HLS. A circular arrangement of hues with a slider for lightness is used by the Apple" Macintosh II"[††] product's color selection/editing tool.

[†] Kodak is a registered trademark of the Eastman Kodak Company.

[‡] Pepsi is a registered trademark of the Pepsi-Cola Corporation.

[††] Apple and Macintosh are registered trademarks of Apple Computer, Inc.

Target						Measured			ΔE
Hue	Value	Chroma	L^*	u^*	v^*	L^*	u^*	v^*	
0.00	10.00	0.00	10.00	0.00	0.00	9.06	0.18	-0.06	0.96
0.00	20.00	0.00	20.00	0.00	0.00	18.58	1.41	0.06	2.00
0.00	30.00	0.00	30.00	0.00	0.00	28.44	1.25	-0.64	2.11
0.00	40.00	0.00	40.00	0.00	0.00	38.29	1.47	-0.66	2.36
0.00	50.00	0.00	50.00	0.00	0.00	49.53	1.34	0.04	1.43
0.00	60.00	0.00	60.00	0.00	0.00	59.91	1.00	-0.30	1.05
0.00	70.00	0.00	70.00	0.00	0.00	70.25	1.48	-0.61	1.62
0.00	80.00	0.00	80.00	0.00	0.00	80.42	1.23	-0.79	1.52
0.00	90.00	0.00	90.00	0.00	0.00	90.81	1.26	-1.00	1.80
0.00	100.00	0.00	100.00	0.00	0.00	99.97	0.33	0.24	0.41
135.00	40.00	14.08	40.00	-17.26	17.23	37.71	-16.06	16.19	2.79
195.00	40.00	8.43	40.00	-14.10	-3.79	37.67	-12.93	-5.37	3.05
255.00	40.00	21.02	40.00	-9.45	-35.14	38.15	-8.73	-36.25	2.27
315.00	40.00	23.18	40.00	28.36	-28.38	38.28	29.13	-28.45	1.89
15.00	40.00	73.99	40.00	123.75	33.17	40.22	126.69	33.82	3.01
135.00	40.00	28.17	40.00	-34.51	34.50	37.92	-32.77	33.51	2.89
195.00	40.00	16.87	40.00	-28.23	-7.56	38.09	-26.44	-8.62	2.83
255.00	40.00	42.04	40.00	-18.86	-70.32	38.63	-17.49	-72.34	2.80
315.00	40.00	46.36	40.00	56.77	-56.76	39.50	57.28	-55.94	1.08
0.00	60.00	32.49	60.00	55.64	-0.08	58.73	57.44	0.20	2.22
120.00	60.00	29.69	60.00	-22.65	39.20	58.40	-22.84	38.74	1.68
180.00	60.00	12.71	60.00	-22.03	-0.01	58.47	-22.20	-1.24	1.97
240.00	60.00	20.19	60.00	-17.52	-30.27	58.49	-17.24	-31.89	2.23
300.00	60.00	37.46	60.00	32.39	-56.16	58.59	31.80	-57.29	1.91
0.00	60.00	64.98	60.00	112.60	0.05	59.07	113.92	1.22	1.99
120.00	60.00	59.38	60.00	-45.29	78.43	58.78	-45.65	78.82	1.33
180.00	60.00	25.42	60.00	-44.00	0.00	59.22	-43.78	-0.77	1.12
240.00	60.00	40.39	60.00	-34.96	-60.54	59.07	-34.31	-63.19	2.88
300.00	60.00	74.93	60.00	64.86	-112.37	59.61	63.71	-113.54	1.69
30.00	80.00	15.65	80.00	23.48	13.55	79.21	22.29	12.94	1.56
90.00	80.00	17.54	80.00	-0.01	30.34	79.18	-0.78	29.74	1.27
150.00	80.00	21.41	80.00	-32.11	18.52	79.06	-32.65	17.29	1.64
210.00	80.00	18.01	80.00	-27.00	-15.61	79.03	-27.23	-17.12	1.81
270.00	80.00	17.19	80.00	-0.01	-29.76	79.10	-0.63	-31.22	1.82
330.00	80.00	14.32	80.00	21.51	-12.38	79.16	20.82	-13.77	1.77
30.00	80.00	31.30	80.00	46.87	27.15	79.25	46.88	28.27	1.35
90.00	80.00	35.07	80.00	0.01	60.72	79.19	-0.65	61.56	1.34
150.00	80.00	42.82	80.00	-64.20	37.06	79.56	-64.50	36.93	0.55
210.00	80.00	36.03	80.00	-53.99	-31.19	79.65	-53.94	-33.63	2.47
270.00	80.00	34.38	80.00	0.05	-59.54	79.19	-0.50	-62.37	2.99
330.00	80.00	28.64	80.00	43.00	-24.78	78.97	43.12	-25.98	1.59

RMS $\Delta E_{u,v}$ = 1.98

Table 1. Preliminary measurement data for selected HVC color samples. CIELUV tristimulus values predicted using the HVC algorithms are compared to values for each display color obtained by spectroradiometric measurement. The resulting color difference, (CIELUV $\Delta E_{u,v}$) is calculated. All calculations were made using the monitor white point, (1976 CIE UCS) u´ = 0.1917, v´ = 0.4416 with a luminance of 51.7 fL, and the 1931 CIE 2° Standard Observer.

While these interfaces go a long way towards rendering a visual representation of a color, they often fail on the attributes of the underlying color model. In the Macintosh II interface , for example, the user is asked to specify colors in triplets ranging from zero to 65,000. Most numeric changes are not accompanied by any immediate visual change on the graphic display.

The HVC Color model presented an interesting challenge to develop a graphic interface. The very nature of the color model necessitates a visual interface as the variations in available chroma and value levels associated with each hue render the model very spatially complex.

The interface must present the system in a way that is straightforward and meaningful, thus it must enhance the user's concept of a color's general appearance, assist in the visualization of the color within the system framework, and then provide a functional means to physically describe and/or access that color.   This needs to be accomplished in both an accurate and timely fashion.

There are many other considerations that are factors in the design of an integrated interface package. For example, possible software, firmware, or hardware constraints, the types of available or practical input devices, the environment in which the product may be utilized, and in particular, the tasks that will most likely be performed by the user. In addition, the interface or limited aspects of it often need to be consistent throughout a series of display products with a variety of capabilities. A need may also exist for compatibility with previously existing or future display implementations.

There is generally not one single, "best interface", and a variety of implementations
may provide a desirable level of functionality and utility to the user. Graphics is a dynamic means of illustration that will aid the user considerably in the visualization of the color system and, as a result, enhance the capability to select colors within the color solid. In addition, graphics applications will be the principal use of the display products in which the HVC system is initially implemented. An interface designed around a graphics implementation will provide a natural extension to the tasks being addressed by these users.

The current implementation of the user interface to HVC employs two-dimensional graphics to systematically illustrate the three dimensional HVC color solid. As a result, the current interface is designed to present constant hue leaves that represent the available value and chroma ranges for any selected hue. This is a natural way to organize a collection of colors, since the process of color selection is most often a procedure in which a color is chosen first on the basis of its color family (i.e. hue). Once a decision is made on the hue, the next task is to decide what particular variant of that color family is desired; should it be dark or light, vibrant or subdued? An interface organized in such a way allows the user to move through the color system in a manner that is similar to the thought process associated with color selection.

Upon initialization of the interface to the HVC system, the first hue page displayed is the H=0 plane, representing a family of red colors. The user may "step around" the hue circle, selecting the desired hue page through the use of function keys.   A representative hue page from the current implementation of the interface is seen in Figure 10. Each hue page is enclosed in a square, with Chroma varying along the horizontal axis from zero on the left to 100 on the right. Value is represented along the vertical axis (at Chroma = zero) with zero at the origin and 100 at the uppermost point. The limits on available value and chroma are denoted by the triangular outline pictured within the square. In the version of the interface portrayed in Figure 10, the range of accessible levels of value and chroma for the 180° hue (cyan) are shown for a video monitor (Tektronix 4319) and a color printer (Tektronix ColorQuick®). The solid line portrays the monitor boundary while the broken line indicates the ranges for the pr inter. Obviously value and chroma levels common to both devices indicate colors common to the monitor and printer.

TekICI™ Tektronix Interactive Color Interface ©Tektronix 1989

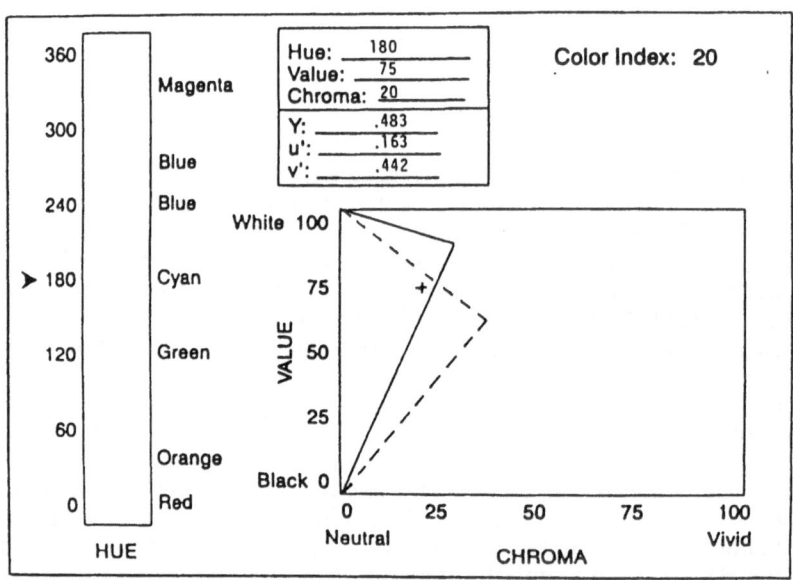

Figure 10. A representative hue page from a current implementation of the HVC interface illustrating the hue bar, value/chroma page, archive color region, and display of HVC and CIE color notations.

The current active location within the color leaf is represented with a flashing cursor, which is denoted as a filled-in square about four times larger than the boundary dots. Movement of the cursor, and thus movement throughout the hue leaf is accomplished using a mouse. A horizontal movement controls position along or parallel to the Chroma axis, while a vertical excursion regulates movement along or parallel to the Value axis. Motion of the cursor invokes instantaneous change to the active color area to reflect the nature and magnitude of the repositioning. In addition, the display also provides interactive data on the appropriate CIE u´ and v´ coordinates for the designated color. Fine adjustment of cursor position, in one unit steps, is accomplished using the SHIFT key in conjunction with mouse movement.

The color of the active color area is currently shown in a square that is positioned above the hue leaf plot. The appearance of this square varies to display the precise color within a given color map index that is defined by the H, V, and C coordinates dictated by the stipulated hue page and cursor position. The current implementation allows movement of the cursor both within and outside of the triangle denoting a hue page's achievable color. When the user moves the mouse in such a way as to cross the triangle boundary and the cursor rests on an area which represents a color outside of the video gamut, the active color area reverts to the color that was last defined for the color map index in question (through a mouse click). This signals that the user has exceeded the bounds on available colors for the display device in question.

2.5.1   Interface - Development Potential: As mentioned previously, there are a number of interfaces and implementations that will provide the user with the desired capability to access and utilize the HVC system. In designing the current interface, the goal was to develop a firmware/software program that illustrated the features and advantages of the HVC system that was relatively easy to implement, thus serving as a prototype. In working to develop this interface, numerous ideas were raised as potential modifications and desirable features that might be incorporated into the final version. The points enumerated in this section are by no means an exhaustive list, but are discussed in order to illustrate the development potential of the color graphics interface to the HVC system.

It is possible to stipulate the hue through the use of a variety of input devices, and not necessarily through the exclusive use of function keys. Stipulation of the hue through the direct keyboard input of numerical designations may also be attempted. The use of numbers via the keyboard would be needed for graphics programming, however, as part of a graphics interface, it is of questionable utility. Another alternative is a separate illustration showing a band or circle of hues that the user can access with a locater device, such as a mouse, thumbwheels, or a joystick. In addition, the hue may be selected using a voice command.

Currently, the hue page is a simple two color graphic consisting of a single color triangle boundary framed by a square. It is possible, however, to display the hue page in such a way as to exploit the color capabilities of different display devices through the use of limited or full color. In the full color implementation, the entire leaf may be displayed in such a way that the color of each pixel is determined by the selected hue and the relative position of that pixel within the hue leaf. The resulting graphic is continuously shaded. When only limited color indices are available, the leaf may contain color at prescribed intervals, or in other assigned locale.

Movement of the cursor may be accomplished through the use of a number of input devices including a mouse, joystick, or thumbwheels. It should be noted that if the same device is to be utilized in the selection of hue, then a means must be available to indicate the different input modes. This might include a button or switch which could be coupled with direct display feedback, such as flashing or reverse video, indicating the current active mode.

3. Color Fidelity

The accurate control of color on a visual display provides only a partial solution to the overall problem of color. Once the correct set of colors has been selected it is desirable, often imperative, that those colors be correctly translated to an output medium such as a printer or film. Again the emergence of an awareness of the problem of matching colors between devices has been strengthened by the distinction between qualitative and quantitative color. A business graphic may lose some of its aesthetic appeal if the screen colors do not match the printer colors but the information portrayed is not damaged so long as colors rendered as distinct in one medium remain distinct in the other. For quantitative colors, however, the information is contained in the color difference and must be rendered faithfully between the devices.

In order to capture the essence of the color fidelity problem this review will concentrate on the specifics of matching the colors on a visual display to those of a printed output. For the display a CRT image is assumed and for the printer the individual characteristics of an ink jet printer and thermal printer will be considered. To understand the fundamental problem a brief review of the underlying processes of color production and mixture in the display and printer is in order.

3.1 Color Mixture

The process by which inks and dyes are combined to produce colors is called subtractive color mixture while the generation of colors through combinations of phosphor emissions follows the process of additive color mixture.

3.1.1 Subtractive color mixture: The perceived color of a surface, such as a sheet of paper, depends upon the capacity of the surface to reflect some wavelengths and absorb others. When a surface is dyed with a particular pigment, a new reflectance characteristic is created based on the capacity of the dye to absorb some wavelengths and reflect others. A surface dyed yellow, for example, might reflect wavelengths above 570 to 580 nm while absorbing most of the longer and shorter wavelengths. Figure 11a diagrams the energy distribution of a yellow pigment. Consider another surface dyed magenta such that wavelengths of 400 to 480nm and 560 to 600nm predominate. This energy distribution is shown in Figure 11b. If one were to mix both pigments and deposit them

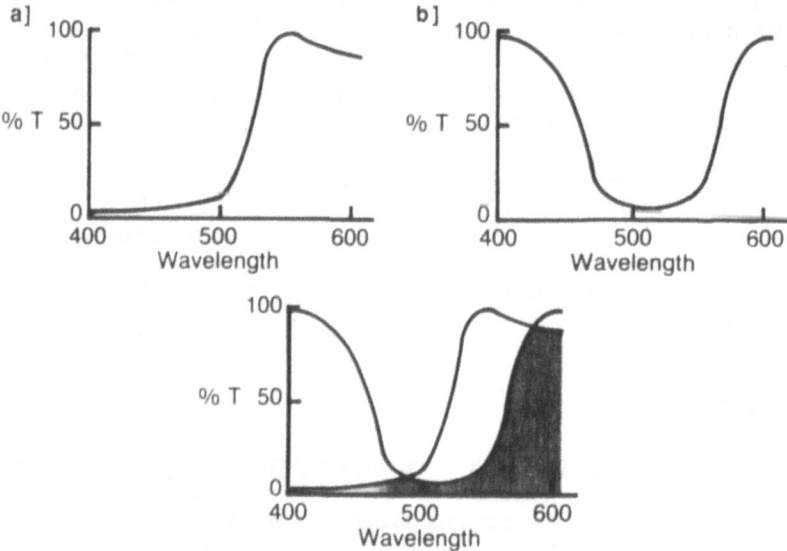

Figure 11. An example of subtractive color mixing. a) representative spectrum of a yellow pigment; b) representative spectrum of a magenta pigment; c) the spectrum of a red color from the mixture of a) and b).

on a surface, the resulting color would be red. The mixture of magenta and yellow produces red because the yellow pigment absorbs all of the short wavelengths (500nm and below) and the magenta absorbs all of the wavelengths between 480 and 560nm. The energy distribution of the mixture is shown in Figure 11c. Thus, the yellow absorbs wavelengths which evoke the sensation of blue while the magenta absorbs those wavelengths associated with green. What is "left over" is a band of wavelengths that evoke the sensation of red. This type of color mixture is called *subtractive color mixture* as bands of wavelengths are subtracted or cancelled by the combination of light-absorbing materials. If we add a third pigment to the mixture of yellow and magenta – one that absorbs the band of lower wavelengths such as cyan – the surface would appear black because all of the light falling upon it would be absorbed. By this process of eliminating parts of the reflectance distribution through varying the amounts of each pigment, intermediate hues can be created. In the example, the resulting red would not be very light as much of the illumination falling on the surface is absorbed. The mixture of two pigments produces a reflectance surface which absorbs more light than either pigment alone.

Color hard copy, then, is produced by the subtractive combination of inks or dyes. In most applications the three primaries used are yellow, cyan (blue-green) and magenta. These three in all possible combinations provide a minimum palette of eight colors as shown in Table 2 below.

TABLE 2   Subtractive Colors

Color	Subtractive Combination
Red	Yellow + Magenta
Green	Cyan + Yellow
Blue	Magenta + Cyan
Yellow	Yellow
Cyan	Cyan
Magenta	Magenta
White	—
Black	Yellow + Cyan + Magenta

Often pure black (notated as K) is included as fourth color simply because the three primaries which produce the best chromatic color usually do not produce the best black. The color set is abbreviated CMYK.

To extend the hard copy palette beyond eight colors requires that different levels of the colors occur in each mixture. Two density levels of each primary increase the palette to 26 colors. An alternative means of extending the color gamut to much larger palettes is to employ a technique known as *half toning* in which colors are placed on the paper as tiny dots that can either vary in frequency or size. Pure red, for example, would require the highest dot frequency (i.e., 200 dots per inch) while a desaturated pink would result when the dot frequency was reduced to 120 dots per inch. In this technique, the resulting hue occurs as a result of the *additive mixture* of red and the white of the paper, whereby the dot frequency defines the density of the color component.

The size of the color palette depends, of course, on the number of perceptually discriminable densities that can be produced for each primary. Currently, it is difficult to obtain more than 15 to 20 discriminable densities which limits the hard copy palette to less than 9261 perceivable colors. Also the density of a given pigment does not increase linearly with increased absorption or dot frequency. That is, the hard copy color system has a "gamma" in which a large change in density occurs with a small initial absorption increase followed by a progressively lower amount of change as maximum density is reached. An uncorrected gamma will produce a number of indiscriminable levels at the higher densities. Additionally, the combination of two discriminable levels, each of which are visible against a third color, may not be discriminable from the third color. The total available palette, then, will always be some number of colors less than the number of color addresses.

3.1.2 Additive color mixture: Colors can be mixed in another fashion in which bands of wavelengths are added to one another. In fact, this method of additive color mixture forms the underlying principle by which the visual system "mixes" colors. Additive color mixture is also the means by which color is produced on a color display.

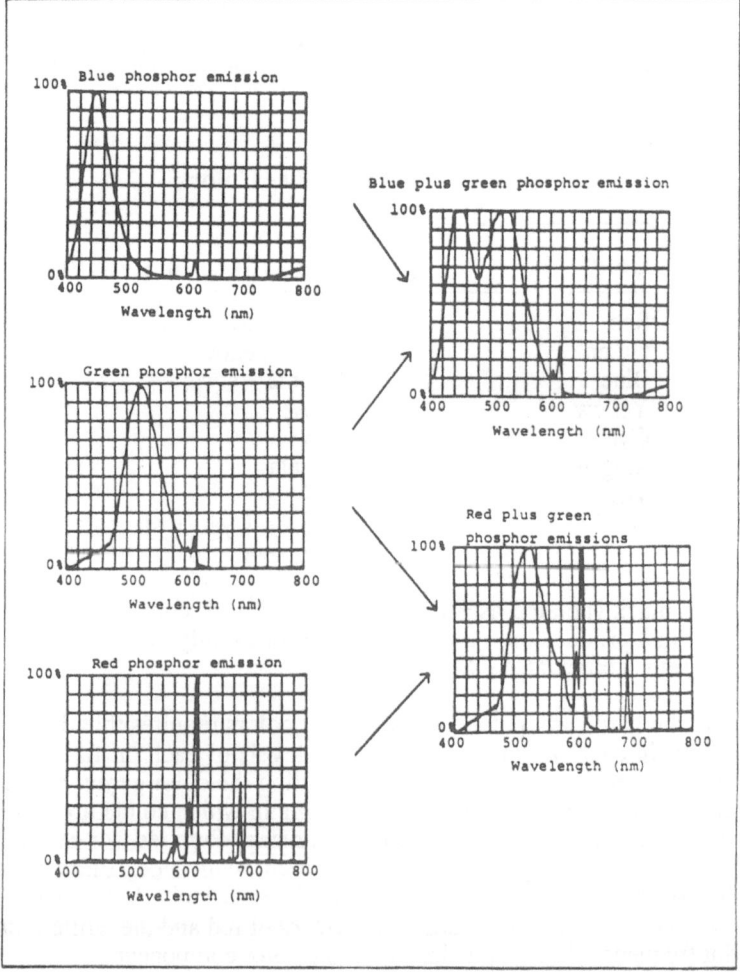

Figure 12. Additive color mixture with phosphor emissions.

The surface of a typical color display is made up of thousands of tiny dots of phosphor. The phosphors on the screen are grouped into threes – called *triads* – with one phosphor emitting long wavelength light (red), one emitting middle wavelength light (green) and the third emitting short wavelength light (blue). To display a red object on the screen, for example, all the red phosphors forming the outline and the interior of the object are made to emit light. A green or blue object would be produced in the same manner.

Intermediate hues to red, green and blue are produced by simultaneously making two or more of the three phosphors in a triad emit light. Because the phosphor dots are very small, when viewed from a distance the output of the three members of the triad fuse together or add to one another. The result is a homogeneous appearing field of color. The principle is shown in Figure 12.

The top left graph shows the energy distribution of a typical blue phosphor while the middle left indicates the energy distribution of a typical green phosphor. When both are additively combined, the mixture shown on the right is produced. The mixture consists of a broader band of wavelengths which means that the mixture will be less saturated than the blue or green alone. The lower left chart shows the emission of a red phosphor which is combined with green in the lower right panel. The resulting hue of the mixture will be yellow. The exact color of the yellow would depend upon the relative intensities of the red and green phosphors. Increasing the amount of red while decreasing green would move the color towards orange. Conversely, increasing the intensity of the green would shift the mixture towards a yellow-green. Note that the mixture of two phosphors does not necessarily produce more energy in the wavelength region corresponding to the perceived hue. In fact, the mixture of two single wavelength, monochromatic lights can be adjusted to match a yellow – a yellow for which no energy is present in the emission spectra of either of the phosphors. Basically the perceived color on a visual display depends upon the ratio of intensities of the primary phosphors.

3.2 Color Matching

As colors are produced in such a different manner by a display and a printer it is not surprising that the output of the devices appears vastly different. There is no simple algorithm to translate from one medium to the other. A blue can be produced on the display by specifying some level of the blue electron gun output and on a printer by requesting some combination of magenta and cyan. While most observers would agree that both colors are blue, they are very dissimilar in hue, lightness and saturation. Before discussing potential solutions to the display and printer color match it is necessary to understand what is implied by the expression color match.

There are two basic classifications of color matches; *invariant* and *conditional*. Invariant color matches are ones that have identical spectrophotometric curves and thus are visual matches for all observers under all illuminants. This is a very strict type of color match that requires colorants, substrates, processing (application), and viewing conditions that are identical for both matched samples. In almost all cases, this type of match is difficult and sometimes impossible to achieve. As a result, it becomes necessary to make close matches under a limited set of illuminating and viewing conditions. This is defined as a conditional match‡‡ . Conditional matches are the ones most often made in

---

‡‡ The term conditional is often used interchangeably with the term *metameric*. If two samples are seen to have the same color or match when viewed under the same light source, yet the samples no longer match under a second source, the spectral response curves of each are different. Even though two colors may have different spectral response curves, they are defined and will appear as a match if their CIE tristimulus values are the same for a given illuminant and observer. Samples that exhibit this behavior are displaying the phenomenon of *metamerism* and are referred to as *metamers*. Metamerism is generally the result of two colored samples being prepared in different ways, (i.e different colorants and/or substrates)

color-dependent industries due to the variability of available raw materials and the high cost that is generally associated with creating invariant matches.

For matches between printer and display, conditional matches are the only option. Several approaches to conditional matching have been offered. The simplest approach is that of the visual match in which observers select printed samples which visually resemble corresponding samples on a CRT (or select CRT colors to match printed samples). The obvious drawback to this approach, the magnitude of the task not withstanding, lies in the lack of any referent standard. The matches obtained, at best, will hold for the particular printer and display used, for the actual observers doing the matches and for the illumination conditions under which the matches were made. A change in any of these elements will produce a lack of color match.

A second approach to matching can be described as *gamut mapping*. This technique has been developed by Xerox[12]. The basic concept lies in the fact that the colors on the display and on the printer can be described colorimetrically by the calculation of the color gamut or space of each device. By measuring the XYZ values for the display and the gamma function relating DAC to light output a three dimensional volume of colors can be created that describes the color palette of the display. Similarly it is possible to create a color volume for the printer. In this case the XYZ values produced by combinations of inks or dyes on a white paper are calculated. The complete volume is formed by assessing the XYZ definitions of the range of colors produced by half toning. The color space thus created is correct only for the specific illuminant under which the measurements were made. Viewing the colors under a different light source changes the relations and shape of the volume. Figure 13 shows a two dimensional representation of the color gamut of a typical CRT and that of a typical ink jet printer. Note that this diagram does not show luminance variations but rather represents a slice at a constant luminance level. Obviously some colors are common to both the printer and display.

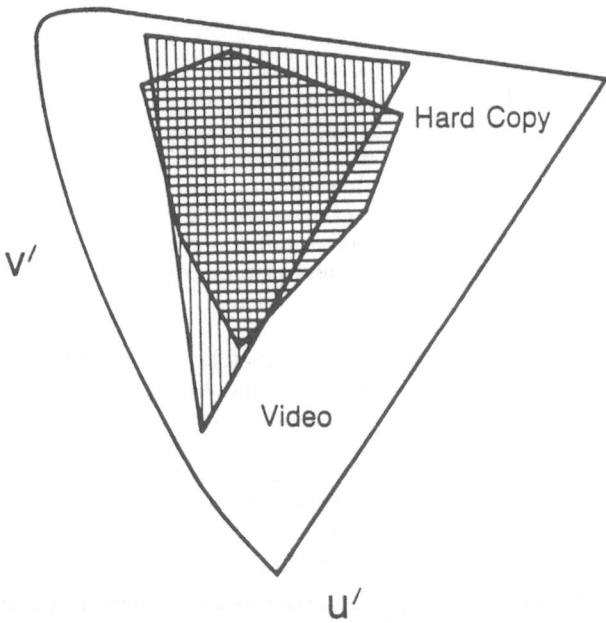

Figure 13. 2D representations of the color gamuts of typical CRT and ink jet printer, relative to the 1976 CIE UCS Diagram.

The process of gamut mapping consists of a transformation of one color space into the other. In practice gamut mapping involves three distinct transformations. The first transformation involves the gray scale range of white through gray to black. The range available on one device is rescaled on the second device so as to match the available range of distinctive gray levels and, at the same time, to maximize the contrast of the resulting image. This transformation also rescales the colors of the printer to fall within the range of the colors of the monitor. The general relationships between colors in terms of the magnitude of color difference is thus maintained. The general form of the process of locating a specific color on the printer becomes:

$$X_p = B_p + csf \times R \times (X_m - B_m)$$

where

X_p is the XYZ value of the printer color
X_m is the XYZ value of the monitor color
B_p is the XYZ value of the printer black
B_m is the XYZ value of the monitor black
R is the rotation matrix
csf is the contrast scale factor

The net result of the process is that the gamut of the monitor has now been mapped to the gamut of the printer. This process is very much like taking one irregular shaped object and deforming it to fit coincidentally into the second, differently shaped object.

The second transformation deals with colors which end up outside the gamut of the printer as a result of the limits placed on the mapping process. This transformation, termed the umbrella transformation, attempts to offset the loss of contrast that occurs in images with highly saturated colors. This is done by increasing or decreasing the saturation levels of the colors to be mapped while keeping luminance contrast as high as possible. The attempt is made to maintain the same hue in the transformed color.

The final transformation in the gamut mapping technique is to allow some colors to actually exist in the monitor image that could not be printed by the output device. These are truncated to the surface of most saturated colors producable by the printer. The result is a preservation of chromatic contrast.

While gamut mapping does provide a means of obtaining palettes of highly similar colors, the degree of similarity depends upon the color ranges of the devices. In fact very few of the gamut matched colors actually match one another. They are just similar. This is because the mapping technique maintains only a few truly conditional matched points and selects sets of nearest neighbors to the desired color. An additional limitation is that the selection of gamut ranges is based on Euclidean distances between the XYZ values. The perceptual non-linearities of the XYZ color space are well documented. The result is that large perceptual differences will occur between pairs of colors which lie at equally distant points in the color space. The gamut mapping concept does attempt to keep the hue of mapped colors the same, again within the limits of the XYZ color space. From the perspective of conditional matching, it is known that humans are more sensitive to variations in hue than in lightness and saturation. Finally the process of gamut mapping does not provide for colorimetric fidelity between devices. That is the two visually similar colors may have different colorimetric (XYZ) values.

The researchers at Xerox who have developed the gamut matching technique point out that an interactive tool must be provided to the user of such a system to facilitate color editing of the resultant images. Clearly the human visual system must be the final judge of the color fidelity between monitor and printer and this system should be capable of performing key modifications to the images.

To date the gamut mapping concept represents the most comprehensive attempt to provide color fidelity between diverse color imaging media. It is a complex system with some drawbacks and strengths as indicated above. The complexity of the required transformations simply underscores the difficulty of the problem.

Another approach to the problem has been advanced by Hewlett-Packard[13]. These researchers point out that the gamut mapping technique remaps colors that were in fact the same between the monitor and printer images. They have advanced a new technique called *adaptive scaling* which is based on the concept that only colors which cannot be reached on the printer need to be rescaled. Several steps are required in adaptive matching. These include an analysis of the image in terms of detail content and a scaling of the lightness range. The compression of saturation is done only for those colors which fall outside the gamut of the printer. The compression allows changes in both hue and lightness and does not provide for all monitor colors to be forced within the bounds of the printer color space. A final image clipping insures that unwanted errors are equally distributed throughout the color ranges.

Adaptive scaling attempts to reduce the role of the operator in judging the effectiveness of the resultant transformation. It does, however, require that the operator understand the characteristics of the image to be printed and th paper and ink combination to be used. The reliance on the XYZ color definitions produces a similar problem to that noted with gamut scaling in that the magnitude of the numeric difference between colors in XYZ does not represent their perceptual difference.

A third approach, developed by Tektronix, is to define a conditional match as the equivalent of a colorimetric match[14]. This means that all common points in the two color gamuts of the devices to be matched that are in fact common to one another (see Figure 14) are mapped directly one into the other. Thus colors that have the same XYZ values will appear on the display and printer. This technique can capitalize on the colorimetric basis of the HVC system described previously. In essense the colors of the display are translated into their HVC equivalents and mapped to the same HVC values created by the printer. As with all matching systems, the maintenance of the illuminant is important as the HVC values will change if the illuminant is changed. The actual number of corresponding HVC values for printer and display will depend upon the technologies being mapped. For ink jet printers approximately 40% of the colors are common with a CRT while thermal printers have a common color space of about 50%.

The HVC approach has the advantage of maintaining common colorimetric definition for colors on different devices. This is, of course, only true for those colors common to both devices. For colors which can be created on one device but not the other a process similar to gamut mapping is used. Again the visual sensitivity to hue shifts is taken into account. To locate a displayable color which does not reside in the printer color gamut, the same hue is maintained and levels of chroma and value are sacrificed. One simple algorithm locates the printable color as the least squares distance in the sum of value and chroma between the desired display color and the nearest printable color of the same hue. Because the HVC system is derived from the CIE Uniform Color Space this Euclidean distance between colors produces a measure of their perceptual difference. One obvious application of this principle is that the user can select two points in the color space and obtain a smooth shaded color or gray scale between the two points. This smooth shaded scale is maintained when the image is shipped to the printer.

All of the algorithmic approaches discussed (gamut mapping, adaptive scaling and HVC) depend upon the ability to characterize the color gamut of the devices. For the CRT display this process is straightforward and involves, as noted, the calculation of the color volume on the basis of XYZ values and display gamma. For printer devices the process is more difficult[12]. This is because the change in XYZ with increasing ink or wax density does not follow a simple progression. Figure 14 shows the changes in color which occur with a thermal wax process as one steps the color from 100% Cyan, Yellow, Magenta, Red, Green and Blue to Black. Note that the progression is not a simple function. This complex relationship makes it very difficult to mathematically describe the colorimetric properties of the printer.

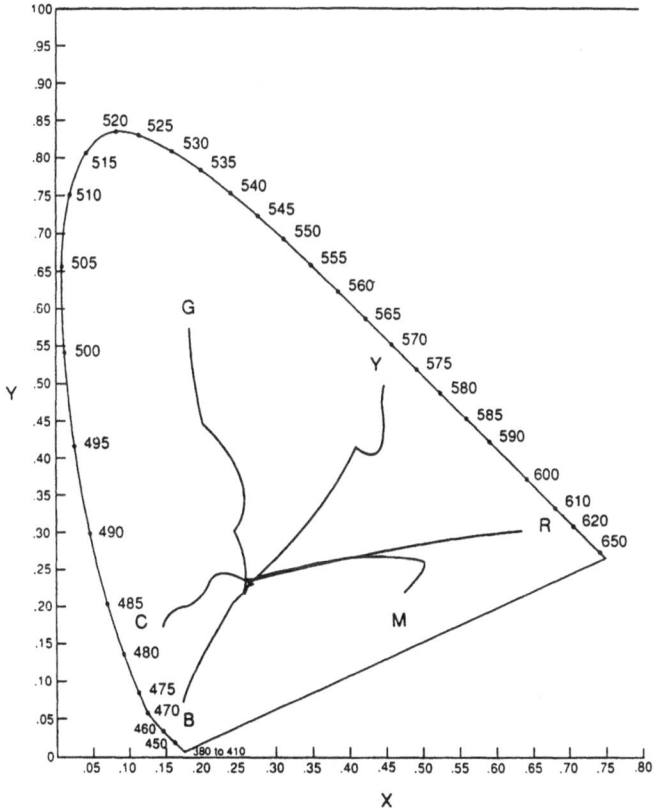

Figure 14. The changes in color which occur in a thermal wax transfer printing process as 100% of the colors, Cyan, Blue, Magenta, Red, Yellow and Green are stepped towards Black.

Color matching between devices which produce colors by very different means is possible to the degree that colors are common to both devices. Algorithms such as the location of nearest printable or displayable neighbor can locate similar colors between the media. One must be aware that certain limitations will always exist for inter-media matching. The illuminant under which a printed copy is viewed is one of the most critical. Of major importance is the recognition that much of human color perception is relational. That is, the appearance of a color depends critically upon the neighboring colors. Yet as we have become more aware of the need for quantitative color and the opportunities for data analysis through visualization, the techniques for improving matches have developed.

Given that the actual appearance of colors will vary dramatically depending upon the nature of other colors in the image it should be obvious that any algorithms designed to map colors between devices must be accompanied by operator interfaces that permit easy editing of the images. The final product is in fact the judgment of the viewer of the display and the printed image which is suggested that a mating to the visual system is imperative. Today's complex color systems, then, must provide the user with an intuitive interface to color, an underlying perceptual color model and a method of translating colors between various imaging devices. A description of the progress in bringing these elements together has been the focus of this review.

TekColor, TekHVC, and TekICI are trademarks of Tektronix, Inc.

REFERENCES CITED

1. Wilhelm Ostwald, Colour Science, (Authorized translation with an Introduction and Notes by J. Scott Taylor), Part I, Colour Theory and Colour Standardization, (1931); Part II, Applied Colour Science (1933); Windsor and Newton, Ltd., London, England.

2. Novia Weiman, Joann M. Taylor, Robert J. Beaton, and Roxanna Rochat, A Human Performance Comparison of Two Color Order Systems: HLS *vs.* RGB Using a Color Matching Task, Internal Technical Report Number HFR - 613 - 01, Tektronix Laboratories, (1986).

3. International Commission on Illumination, *Recommendations on Uniform Color Spaces, Color Difference Equations, and Psychometric Color Terms*, Supplement No. 2 to CIE Publication No. 15, E - 1.3.1 Colorimetry, 2nd ed., TC - 1.3 Colorimetry, Central Bureau de la CIE, Vienna, (1986).

4. Fred W. Billmeyer, Jr., and Max Saltzman, *Principles of Color Technology*, 2nd ed., Wiley Interscience, New York, (1981).

5. Gunter Wyszecki and W. S. Stiles, *Color Science*, 2nd ed., Wiley Interscience, New York, (1982).

6. International Commission on Illumination, *Proceedings of the Eighth Session*, Cambridge, England, Central Bureau de la CIE, Paris, (1931).

7. David L. MacAdam, Maximum Visual Efficiency of Colored Materials, *J. Opt. Soc. Am.*, **25**, 361-367, (1935).

8. Ewald Hering, *Outlines of a Theory of Light Sense*, translated by Leo M. Hurvich and Dorthea Jameson, Harvard University Press, Cambridge, (1964).

9. Gerald M. Murch, Color Display and Color Science, in H. John Durrett, *Color and the Computer*, Academic Press, Orlando, FL. (1987).

10. A.H. Munsell, *A Color Notation*, Munsell Color Company, Baltimore Maryland, (1936-1963).

11. Anders Hard and Lars Sivik, NCS - A Swedish Standard for Color Notation, *Col. Res. Appl.*, 6, 129-138, (1981).

12. Maureen C. Stone, William B. Cowan, and John C. Beatty, Color Gamut Mapping and the Printing of Digital Color Images, *ACM Transactions on Graphics*, 7, 249-292, (1988).

13. John Meyer and Brian Barth, Color Gamut Matching for Hard Copy. *SID Digest of Technical Papers*, Baltimore, MD. (1989).

14. Joann M. Taylor, Gerald M. Murch, and Paul McManus, Tektronix HVC: A Uniform Perceptual Color System for Display Users. *SID Digest of Technical Papers*, Baltimore, (1989).

Chapter 3
Advanced Topics in Solid Modeling

Martti Mäntylä

Abstract

Solid modeling is now a relatively well establihed technology widely used in various areas. Even so, many research problems of solid modeling are still being investigated, and much room for new results seems to exist. The tutorial explores some research directions which are under current study. In particular, advanced techniques for CSG visualization and for manipulating boundary models are described. It is assumed that the reader is familiar with basic techniques of solid modeling as presented in textbooks [29, 30].

1. Introduction

After an intensive research period started in the late 60's and the early 70's, solid modeling has now become a well known and widely used tool for various applications that require manipulation of three-dimensional geometry, including CAD, CAM, robotics, and scientific visualizaton. Besides numerous commercial modeling systems, the relative maturity of the field is indicated by the appearance of first textbooks in the area [29, 30].

Nevertheless, solid modeling is still quite far from being a perfectly mastered area, nor has research work on solid modeling ceased. On the contrary, increased practical interest to solid modeling has opened new research problems as new applications with their new demands emerge. This tutorial is aimed at exploring some areas where there have been recent important developments. It is assumed that the reader is familiar with the "standard" techniques of solid modeling as explained, e.g., in the textbooks refered to in the above, or in the survey [34].

The tutorial is organized as follows: First, some problems of current solid modelers are outlined in Section 2. This section also introduces the terminology used in the rest of the tutorial. The following sections are organized according to the major solid representations currently used in practical and research systems, namely *constructive models* and *boundary models*, and describe some promising developments that address the problems outlined in section 2. Next, we take a brief look into recent work on *feature modeling*, a new modeling paradigm aiming at wider coverage of product information. Finally, some conclusions concerning future modeling systems are drawn.

2. Deficiencies of Solid Modelers

2.1 Basic Approaches to Solid Modeling

Solid modeling can be broadly defined as "the art of designing data structures and algorithms for the creation, manipulation, and analysis of three-dimensional solid objects". Current solid modeling techniques can roughly be divided in three categories:

1.   *Decomposition models* that represent a solid object by means of a subdivision of space either in homogeneous blocks, or recursively in variable-sized blocks, or in curved (free-form) cells. The most common example of these representations is the *octree model* [27]. An octree model is illustrated in Figure 1.

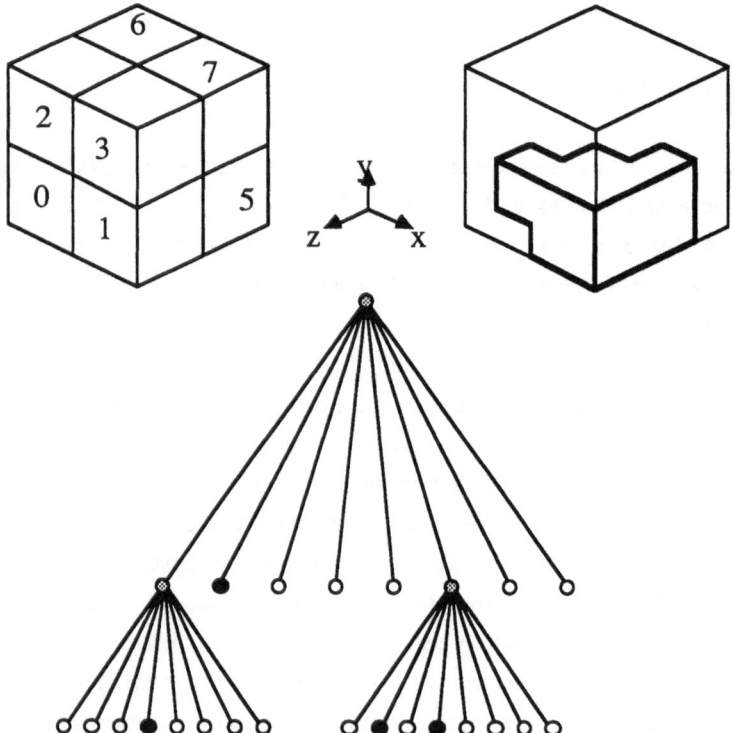

Figure 1: An octree model.

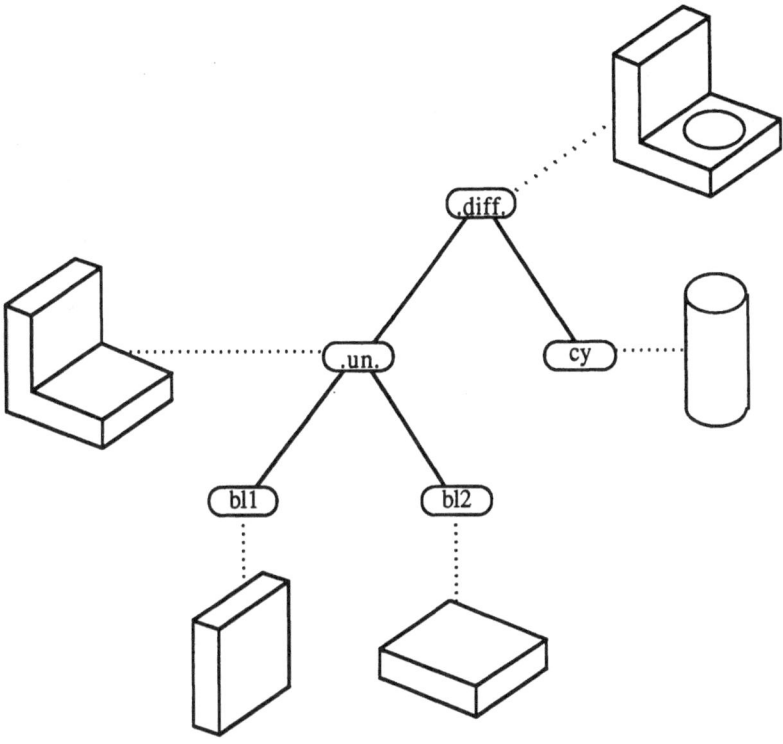

Figure 2: A CSG tree.

2.   *Constructive models* that represent a solid object as a combination of simple geometric shapes, such as blocks, cylinders, and tori (or, more generally, *half-spaces*). The most common case is the *Constructive Solid Geometry* (CSG) model [34], where a solid is described in terms of a *CSG tree* whose leaves represent the various primitives, and whose internal nodes represent either regularized Boolean set operations or rigid motions. The concepts of CSG models are visualized in Figure 2.

3.   *Boundary models* that represent a solid object by means of its bounding surface. Typically, the surface is subdivided into a set of nonoverlapping faces, bounded by edges and vertices; see Figure 3. Boundary models come in many varieties; a typical sample is the *winged-edge representation* originally introduced by Baumgart [2].

All of these models have their strengths and weaknesses. At the risk of oversimplification, we can summarize the characteristics of the typical representatives of the various models as follows [30]:

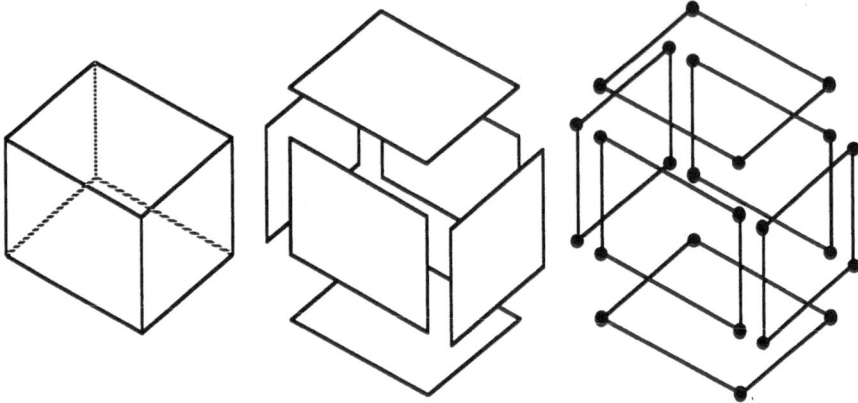

Figure 3: Concepts of boundary models.

1.   Octrees lead to relatively simple algorithms for many tasks, including the creation, visualization, analysis, and many manipulations of octrees. The validity of the models is easy to establish. Nevertheless, octree algorithms are very slow on conventional sequential hardware.

Because of their approximative nature, decomposition models are seldom used as the primary representation except when the original solid information is in voxel form (e.g., medical applications). Therefore, this tutorial will deal with decomposition models only as auxiliary ones used for analysis and visualization purposes.

2.   Constructive Solid Geometry (CSG) models are based on a rigorous mathematical theory that guarantees the validity of the model. The algorithms for CSG models form a well understood family, usually based on so-called *set membership classification* paradigm [47], a generalization of the well known ray tracing algorithm. Nevertheless, the algorithms are inefficient if implemented simplistically and may suffer from numerical accuracy problems.

3.   The creation and manipulation of typical boundary models can be encapsulated into a small set of basic operations — *Euler operators* — that preserve the topological validity of the model. The representation is well suited for many graphics applications and supports directly interactive manipulation typically needed in, e.g., CAD systems. However, boundary models are plagued by numerical problems, leading to independable algorithms for advanced operations such as the Boolean set operations. The numerical inaccuracies become particularly severe because the result of one operation is typically used as input of the next one.

As a result, many practical systems use several simultaneous representations to take advantage of the strengths of each model, and to avoid their inherent problems. Typically, either CSG or boundary models are used as the basic representation of such systems. These *hybrid modelers* suffer somewhat by the fact that some important conversions between various models are not available.

2.2 Characteristic Problems of Solid Modelers

As outlined in the above, some problems of solid modelers depend on the particular modeling technology being used. Other, more fundamental problems result from a mismatch between the original goals set forth for solid modelers and the ways we would like to use them. For reference, let us outline some of the most significant problems as follows:

1. *Numerical inaccuracy:* Numerical problems are unavoidable in all programs that try to represent and manipulate geometrical information in a fixed-precision computer. However, it is clear that boundary modelers suffer more from these problems than the others.

    As important as they are, we shall exclude numerical computation problems from the scope of this tutorial, and concentrate on other issues described in the sequel.

2. *Manipulation of large models:* None of the major solid modeling approaches is naturally suited for the processing of large models — models consisting of thousands of primitives or individual surfaces. Many of the advanced techniques to be described in the following sections address the issue of speed: how to make a solid modeler fast?

3. *Limitations of modeling domain:* All major approaches have limitations as for the kinds of objects that can be represented. CSG models (in principle) are limited to so-called *half-space* surfaces. It is not possible to extend CSG to cover free-form surfaces without simultaneously sacrificing at least some aspects of the algorithmic advantages of CSG.

    Boundary models are somewhat less rigid in this respect. Nevertheless, true integration of free-form surfaces with boundary-type solid modelers is a difficult task; in particular, numerical problems become very severe. In later parts of this tutorial, we shall discuss another extension of the "standard" geometric coverage of boundary modelers, namely techniques for including *implicit blend surfaces* in boundary models. Being of much lower degree, these surfaces are better in the reach of numerical techniques than full-flavored parametric surfaces.

4.   *Representation of non-geometric properties:* Solid models were originally
        introduced as the component of a larger system responsible for geometric
        computation only. Therefore, nongeometric aspects of the things modeled were
        originally a secondary concern.

           Unfortunately, real-world applications require that varying, and often large,
        amounts of nongeometric attribute information must be associated with geometric
        entities of solid models. Often this task cannot be accomplished without a model
        consisting of semantically higher level entities than the simple geometric entities of
        typical solid models. We shall take a brief look at so-called *feature models* that have
        been introduced to deal with the modeling problems of advanved research
        CAD/CAM systems.

5.   *User and application interfaces to solid modelers:* User interface is probably the
        least developed part of current-generation solid modeling systems. This may be
        caused by the emphasis on "pure" geometry of the current generation of modelers:
        without the capability of working with semantically higher-level entities, better user
        interfaces are difficult to create. Almost same notes apply to another neglected area,
        namely *dynamic programming interfaces* intended for application programmers
        wishing to make use of solid modeling in their application programs.

           Currently, a new generation of modelers is being developed based on feature
        models or object-oriented techniques, with the promise of much improved user or
        application interface capabilities. First commercial offerings of this development
        have just started to appear at the time of writing this tutorial (see, e.g., [3]). The real
        significance of these systems still remains to be seen, however.

   A further problem of solid modelers which is not addressed here is the *algorithmic
complexity*: real solid modelers are large and complicated computer programs. Because of the
sheer volume of solid modeler codes, and because algorithmic details of commercial systems are
usually not published, it seems to this author that members of the solid modeling community are
not good enough in learning from the experience of each other.

3. Advanced Techniques for CSG Visualization

Most of the advanced techniques for the processing of constructive models have been originally
developed in the context of viewing CSG models. Even though these techniques often are
applicable to other purposes, such as null object testing [49] or the evaluation of integral
properties [26], it seems natural to concentrate the following discussion around viewing
techniques.

Most viewing techniques proposed for CSG models belong to one of the following categories:

1. CSG ray tracing
2. CSG z-buffer algorithm
3. CSG viewing by conversion.

Each of these will be discussed in the following subsections.

3.1 CSG Ray Tracing

CSG ray tracing is the "classical" way of visualizing CSG models [41]. Ray tracing is based on the idea of intersecting the scene modeled in computer memory with a bundle of rays. The color of a pixel on the screen is determined by firing a ray from the eyepoint through the pixel into the scene, and searching the first surface that the ray intersects. The color is then calculated according to some shading model evaluated at the intersection point. Various visual effects, such as shadows, mirroring, or transparency can be simulated by casting further rays towards the light sources, or along the mirrored and refracted rays of light. The ray tracing paradigm is illustrated in Figure 4.

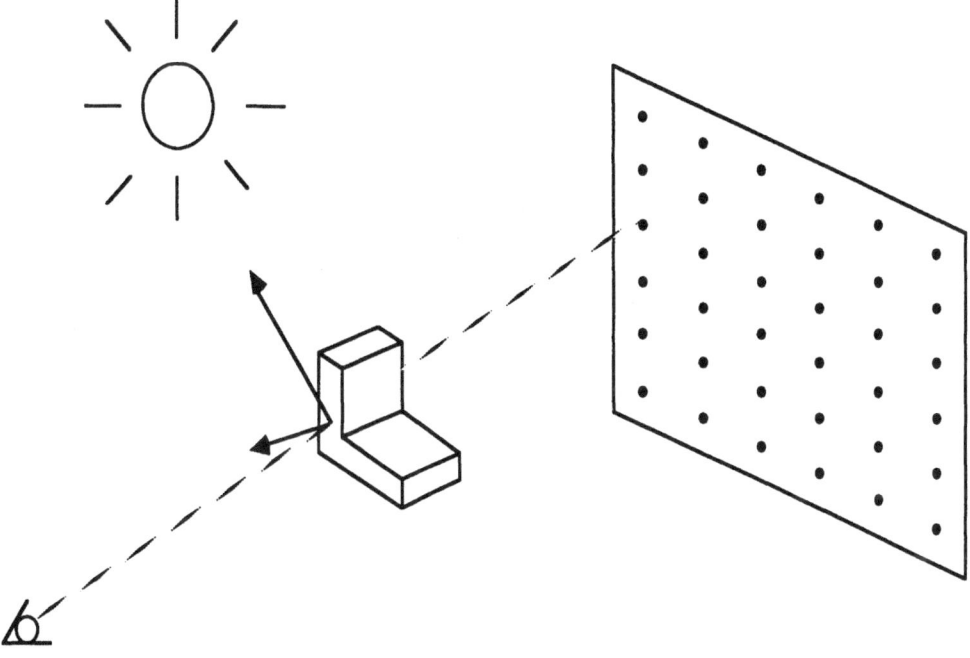

Figure 4: Ray tracing paradigm.

The heart of a CSG ray tracing algorithm is the *line-solid classification algorithm*: given a ray (semi-infinite line) and a solid, determine the first point (if any) where the line intersects the solid. For CSG models, this process typically involves two steps. First, the intersections of the ray and each primitive must be located (see the left part of Figure 5). This computation typically requires the numerical solving of equations of degree 2 (spheres, cylinders, cones) or 4 (tori).

As the second step, the CSG expression describing the part must be evaluated so as to find which intersection (if any) is the first one belonging to the true surface of the part. The right side of Figure 5 displays this computation as described by Roth [41].

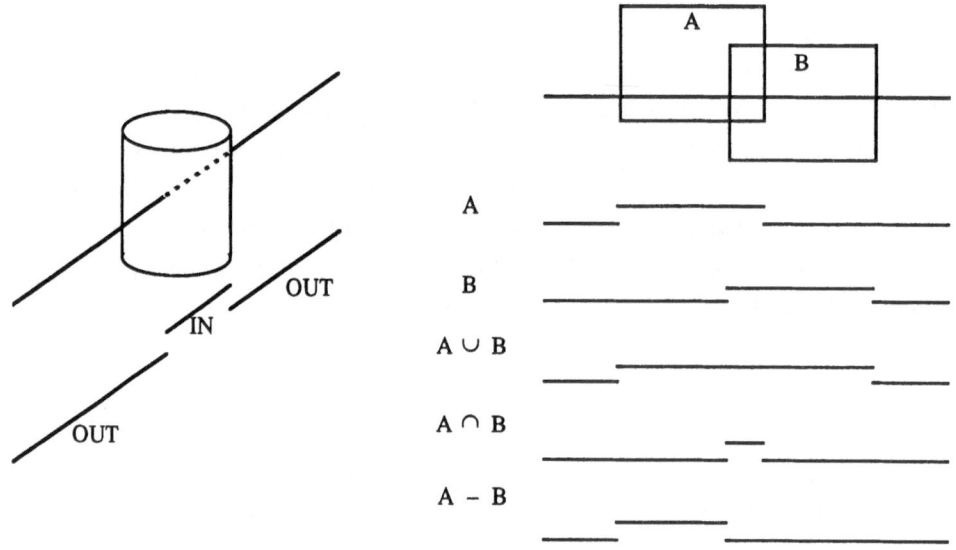

Figure 5: Line-solid classification.

As shown, the result can be formed by effectively evaluating the Boolean set operations on the one-dimensional ray. Alternatively, the middle points of each segment of the ray could be classified by means of a *point classification* routine; the first segment which is classified as being inside the CSG object gives the intersection.

It is clear that in its basic form, the ray tracing approach requires a lot of computation because the algorithm must intersect each ray with each surface. Therefore, much work has been directed towards finding ways of speeding up CSG ray tracing.

Bounding volumes. The basic idea behind using bounding volumes is to enclose complicated objects with simpler ones that are easier to test for intersection. If the ray is found to miss the bounding volume, no further tests are necessary. Usually, some kind of a hierarchy is built of the bounding volumes. For instance, Roth [41] uses boxes whose faces are aligned with the coordinate axes. Each primitive type has a procedure for computing its bounding box; boxes for non-leaves of a CSG tree are determined from the boxes of the subtrees according to the set operation.

Cameron [5] describes an interesting method for refining the bounding volumes of a CSG tree. He shows that if one knows a bounding volume for the whole CSG tree, one can shrink the bounding volumes of the subtrees. Next, a new bounding volume for the whole tree can be evaluated. If this is smaller than the original bound, the process can be repeated.

Space partitioning. Space partitioning has recently become popular in connection with ray tracing. In this approach, the part of space containing the CSG tree is divided into disjoint cells. Each cell has a list of those CSG primitives whose surface intersects it. Hence, the intersection testing can be enhanced by looking at only those cells that are intersected by the ray. When a cell is visited, the active primitives of the cell are intersected by the ray. Those intersection points that lie outside the cell are ignored; the others are sorted, and checked whether they belong to the CSG object.

A problem of space partitioning is that the same primitive can be visited several times for each ray. In the practical sense, several authors have suggested that the unnecessary computation can be avoided by marking each primitive as it is first checked against a ray. Nevertheless, asymptotically the problem still persists.

Various examples of the space partitioning approach are [1, 8, 10, 46]. Fujimoto [10] makes use of a regular 3-dimensional grid, and concentrates on efficient algorithms for accessing the cells occurring along the ray. Amanitides and Woo [1] deal with a similar problem. Glassner [8] uses octrees as the search structure to deal with data whose "spatial density" is variable. Tamminen *et al.* [46] use EXCELL, a multidimensional spatial directory based on extendible hashing, hence avoiding the costly manipulation of pointers of octrees.

Surface approximation. Approximation of curved objects by means of faceted ones can also be viewed as a ray tracing acceleration technique. Recent work into this direction is found in references [4, 18].

Other improvements. Jansen [18] also describes various other ways to speed up CSG line and point classification algorithms. For instance, if a point is found to be inside the left subtree of a union node, it is unnecessary to examine the right subtree. Naturally, these improvements can also be used to speed up the CSG z-buffer algorithm to be descibed in the next section. van Wijk [52] extends CSG ray tracing techniques to cover, for instance, various procedurally described models.

3.2 CSG Z-Buffer Algorithm

The idea of the CSG z-buffer algorithm is described by Rossignac and Requicha [39]. The algorithm is based on the notion of *boundary monotonicity*: the boundary of a CSG object is a subset of the boudaries of its primitives.

In the algorithm of Rossignac and Requicha, each surface of each primitive is scanned sufficiently densely so that at least one point of each surface is projected on each pixel inside the projected image of the surface. Each such point is classified with respect to the CSG model to determine whether it belongs to the boundary of the actual solid. If so, the distance of the point from the viewing plane is compared with the value stored in the z-buffer array to see whether the point obscures the point already stored.

It is useful to observe the differences between the CSG z-buffer algorithm, the traditional z-buffer algorithm for boundary models, and CSG ray tracing. In the traditional z-buffer algorithm, the actual bounding surfaces of the object are scanned, and all points found are "valid" in the sense that they belong to the boundary. In the CSG z-buffer algorithm, the validity of the points must be determined separately. CSG ray tracing differs from the z-buffer algorithm in that instead of the surfaces of the primitives, the pixels of the viewing plane are scanned.

Observe that efficient implementation of the algorithm requires that both implicit and parametric representations of the surfaces are available. Implicit representations are needed for rapid in/out classification of points, while parametric representations are needed for scanning the surfaces. This seems to limit the usefulness of the algorithm.

The CSG display algorithm of the Pixel-Powers system [9] is a hardware implementation of the CSG z-buffer algorithm. The system consists of an "intelligent" frame storage where each pixel has local computing elements that can work in parallell. Using this machinery, the CSG classification for the whole array of pixels can be implemented in a bit-serial manner. The use of a z-buffer algorithm for CSG models with faceted primitives is considered by Jansen [18].

3.3 CSG Viewing by Conversion

A third alternative for rapid CSG viewing is described by Samet, Tamminen and Koistinen [22, 43]. The technique is based on a conversion from the CSG model to a *bintree model*, a decomposition model similar to the octree but based on binary subdivision alternating in x, y, and z.. Like octrees, bintrees can be displayed easily with recursive back-to-front algorithms.

Because the algorithm compactly illustrates several advaced techniques for processing CSG models, we shall describe it to some depth following the exposition of Koistinen [23].

```
typedef struct binnode {
    colortype        color;    /* BLACK, WHITE, GREY */
    struct binnode *left, *right;
} binnode;

StoBin(S, tree, B)
solid        S;
binnode      *tree;
block        B;
{
    if (voxel_size(B))
    {
        if (classify_voxel(B, S) == IN)
            tree->color = BLACK;
        else
            tree->color = WHITE;
    }
    else
    {
        switch (classify_block(B, S))
        {
            case IN:
                tree->color = BLACK;
                break;
            case OUT:
                tree->color = WHITE;
                break;
            case '?':
                tree->color = GREY;
                allocate_children(tree);
                StoBin(S, tree->left, split(B, left));
                StoBin(S, tree->right, split(B, right));
                collapse(tree);
        }
    }
}
```

Figure 6: Converting a solid to a bintree.

Converting Solids to Bintrees. The crucial task in the conversion process is the *block-solid classifier* procedure which is expected to determine whether a rectangular block (a bintree node) is completely outside or completely inside the solid, or intersects the boundary of the solid. As observed by Lee and Requicha [26], ideal classification that produces the exact result immediately is too slow to be practical. Instead, the classifier usually is implemented so as to perform a "lazy" classification that returns one of the values *in, out,* and *?* denoting that the block is in the inside or in the outside of the solid, or that the relation of the block with respect to the solid is unknown. In this final case, the classifier will simply subdivide the large block and try to classify the parts.

Armed with the classifier, we can present in Figure 6 a general-purpose algorithm for converting a solid description into a bintree. The algorithm proceeds recursively; initially, the whole space of interest is classified. The recursion terminates when the smallest voxel size has been reached (function `voxel_size`); in this case, a two-way classification is used. Otherwise, a lazy classification step is performed. If the block is found to be completely in or out the solid, the bintree node is filled with the appropriate information and the recursion terminates. Otherwise, the block is subdivided, and classified against the child nodes of the current bintree node. Because of the nature of the classification, it might happen that both children are classified either `WHITE` or `BLACK`; in these cases, the bintree is simplified by combining the children (procedure `collapse`).

Block Classification for CSG. When applied to CSG, the algorithm presented in Figure 6 requires a method for classifying a block with respect to a CSG tree. One way of producing such a classifier can be based on Tilove's notion of *localization* [48, 49].

A localization of a CSG model S with respect to a block B is defined as another (simpler) model S' such that the intersection of S and B is equal to the intersection of S' and B. That is, within B S and S' are identical (but may differ outside B). Tilove proves that if some primitive P in the definition of S does not occur within B, a candidate S' can be generated by replacing P with the empty set Ø in the expression of S. Similarly, of B is completely within P, P can be replaced by the universal set W.

Tilove's result identifies *redundant primitives* in a CSG expression. This gives us the opportunity of implementing a block classifier according to the following outline:

1.   For each primitive P of the CSG expression, check whether P is redundant within the block B and perform the possible substitutions.

2.   Simplify the CSG expression.

3.   If the simplified expression is Ø, return *out*; else, if it is W, return *in*; otherwise, return '*?*'.

The simplification of the CSG expression is done by applying simple rules of set theory [43]. Rules applied for set unions and intersections are given in the below:

$$\emptyset \cup A \Rightarrow A \qquad\qquad A \cup \emptyset \Rightarrow A$$

$$W \cup A \Rightarrow W \qquad\qquad A \cup W \Rightarrow W$$

$$\emptyset \cap A \Rightarrow \emptyset \qquad\qquad A \cap \emptyset \Rightarrow \emptyset$$

$$W \cap A \Rightarrow A \qquad\qquad A \cap W \Rightarrow A$$

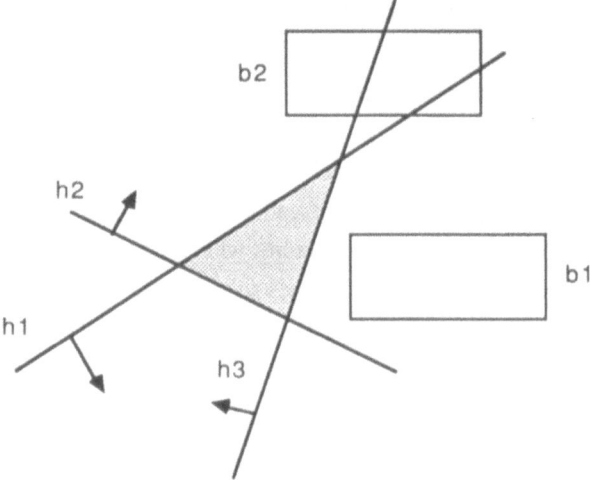

Figure 7: Example of block classification [23].

An example of the block classification is given in Figure 7. In this case, the CSG expression of the shaded triangle is ((h1 ∩ h2) ∩ h3). For block b1, half-space h3 is redundant; hence, inside b1 the valid local CSG expression is ((h1 ∩ h2) ∩ ∅), which can be simplified to ∅. Hence, b1 is found to be outside the triangle. Becase none of the half-spaces is (yet) redundant within b2, no pruning is possible, and the block must be subdivided.

Block vs. Primitive Classification. To determine redundant primitives, we need a block-primitive classification procedure that will tell us whether the primitive is wholly out of the block, completely contains the block, or whether the surfaces of the primitive and the block intersect. Lee and Requicha [26] propose a "geometric" technique based on constructing inner and outer bounds of the primitive, while Samet and Tamminen [43] propose fully "algebraic" techniques. Koistinen [23] solves the problem by using interval arithmetic in order to estimate the range of the defining half-space function within the block.

Other techniques. Tilove's work on detection of redundant primitives and CSG tree pruning has later been extended and improved by Rossignac and Voelcker [40]. They formulate the concept of the *active zone* of a primitive in the CSG tree as the region outside which any change to P does not affect the model of which it is a part. Amongst other things, this concept allows an improvement of Tilove's redundant primitive detection.

Woodwark [54] describes a different technique based on considering the *constituents* of the CSG model that are formed by complementing the primitives in every possible combination and intersecting the results together. For n sets, this leads to 2^n constituents. To avoid this combinatorial explosion, Woodwark makes use of space subdivision.

4. Advanced Techniques for Boundary Models

4.1 Nonmanifold Boundary Models

The most commonly used boundary model representations are based on the notion of a *2-manifold*, which intuitively is a simple surface on which every point sees a simple circular neighborhood. This notion leads to data structures where the whole boundary of the solid is represented by "gluing" together individual faces so that along each edge, exactly two faces meet. A typical representative of these models is the *winged-edge data structure* originally developed by Baumgart [2] and its variants, such as the *half-edge data structure* by Mäntylä [30].

2-manifold models are primarily intended for representing complete solid objects. Unfortunately, practical CAD systems require also representations for other kinds of geometric objects, such as wireframes and "loose" surfaces. In such more advanced modeling tasks, 2-manifold models have the following problems:

1. 2-manifold models are not "closed" under Boolean set operations, that is, a Boolean combination of two 2-manifolds is not necessarily itself a 2-manifold.
2. 2-manifold models are unnatural for the representation of geometric objects other than boundaries of solids.
3. 2-manifold models are not convenient for representing cellular structures, such as composite parts or delta volumes for machining applications.

As a result, several researchers have recently proposed that the 2-manifold-based boundary models should be replaced with a more general concept that allows the precise modeling of cases not conveniently addressed by the ordinary techniques.

In his Ph.D. thesis [51], Weiler describes the *radial edge data structure* which addresses the problems outlined in the above. The radial edge data structure can be viewed as an extension of the winged-edge data structure that allows a single face, loop, edge, or vertex to be shared by several objects. As indicated in Figure 8, this is realized in terms of special "use" entities of the data structure. The figure also includes further high-level entities on top of the "shell" node typically used in boundary models that allow the modeling of cellular structures.

So, if a face separates two neighboring volumes in a cellular structure, there will be two "face_use" nodes in each of the volumes pointing at a single entity. Similarly, an edge shared by several faces would be represented by means of a network of "edge-use" nodes, as illustrated in Figure 9 that displays an object consisting of four faces meeting along an edge and a part of its data structure. Observe that the two "sides" of the face are represented as two "uses" of a single face.

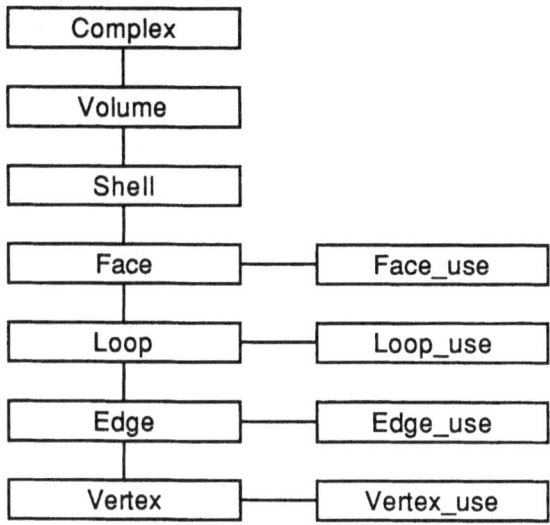

Figure 8: Concepts of the radial edge data structure.

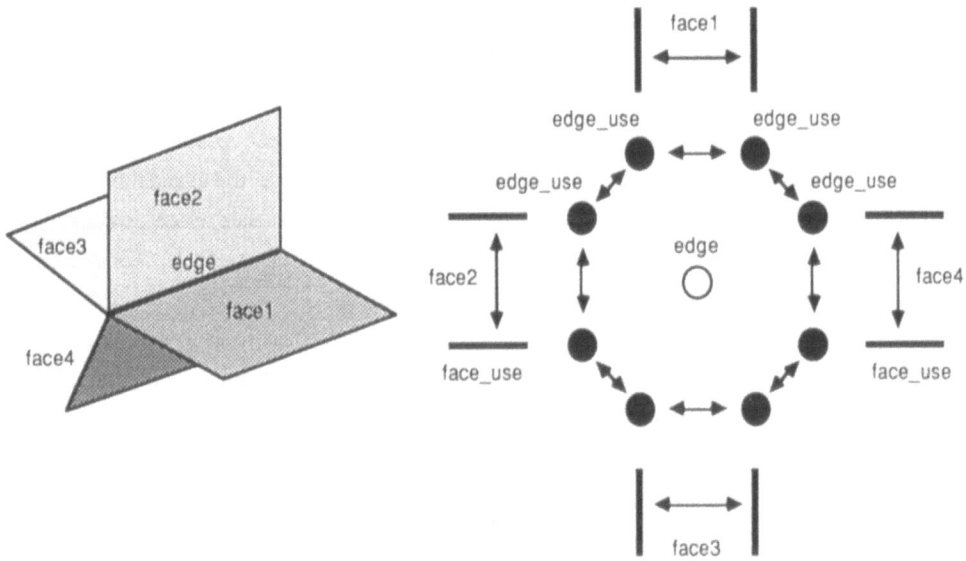

Figure 9: Example of the radial edge data structure.

Weiler's work has been followed by many others. For instance, Kawabe *et al.* [21] refine the mathematical basis of Weiler's work, and discuss various ways the new capabilities of the representation can be used. Nonmanifold models have also recently become recognized as a basis for potential future standardization under the PDES/STEP umbrella.

4.2 Rounding and Blending Techniques for Boundary Models

Boundary modelers that support curved surfaces fall in two categories. First, a growing number of modeling systems makes use of some form of parametric surfaces. Currently, it appears that most of the new development in this group is based on so-called NURBS, non-uniform rational B-spline surfaces. This choice is attractive because of the large family of surfaces that can be represented. In particular, many commonly used surfaces such as cylinders, cones, and spheres can be represented exactly.

Parametric surfaces have certainly many advantages from the point of view of applications such as visualization and machining. However, the high degree of the surfaces causes incurable problems for basic operations of solid modeling such as Boolean set operations.

The second category of modelers follows the more traditional approach of representing curved surfaces implicitly, usually by means of a surface type code, some natural parameters, and a rigid transformation. For instance, a cylinder could be represented by means of a radius and a transformation that moves the cylinder from the default position to its actual position. The usual collection of surfaces supported consists of planes, the natural quadrics (cylinder, cone, sphere) and tori.

Unfortunately, there are applications that require the capability of modeling more complex surfaces than the ones included in this collection. A typical requirement is the modeling of *blend surfaces* that represent a smooth transition between two intersecting surfaces. Such surfaces are required for strength, manufacturability, safety, or aesthetic reasons. While simple blending situations can be delt with the simple surfaces — for instance, the toroidal blending of a cylinder intersecting an orthogonal plane — some others require surfaces which do not belong to the usual collection — for instance, the blending of two intersecting cylinders. For examples of systems providing "simple" rounding operations, see [6, 15].

Of course, modelers with parametric surfaces can be furnished so as to deal with blend surfaces — blending support was actually the original motivation for introducing parametric surfaces in boundary modelers in the first place. However, many people (including the author) feel that introduction of parametric surfaces is an overkill for situations where the full flexibility of the parametric model is not required. As a result, there has been considerable activity in the area of blending techniques for implicit surfaces.

Blend surfaces differ from the ordinary surface modeling situations in that the surface is not constructed indepedently, but with reference to two or more existing surfaces. The actual shape of the blending surface is usually not of direct interest, provided that it satisfies some overall requirements such as the smoothness of the transition.

Various blending techniques differ in how the blend is specified in terms of the original surfaces. In his extensive overview, Woodwark [53] classifies the various techniques on the basis of how they control the extent of the blend:

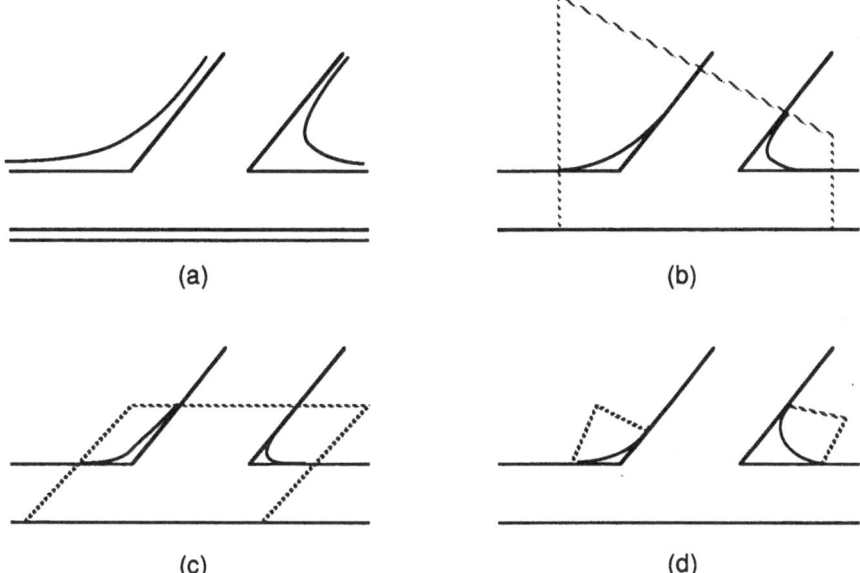

Figure 10: Alternative blend control techniques [53].

1. *Unbounded blends:* Some blending techniques affect all of the original surfaces, with decaying effect. These techniques are mainly applicable to aesthetic situations such as image generation, and are not generally felt as being appropriate for engineering applications. See Figure 10 (a).

2. *Volume-bounded blends:* The blending surface is controlled by a volume by which the blend is bounded. Recent examples of volume-oriented blending techniques are given by Hoffman and Hopcroft [13], and van Wijk [52]. See Figure 10 (b).

3. *Range-controlled blends:* The blend is controlled by a desired range of the blend, either in terms of the distance from the original edge, or from each of the surfaces being blended. Various approaches to range-controlled blends have been developed by Hoffman and Hopcroft [11, 12], Middleditch and Sears [28], and Rockwood and Owen [37]. See Figure 10 (c).

4. *Radius-controlled blends:* The blend is specified in terms of the (minimum) radius of curvature of the blend. This leads to the so-called *rolling ball analogy* : the result of the blending operation approximates the surface swept by a ball rolling through the region to be blended. An example of this approach is given by Rossignac and Requicha [39]. See Figure 10 (d).

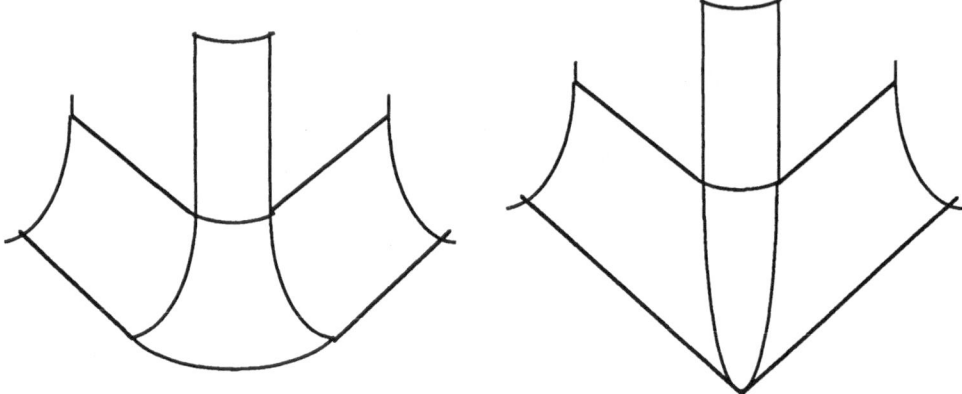

Figure 11: Examples of three-surface blends.

Description of the actual mathematical formulations of the various techniques is beyond the scope of this survey; for an in-depth analysis, see [53]. As perceived from the user's point of view, the differences are particularly apparent in the area of simultaneous blending of several surfaces. Some methods do not cover this problem at all (such as van Wijk's). Some others require that the situation is treated in two steps, where the final blend is created by reblending an intermediate situation where two surfaces have been blended.

So, for instance, the situation of Figure 11 left cannot be produced by the multi-surface version of Middleditch-Sears technique without reblending, whereas Hoffman and Hopcroft's method, and Holmström's method can create the situation on the right directly. Apart from user convenience, the situation on the right can be realized with lower degree surfaces, thus reducing the cost of e.g. visualizing the blend. Nevertheless, because blend surfaces have no straightforward parametric formulations, operations such as ray tracing may become nontrivial; see, e.g., [17].

Most of the cited methods have been developed in the context of CSG modelers. Exceptions are the blending methods of Rockwood and Owen [37], which was developed in the ROMULUS boundary modeler, of Holmström [14, 16], which has been implemented in the GWB boundary modeler [30], and of Varady *et al.* [50], whose method is being implemented in FFSolid, a modeler based on Build. The reason for the lesser amount of work with boundary models is the complex case analysis that blending methods for boundary modelers must undertake in order to work out the proper treatment of corners where several blend surfaces meet. The description of the as for yet only partially implemented blending facility of Varady *et al.* [50] illustrates well this complexity.

5. Beyond Solid Models: Features

By their very nature, all solid models emphasize the geometric aspects of objects. Unfortunately, real world applications deal with objects made of steel or plastics, not of abstract geometric entities. Conversely, a modeling system limited to the geometric aspects of a product only is inherently in mismatch with the requirements posed by the applications.

Many modelers provide some ways for associating nongeometric attribute information to the entities of the model, such as to CSG primitives or to faces, edges and vertices of a boundary model. While this is certainly vital for extending the utility of solid modelers, many researchers feel that mere attributes do not offer a sufficient basis for future applications.

One of the problems of solid models is that some properties of objects cannot be associated to single entities of the model, but rather belong to a group of entities. For instance, the fact that a hole consisting of syme cylindrical and planar faces will be manufactured with a certain milling tool should properly be associated with the "hole", not with some geometric entities of it.

Another example is the modeling of dimensioning and tolerancing information. For instance, as shown in Figure 12, a cylindrical hole would ordinarily be dimensioned by stating the position of its centerline (U) from two planes (Q, P). This results in considering the centerline as the intersection of two planes (R, S). However, these planes are not entities of the solid model at all!

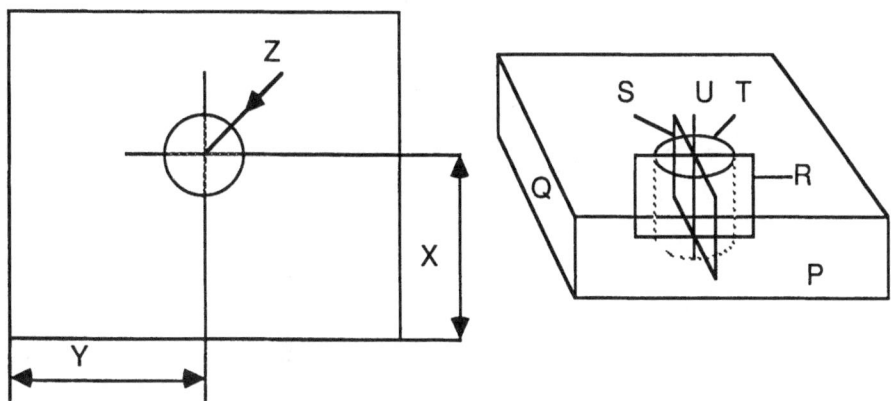

Figure 12: Dimensioning a hole.

A more subtle, but still severe problem of ordinary solid models is that they have a single level of precision: all geometric information is represented exactly even when it would be better to leave something vague. Solid models cannot make a distinction between vital functional

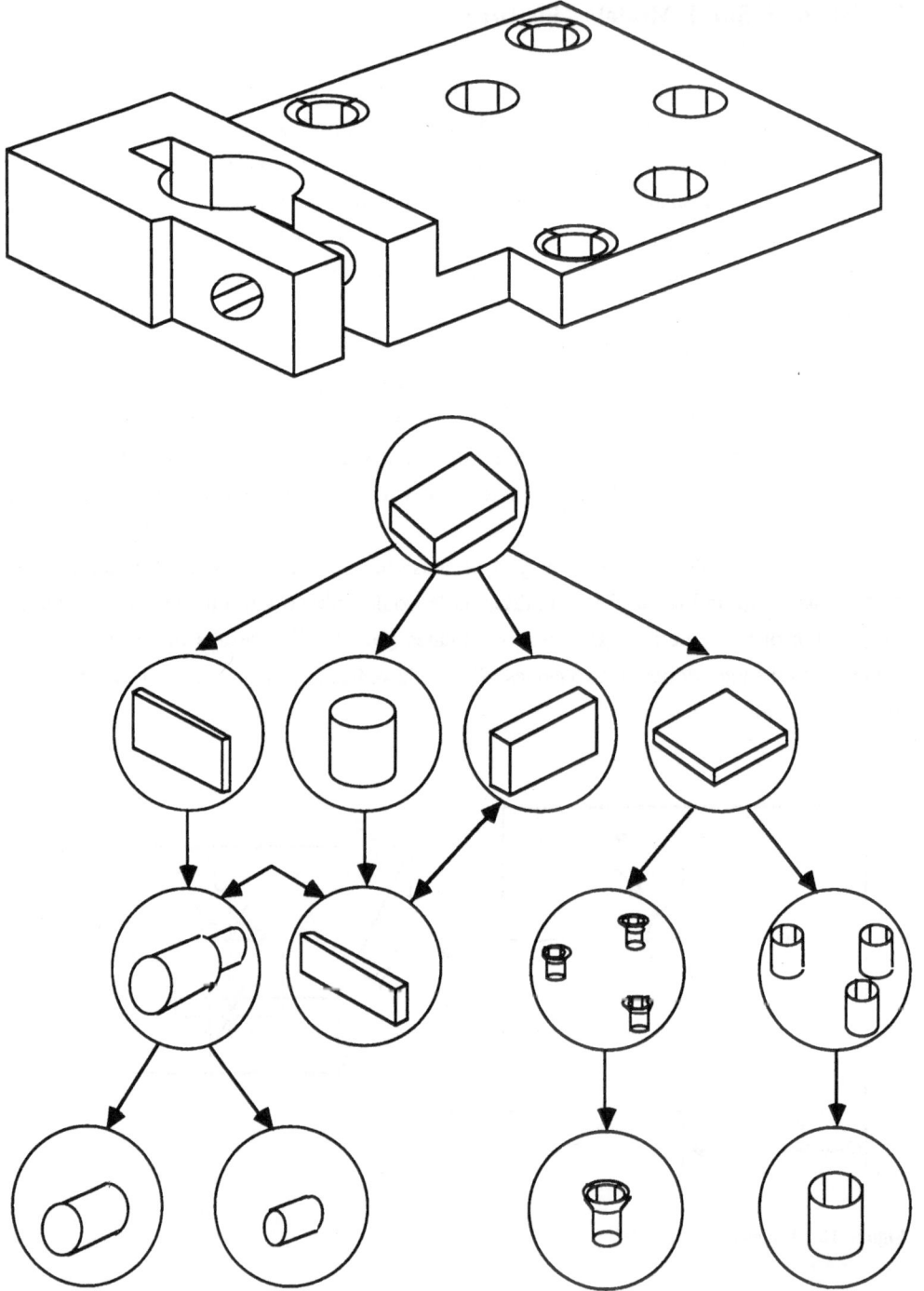

Figure 13: Manufacturing features of a machined part [32].

shapes of a mechanical part and relatively insignificant shapes such as fillets and blends. Advanced applications such as machining process planning could take advantage from representing insignificant details of a part vaguely.

Definition of features. Feature models [33] seek to provide a solution to these problems. A "feature" is simply a collection of geometric elements that forms a significant whole — a whole that may have some attribute information of its own. Obviously, this "definition" makes features entirely view-dependent; features are in the eye of the beholder. Hence, there might be a set of features relevant for product design, another for assembly studies, and a third for manufacturing planning. Dixon *et al.* [7] suggest that eventually the term "feature" must become a rigorously defined notion.

Perhaps best understood are manufacturing features that represent a machined part in terms of simple machinable shapes such as holes, grooves, slots, and pockets. A part and its representation in terms of manufacturing features is shown in Figure 13 [31]. Features are organized into a tree, where leaves denote individual features and inner nodes either "parent" features or various kinds of compounds. The root of the tree is the blank part, from which all other features are subtracted. (It should be noted the subtractive nature of the example is a property of this particular collection of features, not of manufacturing features in general.) This model has been used for generative computer-aided process planning [32].

Ordinarily, features are organized in some form of a taxonomy that helps to organize a large collection of feature types. The taxonomy can help the recognition of feature families that may share some common characteristics or properties and may also help the introduction of new feature types into a feature-based system. In particular, the taxonomy can be mapped onto the class mechanism of an object-oriented environment.

Feature recognition. From the point of view of solid modeling, features pose the problem of interpreting an existing solid model as a feature model, i.e., the problem of feature recognition. Most of the techniques being investigated at the present are somehow related to Kyprianou's Ph. D. thesis [24]. Essentially, his method is based on classifying the edges of a boundary model as being convex or concave, and recognizing various kinds of features (such as pockets and bosses) by means of patterns of edges of different kinds. Representative samples of current work in feature recognition following this pattern of thought includes [19, 20, 42].

Feature recognition on the basis of CSG models is a more challenging task, because data on faces, edges, and vertices used by the above methods is not available. Nevertheless, Woodwark [55] presents the view that feature recognition on the basis of CSG may ultimatelly be more fruitful than boundary model techniques.

Many more references on feature recognition are available in the extensive review of Shah *et al.* [45].

Design by features. As an alternative to feature recognition, parts could be modeled initially in terms of features, not as just solid models. Feature-based modeling systems are just entering the real world from research laboratories, and we can expect to hear much more of them in the near future.

Dixon *et al*. [7] discuss the research issues involved in design-by-features systems. For instance, they observe that a true design system should provide support for the top-down design of complete assemblies of parts with the capability of manipulating the models with different levels of precision and from varying points of view. We do not yet know how to capture designer's intent into such models and how to make it available to other computer-aided systems. They conclude that feature-based modeling systems will need a similar research and development investment as solid modelers did during the last 15 years.

Krause *et al*. [25] give an interesting example of representing assemblies with very high-level, symbolic models. In their approach, assemblies are initially described with an essentyially nongeometric graph notation, which is then mapped into geometric objects. As for system architecture, the problems of implementing a full-scale modeling system supporting features are discussed by Shah and Rogers [44].

6. Next Generation of Solid Modelers

In their surveys of solid modeling techniques, Requicha and Voelcker [35, 36] observe that the various approaches to geometric modeling (sculptured surface models, polyhedral models for computer graphics, drafting models for CAD, solid models) were originally developed in separation from each other. They also predict that these lines of work will merge in future modeling systems, leading to a more integrated combination of functionality.

Indeed, during the last five years, many steps to this direction have been made, such as integration of parametric surfaces to solid models, various hybrid modeling approaches based on combinations of decomposition, CSG and boundary models, and nonmanifold boundary modelers that can represent a wide variety of geometric objects.

What will the next generation of solid modelers be like? Looking at my personal crystal ball, I am seeing the following things for the 90's:

- object-oriented modelers that effectively hid to underlying representation from the applications will emerge
- on the basis of the improved data abstraction mechanisms of object-oriented modelers, various high-level interfaces to solid models (parametric models, features, assembly models, kinematics) will be developed; it will be viable to define application-specific modeling primitives
- many of the advanced techniques discussed in this tutorial will find their way to

mainstream systems (nonmanifold boundary modelers, space decomposition techniques)

- symbolic algebra techniques will be developed to partially solve the current problems of numerical computation
- there will be advanced graphical / scientific workstations that have special support e.g. for ray tracing on the basis of advanced parallel computer architectures
- increasingly more research effort will be invested into very high level product models providing support for multilevel, multiview modeling of complex products.

So, my personal conclusion is that there will be room for a lot of new progress and work in solid modeling in the next few years to come.

References

[1]   J. Amanitides and A. Woo. A fast voxel traversal algorithm for ray tracing. *Proc. Eurographics '87*, North-Holland Publ. Co, Amsterdam, 1987, pages 3–10.

[2]   B. Baumgart. A polyhedron representation for computer vision. *AFIP Conf. Proc.*, Vol. 44, 1975.

[3]   I. C. Braid. Improving product models and kernel modellers. *Proc. 2nd Toyota Conference*, Aichi-ken, Japan, 1988. Elsevier Science Publishers, Amsterdam, to appear.

[4]   W. F. Broonsvoort. Techniques for reducing Boolean evaluation time in CSG scan-line algorithms. *Computer-Aided Design*, Vol. 18, No. 10, 1986, pages 533–538.

[5]   S. A. Cameron. *Modelling Solids in Motion*. Ph.D. thesis, University of Edinburgh, 1984.

[6]   H. Chiokura. An extended rounding operation for modeling solids with free-form surfaces. In: T. L. Kunii, ed.: *Computer Graphics 1987*, Springer Verlag, Tokyo, 1987, pages 249–268.

[7]   J. R. Dixon, E. C. Libardi, and E. H. Nielsen. Unresolved research issues in development of design-with-features systems. *Geometric Modeling for Product Engineering*. Proc. 1988 IFIP/NSF/RPI Workshop on Geometric Modelling. North-Holland, Amsterdam, to appear.

[8]   A. S. Glassner. Space subdivision for fast ray tracing. *IEEE Computer Graphics and Applications*, Vol. 4, No. 10, 1984, pages 15–22.

[9]   J. Goldfeather, J. P. M. Hultquist, and H. Fuchs. Fast constructive-solid geometry display in the Pixel-Powers graphic system. *Computer Graphics*, Vol. 20, No. 4, 1986, pages 107–116. Proc. SIGGRAPH '86.

[10] A. Fujimoto, T. Tanaka, and K. Iwata. ARTS: accelerated ray-tracing system. *IEEE Computer Graphics and Applications*, Vol. 6, No. 4, 1986, pages 16–26.

[11] C. Hoffman and J. Hopcroft. Automatic surface generation in computer aided design. *The Visual Computer*, Vol. 1, 1985, pages 92–100.

[12] C. Hoffman and J. Hopcroft. Quadratic blending surfaces. *Computer-Aided Design*, Vol. 18, 1986, pages 301–306.

[13] C. Hoffman and J. Hopcroft. The potential method for blending surfaces and corners. In: G. E. Farin, ed.: *Geometric Modeling: Algorithms and New Trends*, SIAM Press, Philadelphia, 1987.

[14] L. Holmström. Piecewise quadric blending of implicitly defined surfaces. *Computer Aided Geometric Design*, Vol. 4, 1987, pages 171–189.

[15] L. Holmström and T. Laakko. Rounding facility for solid modelling of mechanical parts. *Computer Aided Design*, Vol. 20, No. 6, 1988.

[16] L. Holmström and T. Laakko. A blending facility for solid modelling of mechanical parts. Unpublished report, Helsinki University of Technology, 1988. Submitted for publication.

[17] L. Holmström, T. Laakko, M. Mäntylä, and P. Rekola. Ray tracing of boundary models with implicit blending surfaces. In: *Proc. Theory and Practice of Geometric Modeling*, Tübingen, 1988.

[18] F. W. Jansen. *Solid Modelling with Faceted Primitives*. Ph.D. thesis, Delft University of Technology, 1987.

[19] G. Jared. Feature recognition in geometric modeling. *Proc. 4th Anglo-Hungarian Conference on Computer-Aided Geometric Design*, 1985.

[20] S. Joshi and T. C. Chang. Graph-based heuristics for recognition of machined features from a 3-D solid model, *Computer Aided Design*, Vol. 20, No. 2, March 1988, pages 58–66.

[21] S. Kawabe, K. Shimada and H. Masuda. Advanced 3D modeling for product definition. *Proc. 2nd Toyota Conference*, Aichi-ken, Japan, Oct. 4, 1988. Elsevier Science Publishers, Amsterdam, to appear.

[22] P. Koistinen, M. Tamminen, and H. Samet. Viewing solid models by bintree conversion. *Proc. Eurographics '85*, Elsevier Science Publishers, Amsterdam, 1985, pages 147-157.

[23] P. Koistinen. *Interval Methods for Constructive Solid Geometry: Display via Block Model Conversion*. Diploma thesis, Helsinki University of Technology, 1988.

[24] L. Kyprianou. *Shape Classification in Computer Aided Design*. Ph.D. thesis, University of Cambridge, 1980.

[25] F.-L. Krause, M. Bienert, F. H. Vosgerau, and N. Yaramanoglu. Feature oriented system design for geometric modeling. *Proc. Theory and Practice of Geometric Modeling*, University of Tübingen, Oct. 6–8, 1988. North-Holland, Amsterdam, to appear.

[26] Y. T. Lee and A. A. G. Requicha. Algorithms for computing the volume and other integral properties of solid objects. II. A Family of algorithms based on representation conversion and cellular approximation. *Comm. ACM*, Vol. 25, No. 9, Sep. 1982, pages 642–650.

[27] D. Meagher. Geometric modeling using octree encoding. *Computer Graphics and Image Processing*, Vol. 19, 1982, pages 129–147.

[28] A. E. Middleditch and K. H. Sears. Blend surfaces for set theoretic volume modelling systems. *Computer Graphics*, Vol. 19, No. 2, 1985, pages 161–170. Proc. SIGGRAPH '85.

[29] M. E. Mortenson. *Geometric Modeling*. John Wiley, New York, N. Y., 1985.

[30] M. Mäntylä. *An Introduction to Solid Modeling*. Computer Science Press, College Park, MD, 1988.

[31] M. Mäntylä. Feature-based product modeling for process planning. *Proc. 2nd Toyota Conference*, Aichi-ken, Japan, Oct. 4, 1988. Elsevier Science Publishers, Amsterdam, to appear.

[32] M. Mäntylä, J. Opas, and J. Puhakka. A prototype system for generative process planning of prismatic parts. In: A. Kusiak, ed., *Modern Production Management Systems*, North-Holland Publ. Co., Amsterdam, 1987, pages 599–611.

[33] M. J. Pratt and P. R. Wilson. *Requirements for Support of Form Features in a Solid Modelling System, Final Report.*. Report no. R-85-ASPP-01, CAM-I, Inc., Arlington, Texas, 1985.

[34] A. A. G. Requicha. Representations of rigid solids: theory, methods, and systems. *ACM Computing Surveys*, Dec. 1980, pages 437–464.

[35] A. A. G. Requicha and H. B. Voelcker. Solid modeling: a historical summary and contemporary assessment. *IEEE Computer Graphics and Applications*, Vol. 2, No. 2, March 1982, pages 9–24.

[36] A. A. G. Requicha and H. B. Voelcker. Solid modeling: current status and research directions. *IEEE Computer Graphics and Applications*, Vol. 3, No. 10, Oct. 1983, pages 25–37.

[37] A. Rockwood and J. Owen. Blend surfaces in solid modeling. In: G. E. Farin, ed., *Geometric Modeling: Algorithms and New Trends*, SIAM Press, Philadelphia, 1987, pages 367–383.

[38] J. R. Rossignac and A. A. G. Requicha. Constant radius blending in solid modeling. *Computers in Mechanical Engineering*, July 1985, pages 65–73.

[39] J. R. Rossignac and A. A. G. Requicha. Depth-buffering display techniques for constructive solid geometry. *IEEE Computer Graphics and Applications*, Vol. 6, No. 9, 1986, pages 29–39.

[40] J. R. Rossignac and H. B. Voelcker. Active zones in Constructive Solid Geometry for redundancy and interference detection. *Transactions on Graphics*, Vol. 8, No. 1, January 1989.

[41] S. D. Roth. Ray casting for modeling solids. *Computer Graphics and Image Processing*, Vol. 18, No. 2, 1982, pages 109–144.

[42] H. Sakurai and D. C. Gossard. Shape feature recognition from 3-D solid models. *Proc. 1988 ASME International Computers in Engineering Conference*, San Fransisco, August 1988, pages 515–519.

[43] H. Samet and M. Tamminen. Bintrees, CSG trees, and time. *Computer Graphics*, Vol. 19, No. 3, 1985, pages 121–130. Proc. SIGGRAPH '85.

[44] J. J. Shah and M. T. Rogers. Functional requirements and conceptual design of the Feature-Based Modelling System. *Computer-Aided Engineering Journal*, Feb. 1988.

[45] J. J. Shah, P. Sreevalsan, M. T. Rogers, R. Billo, and A. Mathew. *Current Status of Features Technology*. Report R-88-GM-04, CAM-I, Arlington, Texas, Aug. 1988.

[46] M. Tamminen, O. Karonen, and M. Mäntylä. Ray-casting and block model conversion using a spatial index. *Computer-Aided Design*, Vol. 16, No. 4, July 1984, pages 203–208.

[47] R. B. Tilove. Set membership classification: a unified approach to geometric intersection problems. *IEEE Trans. on Computers*, Vol. C-29, No. 10, October 1980, pages 874–883.

[48] R. B. Tilove. *Exploiting Spatial and Structural Locality in Geometric Modeling*. Ph.D. thesis, University of Rochester, 1981.

[49] R. B. Tilove. A null object detection algorithm for Constructive Solid Geometry. *Comm. ACM*, July 1984, pages 684–694.

[50] T. Varady, R. R. Martin, and J. Vida. Topological considerations in blending boundary representation solid models. *Proc. Theory and Practice of Geometric Modeling*, University of Tübingen, Oct. 6–8, 1988. North-Holland, Amsterdam, to appear.

[51] K. Weiler. *Topological Structures in Geometric Modeling*. Ph.D. thesis, Rensselaer Polytechnic Institute, Aug. 1986.

[52] J. J. van Wijk. *On New Types of Solid Models and their Visualization by Ray-Tracing*. Ph.D. thesis, Delft University of Technology, 1986.

[53] J. Woodwark. Blends in geometric modelling. In: *Proc. 2nd IMA Conference on the Mathematics of Surfaces*, Cardiff, September 8–10, 1986.

[54] J. Woodwark. Eliminating redundant primitives from set-theoretic solid models by a consideration of constituents. *IEEE Computer Graphics and Applications*, May 1988, pages 38–47.

[55] J. Woodwark. Some speculations on feature recognition. *Computer-Aided Design*, Vol. 20, No. 3, May 1988, pages 189–196.

Chapter 4

Computational Geometry and its Application to Computer Graphics

Mark H. Overmars

1 Introduction

The area of *computational geometry* deals with the study of algorithms for problems concerning geometric objects like e.g. lines, polygons, circles, etc. in the plane and in higher-dimensional space. Since its introduction in 1976 by Shamos the field has developed rapidly and nowadays there are special conferences and journals devoted to the topic.

A recently produced bibliography contained over 2000 entries and this is only a small portion of the material actually published. Although so much work has been done and although computational geometry is rich with results only a very small number of textbooks exists. The most well-known are the works of Mehlhorn [57], Preparata and Shamos [67] and Edelsbrunner [22].

Clearly, a large number of problems in computer graphics deal with geometric objects as well. Examples are hidden surface removal, windowing problems, intersection problems, etc. Hence, computer graphics can benefit from the techniques developed in computational geometry.

Algorithms in computational geometry normally work in *object space*, i.e., objects are stored and treated in a structural way rather than being broken down to e.g. pixels as often happens in the *image space* algorithms that are mostly used in graphics. Treating objects in a structural way has a number of advantages. The most important advantage is that results and time complexity are independent of image sizes. Moreover, treating objects in object space normally gives more flexibility (e.g. rotating a scene is easy).

This paper gives a basic introduction into some of the techniques and data structures developed in computational geometry with emphasis on their use in computer graphics applications. Due to the limited space only global ideas are outlined and no details are presented. References are added, in particular in a subsection "Further Reading" at the end of each section, for those that are interested in learning more about the topics treated.

The paper is organized as follows.

In section 2 we consider problems concerning shapes of sets of objects. In particular we look at the problem of determining the convex hull of a set of points. This is a basic problem in computational geometry with many applications. We give a number of different algorithms for this problem, introducing different algorithmic techniques. As a second problem we look at triangulating pointsets and polygons.

In section 3 we concentrate on proximity problems where distance plays an important role. We introduce the Voronoi diagram, a powerful structure that stores distance information, and use it to solve the nearest neighbor searching problem. To obtain this solution some point location techniques are introduced.

In section 4 we consider the well-known windowing problem where we ask which part of a picture is visible inside a given window. Data structures like k-d trees, range trees and segment trees are introduced for solving this problem.

In section 5 we treat intersection problems. First we concentrate on finding intersections between axis-parallel line segments and rectangles. Next we treat arbitrary line segments and other objects.

In section 6 we look at the hidden surface removal problem. We present two different object space algorithms. The first solution is based on projecting the objects and computing all intersections. The disadvantage of this method is that the number of intersections can be very large. The second solution avoids this problem. This surprisingly simple technique is purely dependent on the complexity of the visible scene.

Finally, in section 7, we give an overview of some important other directions of research in computational geometry and results obtained there.

2 Shape of objects

Given some object, e.g. a polygon, or a set of objects, e.g. points, it is often important to obtain information about the shape of such an object or a set. For example, one might want to obtain a bounded part of space that contains all the objects, or one might want to have a subdivision of the object in a set of smaller, simpler objects. In this section we deal with these two problems. First we concentrate on convex hulls of sets of points and of polygons. Next we look at triangulations, that subdivide pointsets or polygons into a number of non-overlapping triangles.

2.1 Convex hulls

Let V be a set of points or other objects in the plane, the *convex hull* of V is the smallest convex object containing all the points or objects. (An object is convex iff for any two points in the object the line segment connecting the points lies completely inside the object.) The convex hull bounds the set of objects from the outside. See figure 1 for an example of the convex hull of a set of points.

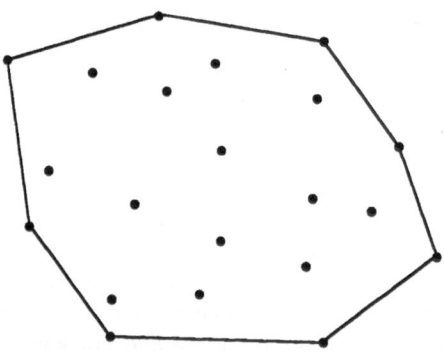

Figure 1: The convex hull.

Convex hulls play an important role in many applications. First of all they give some information about the shape of a set of objects. Secondly, convex objects are easy to deal with. Hence, in many applications the convex hull of objects is often a good first approximation. For example, if a line segment does not intersect the convex hull, it surely does not intersect the object. So the convex hull is a good alternative for the *bounding box* that is often used in graphics. It is easy to compute, easy to use and it gives a better approximation for the object (e.g., the convex hull of a line segment is the segment itself).

For the moment let V be a set of points. Many algorithms are known for computing convex hulls of sets of points. We will mention a few different methods that use completely different techniques.

The first technique is based on one of the earliest methods by Graham [33]. First we sort all points by x-coordinate. This can be done in $O(n \log n)$ time. Clearly, the leftmost point p_l and the rightmost point p_r belong to the convex hull. The convex hull now consists of an upper chain UC that runs from p_l to p_r having all points below it, and a lower chain LC having all points above it. (See figure 2.)

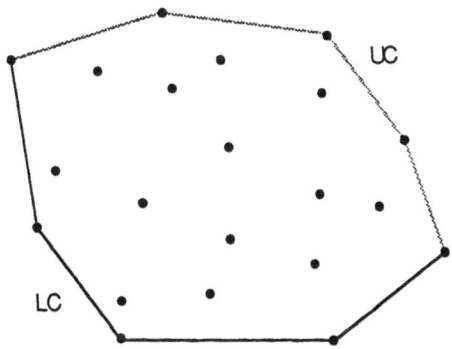

Figure 2: Convex chains.

We will only show how to compute UC. LC can be computed in exactly the same way. We will describe the method without much details. For detail see [33]. We walk from p_l to p_r. We will take care that when we are at some point p_i we found a convex arc from p_l to p_i with all points in between below it. Assume we have reached some point p_i. Now look at the angle $p_{i-1} p_i p_{i+1}$. If this angle is convex we can continue with $i := i+1$. Otherwise, p_i will not belong to the upper convex hull and can be removed. We backup and continue with $i := i - 1$, i.e., we consider the angle $p_{i-2} p_{i-1} p_{i+1}$. Again we check whether it is convex. If it is we can continue with p_{i+2}. Otherwise we throw away p_{i-1} and backup. It is easy to see that is this way we find the upper convex chain. This takes time $O(n)$ because at each step we either consider the next point or we throw away a point. This leads to the following result:

Theorem 2.1 *The convex hull of a set of n points in the plane can be computed in time $O(n \log n)$. When the points are sorted by x-coordinate the problem can be solved in linear time.*

This result is worst-case optimal, i.e., any convex hull algorithm takes time $\Omega(n \log n)$ in the worst case (see Yao [82]).

The following algorithm which is due to Jarvis [39] has a worst-case running time of $O(n^2)$ but works very good when the number of points on the convex hull is small (which is normally the case). Moreover, the method is very simple.

Let p_0 be the bottommost point in the set V. Clearly p_0 is part of the convex hull. Now let l be a horizontal line through p_0. We rotate l counterclockwise around p_0 until it hits a point p_1 of the set V. p_1 can be found by simply checking all points p_i and looking at the angle between $p_0 p_i$ and l. p_1 will also lie on the convex hull. Now we continue rotating l but this time around p_1. In this way we find a point p_2 that lies on the convex hull. Next we rotate around p_2, etc., until we finally get back to p_0. This algorithm is often called the gift-wrapping algorithm because we wrap a line around the set of points.

Theorem 2.2 *The convex hull of a set of n points can be found in time $O(k.n)$ where k is the number of points on the convex hull.*

Proof. For each next point on the convex hull we have to spend $O(n)$ work on checking all points in the set. The bound follows. $\square$

When the points are distributed in some uniform way the following algorithm of Overmars and van Leeuwen [63] based on an idea of Bykat [10] is useful. First determine the highest, bottommost, leftmost and rightmost point. Let these points be p_h, p_b, p_l and p_r. These points clearly belong to the convex hull. Now all points lie inside the axis-parallel rectangle R with p_h on the top boundary, p_b on the bottom boundary, etc. R is suddivided in five regions: V_{ins} being the central quadralateral and four triangle $V_1...V_4$. See figure 3. Clearly, all points in V_{ins} do not belong to the convex hull and can be removed. So we are left with the points in the four triangles $V_1...V_4$.

Now consider such a triangle V' with bottom line $\overline{p_i p_j}$. Find the point p_k in the triangle furthest away from $\overline{p_i p_j}$. This point must belong to the convex hull. This splits the triangle in four regions V'_{out} that lies further away than p_k, V'_{ins} being the triangle $\triangle p_i p_j p_k$ and the two other triangle V'_1 and V'_2. See figure 4. V'_{out} must be empty. The points in V'_{ins} cannot lie on the convex hull. So we are left with two new triangles V'_1 and V'_2 that are treated in the same way. Clearly, at each step of the algorithm a new point of the convex hull is found. Each such step takes time $O(n)$ in the worst case, so the worst-case total time is $O(k.n)$. (And indeed the method might take that many steps if every time all points lie in one of the remaining triangles.) But the expected time bound is a lot better. Note that the area of V_{ins}, the part that is removed in the first step, is of the same size as the remaining parts. Similar, when treating a triangle, the area of V'_{ins} is larger than the sum of the areas of V'_1 and V'_2. Hence, when the points are uniformly distributed in a convex region, the expected number of points remaining after each step of the algorithm is at least halved. This leads to an expected time of $O(n)$.

Theorem 2.3 *Given a set of n points uniformly distributed in a convex region of the plane, the convex hull can be found in expected time $O(n)$.*

Rather than taking convex hulls of sets of points, one can as well compute convex hulls of objects. An important case is the convex hull of a non-convex polygon. It is simple to see that the convex hull of a polygon is equal to the convex hull of the set of vertices of the polygon. Hence, we can compute the convex hull in the ways described above, yielding a worst-case time bound of $O(n \log n)$.

But one can do better. Using a clever way of walking around the polygon, starting at a vertex that lies on the convex hull, the convex hull can be wrapt around the polygon

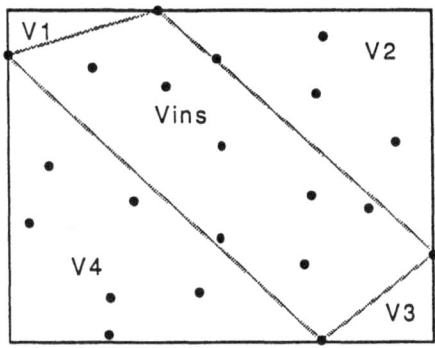

Figure 3: The initial situation.

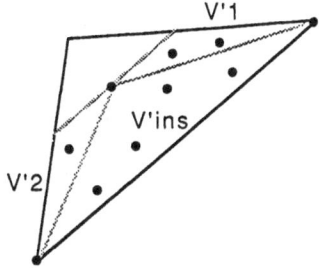

Figure 4: Treating a triangle.

in linear time. This technique was designed by Lee [50] (see also [67] section 4.1.4 for a description). Another technique has been developed by Graham and Yao [34]. We just state the result.

Theorem 2.4 *Given a simple polygon in the plane with n vertices, the convex hull can be determined in time $O(n)$.*

2.2   Triangulation

As a second shape problem we consider the problem of subdividing a pointset or a polygon into small simple pieces, in our case triangles. In the case of a polygon we want to subdivide the interior into triangles using only the vertices of the polygon as vertices of triangles. When triangulating a set of points we want to subdivide the convex hull of the set into triangles such that all points are used as vertices of triangles. See figure 5 for examples of triangulations of a polygon and of a set of points. (Note that triangulations are not unique. The same polygon or set of points can be triangulated in many different ways.)

Triangulating a polygon or a pointset plays an important role in many applications. For example, once a polygon is triangulated many problems can be solved more efficiently.

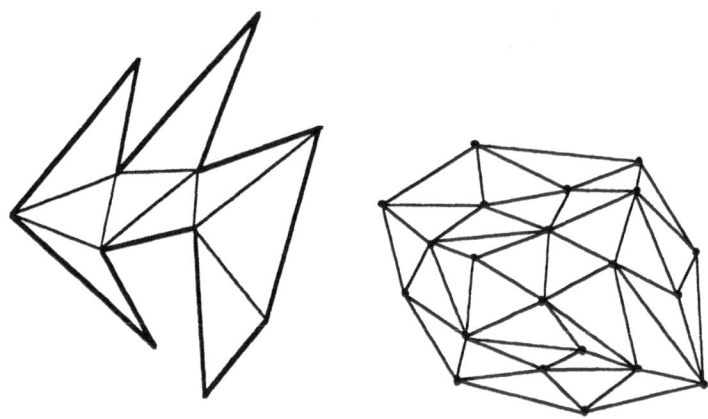

Figure 5: Triangulations.

In particular one can easily determine whether a point lies inside or outside the polygon. Triangulating sets of points is in particular important for interpolating information. When the points are places where some value is computed one can use a triangulation to decide between which values to interpolate when the value at another position is required. Simply determine the triangle the point lies in and interpolate between the vertices of the triangle.

To triangulate a set of points we use a scanline algorithm. We move a scanline from left to right over the set of points. At any moment we will take care that we have the subset to the left of the scanline triangulated. Moreover we maintain the convex hull of the points passed. Now assume the scanline stops at a point p_i. Let p_{i-1} be the last position where the scanline did stop. Connect p_i with p_{i-1}. p_{i-1} will lie on the convex hull of the points passed. Now walk along this convex hull starting at p_{i-1} in both directions connecting p_i with the points on the convex hull, until we reach the tangents from p_i to the convex hull. In this way we have updated the triangulation and the convex hull.

The amount of time spend is an initial $O(n \log n)$ to sort all the points by x-coordinate plus for each step an amount of work in the order of the number of edges added to the triangulation. As the triangulation is a planar graph the number of edges is linear and, hence, after sorting, we spend only $O(n)$ time in total.

Theorem 2.5 *Given a set of n points in the plane, they can be triangulated in time $O(n \log n)$. If the points are sorted by x-coordinate the method takes only linear time.*

Note that this also gives us an alternative method to computed the convex hull of a set of points.

Computing a triangulation of a polygon is more difficult. One way of solving the problem is to use a more general method that produces a so-called *constrained triangulation*. Here we are given a set of line segments (non-intersecting) and ask for a triangulation of the set of endpoints where the line segments must be edges of the triangulation. (This will also triangulate the outside of the polygon but this part can easily be removed.) We will only describe the basic ideas behind the method. For details see e.g. [67] section 6.2.2.

The method consists of two parts. First we split the region into monotone polygons that consist of two vertically monotone chains of edges, i.e., any horizontal line intersects the polygon in one segment. Next each of these subpolygons is triangulated. This triangulation can be done in linear time during one simultaneous walk along the two monotone chains (see [31]).

To form the monotone polygons we first compute the convex hull of all the vertices. These will clearly be edges of the triangulation. Next we use a scanline technique. We move a scanline from the bottom to the top, stopping at each vertex. At any moment the scanline intersects a number of edges. For each part between two such edges we maintain the highest vertex in this part. Now assume we reach some vertex p. If p has both edges running downwards and upwards we simply adapt the information at the scanline and continue. If p has no edges above the scanline we also simply adapt the information at the scanline. If p has only edges above the scanline we connect p with the highest point in the interval p lies in. Next we adapt the information. It is easy to see that this takes time $O(n \log n)$ in total. After this step each vertex will have edges going downwards. In a second sweep, but this time from top to bottom we take care that each vertex also gets edges going upwards. As a result we will have only monotone polygons left.

Theorem 2.6 *Given a polygon with n edges, the inside of P can be triangulated in time $O(n \log n)$. If P is monotone the algorithm takes time $O(n)$.*

This is not the best possible. Tarjan and Van Wijk [75] have given a very complicated algorithm that runs in time $O(n \log\log n)$. The question whether an $O(n)$ algorithm exists is still open.

2.3   Further reading

The most efficient convex hull algorithm for a set of points know today is by Kirkpatrick and Seidel [46] and runs in time $O(n \log k)$ where k is the number of points on the convex hull.

Algorithms for dynamically maintaining convex hulls under insertions and deletions of points can be found in [65, 59].

A generalization of convex hulls are the *alpha hulls* as defined by Edelsbrunner, Kirkpatrick and Seidel [24]. Alpha hulls resemble the shape of the set of points much better than convex hulls, allowing e.g. holes.

Many other triangulation methods for pointsets do exist, all obtaining triangulations with different properties. See section 3.2 for a different method.

There are also many different ways of subdiving polygons in smaller pieces. Sometimes additional vertices (called *Steiner points*) are allowed to obtain decompositions with particular properties. See e.g. Keil and Sack [43] or O'Rourke [58] for a number of different techniques.

3   Proximity

A number of problems in computational geometry deals with notions of *distance*, in other words, they are proximity problems. For example, one might ask for the two points in a set that lie nearest to one another (important in e.g. checking VLSI design constraints) or the points farthest away from one another. Another problem asks to store a set of points or other objects such that for a given query point the point in the set nearest to this query point can be determined efficiently. This plays an important role in planning shortest routes for robots, picking graphical objects, finding the object in a database that satisfy some constraints as good as possible, etc.

In this section we will introduce the Voronoi diagram that can be used for solving many types of proximity problems. Next we will look at point location techniques that are neccessary to be able to use Voronoi diagrams but can be used in many other applications as well.

3.1 Voronoi diagram

Let V be a set of n points in the plane. Now subdivide the plane in n regions $R_1...R_n$ such that R_i consists of those points q for which $p_i \in V$ is the nearest neighbor. The subdivision we obtain is called the *Voronoi diagram* of the set of points, named after Voronoi [76]. See figure 6 for an example.

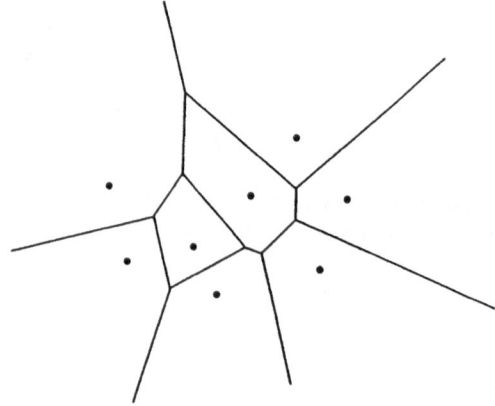

Figure 6: A Voronoi diagram.

A Voronoi diagram has a number of interesting properties. All regions are convex and the region R_i contains p_i and no other point of V. Some of the regions are unbounded. These correspond to the points on the convex hull of V. An edge of the Voronoi diagram is a part of the bisector between the points in the two region on both sides of the edge. The number of edges and nodes in the Voronoi diagram is linear. When no three points lie on a circle the nodes have degree 3. A node corresponds to a point that lies on the same shortest distance from three points in V.

Shamos and Hoey [73] were the first to realize that the Voronoi diagram is a powerful tool in computational geometry. They gave the first algorithm to compute the Voronoi diagram of n points in time $O(n \log n)$. The basic idea of the method is a divide and conquer approach. We will only briefly sketch the algorithm. For details see e.g. [67] chapter 5. We split the set of points with a vertical line in two equal sized subsets V_1 and V_2 and recursively construct the Voronoi diagram VD_1 of V_1 and VD_2 of V_2. To merge the two Voronoi diagrams, note that all edges in VD are either edges of VD_1 or of VD_2 or are bisectors between points in V_1 and V_2. These new edges will form a chain that is monotone in the y-direction. We first determine the half-infinite edges that have to be added. To this end we compute the two tangents to the convex hulls of V_1 and V_2 and take the perpendicular bisectors of these tangents. Let l be the top bisector. l will lie in a region R_i of VD_1 and a region R_j of VD_2. Hence, l is the bisector of p_i and p_j. Determine the first place where l intersects the boundary of R_i or R_j. When l first intersects R_i determine the new region R_k of VD_1 we come in. Adapt l and make it the bisector of p_k and p_j. Similar when we hit a region of VD_2 first. In this way we continue until we reach the bottom half-infinite ray. The new edges can be calculated in time $O(n)$ total.

Theorem 3.1 *The Voronoi diagram of a set of n points in the plane can be determined in time $O(n \log n)$.*

As a first application consider the nearest neighbor problem in which we are interested in finding the two points in the set that lie nearest together. It is easy to see that the Voronoi regions of the two nearest points must share an edge. Hence, we simply check for each edge the distance between the two points on both sides and take the minimum of all pairs. This clearly takes $O(n)$ once the Voronoi diagram has been constructed because the number of edges in the Voronoi diagram is linear.

In fact, for each point p in the set, the nearest neighbor of p must share an edge with p. Hence, in the same way, we can find the nearest neighbor for each point in V.

Theorem 3.2 *Let V be a set of n points in the plane. One can determine for each point in V its nearest neighbor in V in time $O(n \log n)$.*

Using Voronoi diagrams is very practical. The algorithms to construct them are not hard to implement (although they might look that way). Guibas and Stolfi [36] show how to do this implementation. Another approach is to use a quite different method (using the plane sweep technique) that was designed by Fortune [30].

3.2   Delaunay triangulation

Let V be a set of points. We call two points *neighbors* when their Voronoi regions share an edge. Now assume that no four points in V lie on a circle. As a result, if we connect all neighbors with straight line segments we get a triangulation of the pointset. This triangulation is called a *Delaunay triangulation* after Delaunay who studied such triangulations already a long time ago ([18]).

Theorem 3.3 *The Delaunay triangulation of a set of points can be constructed in time $O(n \log n)$.*

The Delaunay triangulation has a number of interesting properties. The most important one is probably that the circle with the three vertices of a triangle of the triangulation on its boundary contains no other point of the set. This follows from the fact that this circle has one of the vertices of the Voronoi diagram as its center and, hence, this center lies on the same minimal distance to the three points. This property makes the Delaunay triangulation useful in interpolation applications (see section 2.2).

3.3   Point location

One important proximity problem is the *nearest neighbor searching problem* (also called the post office problem): Given a set of points (post offices) V store them such that for a given point p we can efficiently determine the point (post office) nearest to p.

To solve this one could construct the Voronoi diagram of the set V. Now the problem reduces to: given a subdivision of the plane in convex regions, store this subdivision such that for an arbitrary point p we can efficiently determine the region p lies in. Storing with each region the nearest neighbor, this immediately solves the post office problem.

Searching in a planar subdivision, also called *point location*, is a very general problem and has many other applications as well. For example, to determine whether a point lies inside a non-convex polygon one can triangulate the polygon and perform point location on the set of triangles. Many techniques have been developed to solve the problem. The simplest one, called the slab method, draws a vertical line through each vertex of the subdivision. In this way we obtain $O(n)$ vertical slabs. We construct a balanced tree on the x-coordinates of the vertical lines to be able to determine for each point in which slab it lies. Next, for each slab, we construct a balanced tree storing all the edges that intersect the slab from top to bottom. Searching in this tree we can determine between which two edges a point lies and this tells us in which region the point lies. The query time will be $O(\log n)$ but the preprocessing time and amount of space required are $O(n^2)$.

The first optimal point location technique requiring $O(n)$ storage with a query time of $O(\log n)$ was given by Kirkpatrick [44]. The method is based on *triangular refinement*. First we triangulate all the regions. Hence, we are left with a subdivision of triangles. Now we remove a number of independent vertices and their edges and retriangulate the holes that appear. In this way we get a new triangulation with less triangles. We continue in the same way until we are left with one big triangle. In [44] it is show that this can be achieved in $O(\log n)$ steps. The different levels of triangulation look a lot alike. As a result, if one knows the position of a point in one level one can find in constant time the position of the point in the next level. To perform a query with a point p we start at the smallest triangulation. From here we step to the next triangulation and continue until we reach the original triangulation. Because each step takes $O(1)$ time and there are $O(\log n)$ levels the query time becomes $O(\log n)$. For details see [44] or [67] chapter 2.2.2.

Theorem 3.4 *Given a planar subdivision consisting of convex polygonal cells with a total of n edges, one can store the subdivision using $O(n)$ storage such that, given a point p, one can determine in time $O(\log n)$ the cell p lies in.*

From this the following result immediately follows.

Theorem 3.5 *One can store a set of points in the plane using $O(n)$ storage such that a nearest neighbor query can be answered in time $O(\log n)$.*

Although theoretically optimal the constants in the triangular refinement method are very high which makes the algorithm unpractical. Hence, people have worked on designing other techniques that are also fast in practice. The best method known today is probably the technique of Edelsbrunner, Guibas and Stolfi [23] (see also [22] chapter 11).

3.4   Further reading

Many different types of Voronoi diagrams do exist. The diagram presented in section 3.1 is just the simplest one. First of all one can usedifferent distance functions. Lee and Wong [52] showed how to compute Voronoi diagrams for the L_1 and L_∞ metric. Lee [48] generalized this to L_p metrics. Chew and Drysdale [13] generalized this further to *convex distance functions*.

A second generalization is to allow other types of objects instead of points. Lee and Drysdale [51] introduced Voronoi diagrams of line segments. Yap [82] extended this further to curved segments.

Another direction of research involved *higher order Voronoi diagrams*. A kth-order Voronoi diagram divides the plane into regions in which the point of the set that is the kth nearest is the same. So the first-order Voronoi diagram is the standard Voronoi diagram. On the other hand, in the nth-order Voronoi diagram we split the plane in regions such that the furthest point is the same. (This diagram is also called the *furthest point Voronoi diagram*). First algorithms to construct kth-order Voronoi diagrams were given by Lee [49]. Better results where obtained by Chazelle and Edelsbrunner [11] (see also [22]).

A survey on Voronoi diagrams together with a large bibliography can be found in Aurenhammer [1].

4 Windowing

The *windowing problem* asks for computing the part of a picture (or 2-dimensional scene) that lies inside a given axis-parallel rectangle. In database applications the problem is often refered to as the *range searching problem*. Many data structures have been proposed for storing a scene such that windowing with different windows can be performed efficiently. The type of data structure and efficiency highly depend on the type of objects in the scene. We will first look at the (in graphics unrealistic) situation where the scene consists of a collection of n points only. Later we will consider scenes of line segments and other objects.

An important property of data structures is whether they are static or dynamic. *Static* data structures are once constructed for a fixed set of objects and can be used only for queries with different windows. *Dynamic* data structures allow for both queries and insertions and deletions of objects. Dynamic data structures are much more flexible and are often required in graphics applications.

4.1 k-d trees

One of the data structures used very often in graphics is the *quad tree*. This structure, originally proposed by Finkel and Bentley [29] but in fact already known for a long time in computer graphics, recursively splits the set of objects in four subsets, corresponding to four quadrants of the plane. In graphics the structure is mostly use as an image space data structure. Here the splitting continues until the regions have the size of one pixel. Quad trees can also be used as object space data structures. In this case one continues splitting the plane (and, hence, the set of object) until the subsets get some small size.

In object space applications quad trees tend to become quite unbalanced. To avoid this another structures, called a *k-d tree* was introduced by Bentley [2] (see also [3]).

A 2-dimensional k-d tree is a binary tree that is constructed as follows: Let V be a set of points in the plane. Choose a point $p \in V$. $p = (p_1, p_2)$ will be stored in the root of the tree. Now split the set V in two subsets V_1 of points with x-coordinate $\leq p_1$ and V_2 of points with x-coordinate $> p_1$. V_1 will be stored in the left subtree of p and V_2 in the right subtree. Now in each subset again take a point. This will become the root of the subtree. Again split the set in two halves but this time with respect to the y-coordinate. On the next level of the tree we again split with respect to x-coordinate, etc. We continue this way until a subset contains only one point. This point we store in a leaf. See figure 7 for an example of a k-d tree.

The main advantage of k-d trees over quad-trees is that we always can split the set in an optimal way by taking as a splitting point the median for the particular coordinate of

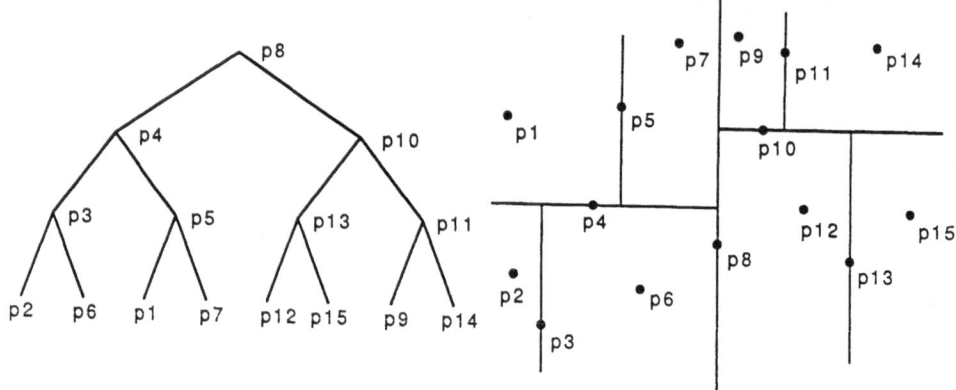

Figure 7: A k-d tree.

all the points. This means that we can always construct k-d trees of depth $\lceil \log n \rceil$. The construction can easily be carried out in time $O(n \log n)$.

To perform a windowing query on a k-d tree we search with the window in the tree. Note that each node in the k-d tree corresponds to a part of the plane as shown in figure 7. Now assume we are at some node v in the tree. First we check whether the point stored at v lies in the set. If so we report it. Next we look at the cell C of the plane corresponding to v. If the window completely covers C all points in the subtree below v lie in the window and we report them all (by traversing the subtree). If the window does not intersect C we don't have to continue in this subtree. Otherwise we continue the search at both sons of v (unless v is a leaf).

It can be shown that such a windowing query will take time at most $O(\sqrt{n} + k)$ where k is the number of answers found. This is based on the fact that any horizontal or vertical line intersects at most $O(\sqrt{n})$ cells of nodes. This leads to the following result:

Theorem 4.1 *There exists a structure, the k-d tree, for storing n points that can be constructed in time $O(n \log n)$, such that a windowing query takes time $O(\sqrt{n} + k)$. The structure uses $O(n)$ storage.*

One of the problems of k-d trees (and of quad trees) is that they are static. Insertion and deletion routines such as the ones for normal binary trees do not work on k-d trees because it is impossible to perform rotations in the tree. A way to avoid this is to redefine k-d trees in a different way.

Kreveld and Overmars [47] define a so-called *divided k-d tree*. Let V be a set of points in the plane. Sort the points on x-coordinate. Now divide this sorted set in $\sqrt{n}$ groups of each $\sqrt{n}$ points. We construct a simple balanced binary search tree on x-coordinate with each leaf corresponding to one of these groups. This tree is called the top tree. For each group we construct a balanced binary search tree on y-coordinate. These are called the bottom trees. So in the top tree we split on x-coordinate and in the bottom trees on y-coordinate (in contrast to a normal k-d tree where we split on each level according to a different coordinate). See figure 8 for an example of a divided k-d tree.

Clearly the structure takes $O(n)$ storage and can be constructed in time $O(n \log n)$. To perform a window query, let the query window be $([A_1 : B_1], [A_2 : B_2])$, i.e., we want to find all points with x-coordinate between A_1 and B_1 and y-coordinate between A_2 and

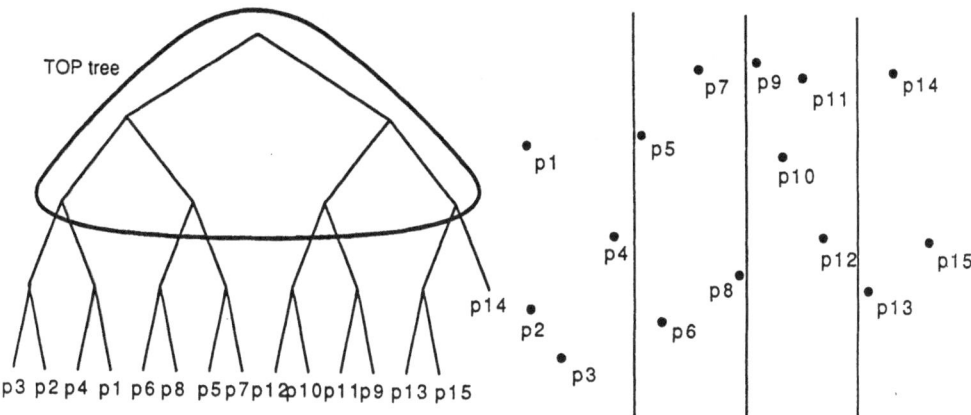

Figure 8: A divided k-d tree

B_2. We search with both A_1 and B_1 in the top tree. Let the leaves we end in be δ_1 and δ_2. For each leaf between δ_1 and δ_2 we know that all points stored in the corresponding bottom tree have x-coordinate between A_1 and B_1. Hence, in each of these bottom trees we simply search with A_2 and B_2 and report all points with y-coordinate between them (remember that the bottom trees are sorted on y-coordinate). Now we are left with the subtrees below δ_1 and δ_2. For the points in these subtrees we do not know whether their x-coordinate lies in the range. So we search in them with A_2 and B_2 but for each point found we also check whether it lies between A_1 and B_1 with respect to its x-coordinate.

Theorem 4.2 *Divided k-d trees of n points can be constructed in time $O(n \log n)$ and use $O(n)$ storage. Windowing queries can be performed on them in time $O(k + \sqrt{n} \log n)$, where k is the number of answers found.*

Proof. Searching with A_1 and B_1 in the top tree takes $O(\log n)$ time. We find at most $O(\sqrt{n})$ bottom trees in between the two leaves in which we have to search. Searching such a bottom tree takes time $O(k' + \log n)$ where k' is the number of answers found in this bottom tree. Searching the trees below δ_1 and δ_2 takes at most time $O(\sqrt{n})$ because this is a bound on the size of the bottom trees. $\square$

To be able to perform insertions and deletions efficiently we relax the conditions on the divided k-d tree slightly. We allow the bottom trees to grow as long as their size remains smaller than $2\sqrt{n}$ and also the top tree may get a size of $2\sqrt{n}$. This does not increase the query time in order of magnitude. To insert a point p we search in the top tree to find the correct bottom tree and insert p in this bottom tree. This takes time $O(\log n)$. If the bottom tree remains smaller than $2\sqrt{n}$ we are done. Otherwise we split the bottom tree in two bottom trees each of size $\sqrt{n}$ and insert a new leaf in the top tree. This takes time $O(\sqrt{n})$ but this time can be charged to $\sqrt{n}$ preceeding insertions in the bottom tree at which it did not need to be split. Hence, this is an average of $O(1)$ per insertion. When the top tree gets too big we rebuid the complete tree. This takes time $O(n \log n)$ but this can be charged to n updates that must have taken place since the last rebuilding. Hence, the average insertion time is $O(\log n)$. Deleting a point p is even simpler. We search in the top tree to find the bottom tree that contains p. Next we delete p from this bottom tree and we are done. (When the number of deletions gets too big we have to rebuild the whole tree to maintain the balance conditions. See [47] for details.) Hence, the deletion time is also $O(\log n)$.

The structure can in fact be improved slightly. Rather than splitting into $\sqrt{n}$ groups we had better split into $\sqrt{n/\log n}$ groups, each of size $\sqrt{n\log n}$. It can easily be seen that this improves the query time to $O(k + \sqrt{n\log n})$.

Theorem 4.3 *In a divided k-d tree updates can be performed in amortized time $O(\log n)$. A windowing query can be performed in time $O(k + \sqrt{n\log n})$ where k is the number of answers found. The structure can be constructed in time $O(n\log n)$ and uses $O(n)$ storage.*

When the window is small the query time is normally a lot better because the number of bottom trees we have to search will be small as well.

4.2 Range trees

We will now concentrate on another structure, called a *range tree*, that has a much faster query time at the cost of a slight increase in storage. The structure was designed independently by a number of researchers (see e.g. [4, 53, 78, 80]).

Let us first consider the one-dimensional problem. So we are given a set of points on the real line and we want to store them such that for a given "window" $[A_1 : B_1]$ we can efficiently determine the points lying in between A_1 and B_1. To this end we store the points in the leaves of a balanced binary search tree, in sorted order. Moreover we link the leaves in this order in a double linked list. The structure clearly uses $O(n)$ storage. We call this structure a one-dimensional range tree.

To perform a query with window $[A_1 : B_1]$ we search with A_1 in the tree to locate the smallest point $\geq A_1$. Let this point be K. If K does not exist or $K > B_1$ we are done. Otherwise, we report K and look at the right neighbor of K in the tree and repeat the test here. It is clear that such a query takes time $O(\log n)$ to search with A_1 plus the number of answers found.

Theorem 4.4 *Given a set of n points on the real line, the one-dimensional windowing problem can be solved in a query time of $O(k + \log n)$ using $O(n)$ storage, where k is the number of answers found.*

Now let us look at the two-dimensional problem. So V is a set of points in the plane. A two-dimensional range tree of V has the following form. We sort all point with respect to their x-coordinate and store them in the leaves of a balanced binary search tree in this order. To each internal node δ we associate a one-dimensional range tree T_δ of the points in the subtree rooted at δ, on their y-coordinate (see figure 9). Hence, in the main tree points are sorted with respect to their x-coordinate and in the associated structures points are sorted with respect to their y-coordinate.

To perform a query with window $([A_1 : B_1], [A_2 : B_2])$ we search with both A_1 and B_1 in the main tree. For some time A_1 and B_1 will follow the same search path but at some internal node δ A_1 will go to the left son and B_1 will go to the right son. Let $\beta_1 \ldots \beta_i$ be the nodes that are rightson of a node on the search path of A_1 below δ and do not lie on the search path themselves. Silmilar, let $\gamma_1 \ldots \gamma_j$ be the nodes that are leftson of a node on the search path of B_1 below δ that do not lie on the search path themselves. See figure 10 for the situation.

All points with x-coordinate between A_1 and B_1 lie in exactly one of the subtrees rooted at the β and γ nodes. Of these points we have to find the ones whose y-coordinate

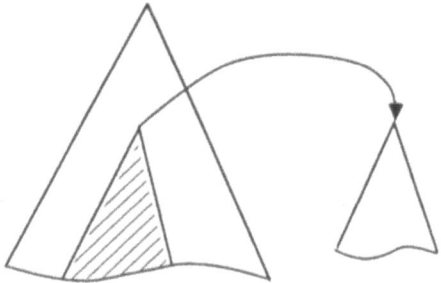

Figure 9: Associated trees.

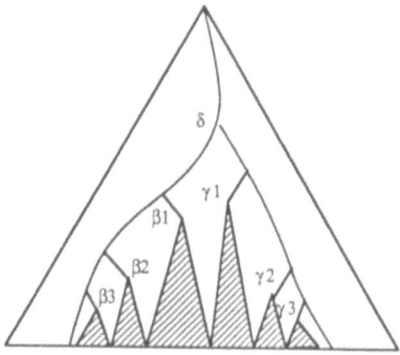

Figure 10: The β and γ nodes.

lies between A_2 and B_2. For this we use the structures $T_{\beta_1} \ldots T_{\beta_i}$ and $T_{\gamma_1} \ldots T_{\gamma_j}$. All points in the x-range are stored in exactly one such structure and all points in these structures lie in the x-range. On each of these T-structures we perform a one-dimensional windowing query with window $[A_2 : B_2]$.

Theorem 4.5 *Given a set of n points in the plane, the two-dimensional windowing problem can be solved in a query time of $O(k + \log^2 n)$ using $O(n \log n)$ storage, where k is the number of answers found.*

Proof. Let us first consider the amount of storage required. The main tree uses only $O(n)$ storage. On each level of the main tree each point in V occurs exacly once in an associated structures. As an associated structure of n' points uses storage $O(n')$, the associated structures on one level together use $O(n)$ storage. As the tree has $O(\log n)$ levels the storage bound follows.

To perform a query we first seach in the main tree with A_1 and B_1 which takes time $O(\log n)$. In this way we locate $O(\log n)$ T_β and T_γ structures that each have a query time of at most $O(\log n)$ plus the number of answers found. Hence, the total query time is bounded by $O(\log^2 n)$ plus the total number of answers found. $\square$

The two-dimensional range tree can be made dynamic but the update algorithms are quite complicated (see e.g [78, 80]).

4.3 Segment trees

Range trees are only capable of storing points. In many applications, especially in computer graphics, objects are not points but, for example, rectangles, line segments, etc. In this section we will treat a second data structure, the segment tree, that can, in combination with e.g. range trees, be used for storing other geometric objects.

The *segment tree* was introduced by Bentley and Wood[8] to solve some rectangle problems. Although used for solving many two-dimensional problems, the segment tree is a one-dimensional data structure.

Let $V = \{[a_1 : b_1], [a_2 : b_2], \ldots, [a_n : b_n]\}$ be a set of n intervals (segments) on the real line. (Intervals are allowed to intersect, overlap, etc.) All left and right endpoints of the intervals we sort. Let the sorted list be $x_1, x_2, \ldots, x_{2n}$. These endpoints split the real line in a number of so-called elementary intervals $(-\infty : x_1), [x_1 : x_2), [x_2 : x_3), \ldots, [x_{2n} : \infty)$. These elementary intervals we store in the leaves of a balanced binary search tree. With each internal node δ we associate the interval I_δ that is the union of the intervals associated to the sons of δ. (In other words, I_δ in the interval spanned by the subtree rooted at δ.) With each node δ we store a structure T_δ containing all intervals in V that contain I_δ but do not contain $I_{\text{father}(\delta)}$. The form of T_δ depends on the problem we want to solve using the segment tree. See figure 11 for an example of a segment tree. With each node δ the intervals stored in T_δ are indicated.

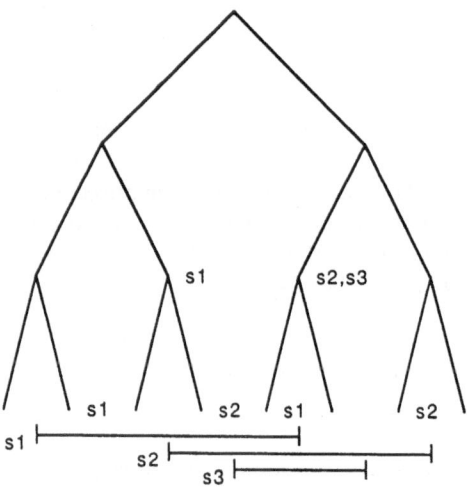

Figure 11: A segment tree.

The segment tree is mostly used for so-called *stabbing queries*. Let p be a point on the line, we want to report all intervals that contain p. To solve this problem we structure T_δ as a simple list of the intervals. To find all intervals containing p, we search with p in the tree, starting at the root. Assume we are at some node δ. We report all intervals stored in T_δ. Next we look at the two sons δ_1 and δ_2 of δ. When p lies in I_{δ_1} we continue the search in δ_1. Otherwise we continue the search in δ_2.

The correctness of the algorithm can be seen as follows. Clearly all intervals reported contain p, because for each node δ visited, p lies in I_δ and the reported intervals contain

I_δ. No interval is reported more than once, because on each path from the root to a leaf an interval can occur at most once. Finally, if interval i contains p it clearly contains the elementary interval stored in the leaf p ends in during the search. As i does not contain I_{root} there must be some node δ on the search path towards this leaf such that i contains I_δ but not $I_{\text{father}(\delta)}$. i will, hence, be reported when the search passes this node. (In fact, this is not completely correct. When p is the right endpoint of i, i will not be found. This case can easily be solved by either treating endpoints in a special way, or by adding some extra information in the segment tree.)

Theorem 4.6 *Given a set of n intervals, they can be stored in a segment tree, using $O(n \log n)$ storage, such that stabbing queries can be answered in time $O(k + \log n)$ where k is the number of reported answers.*

Proof. The query time follows immediately from the above discussion. It remains to prove the bound on storage required. On each level of the segment tree, each interval can be stored at at most 2 nodes. (This follows from the definition.) Hence, at each level the T-structures together use at most $O(n)$ storage. The bound follows. $\square$

Segment trees are (depending on the choice of T_δ) dynamic. See e.g. [8] for details.

In the same way as in range trees, we can construct two-dimensional segment trees. Let V be a set n of axis-parallel rectangles in the plane. (For example, bounding boxes of a set of graphical objects.) To store them, we project all rectangles on the x-axis. In this way we obtain a set of intervals. These intervals we store in a segment tree. For each node δ we have a number of intervals that have to be stored in T_δ. These intervals correspond to rectangles. These corresponding rectangles we project on the y-axis and we make T_δ into a segment tree that stores these y-intervals. In T_δ we store at each internal node a list of rectangles to which the y-intervals, that should be stored there, belong. It is easy to see that the structure obtained requires $O(n \log^2 n)$ storage.

A two-dimensional stabbing query asks for all rectangles that contain a given point p. In graphics, this is for example important when picking an object. To perform a stabbing query we use the two-dimensional segment tree. Let $p = (p_1, p_2)$. We search with p_1 in the main segment tree. The nodes on the search path together contain all rectangles that contain p_1 in the x-projection. Among them we have to find those whose y-projection contains p_2. To this end we use the T-structures. For each node δ on the search path of p_1 we search with p_2 in T_δ, reporting all rectangles stored at nodes on the search path of p_2. As we have to query $O(\log n)$ T-structures, each requiring time $O(\log n)$ plus the number of answers found, we obtain the following result:

Theorem 4.7 *Given a set of n axis-parallel rectangles, they can be stored in a two-dimensional segment tree, using $O(n \log^2 n)$ storage, such that stabbing queries can be answered in time $O(k + \log^2 n)$ where k is the number of answers found.*

Now let us return to our windowing problem. But this time let us assume that our picture consists of (non-intersecting) line segments rather than points. For example, a large map stored in a database. We will show how to store the picture in a two-dimensional data structure based on the segment tree such that for each given window we can efficiently determine what part of the picture is visible in the window. (These results are based on work by Overmars [60, 61]).

To solve the windowing problem, we split it in two parts. The first part asks for all line segments that lie completely in the window. The second part asks for all line segments that intersect the boundary of the window.

To solve the first problem we can use the solution for range searching described in the previous section. When a line segment s lies completely in the window surely its left endpoint lies in the window. So we can store all left endpoints in a range tree and perform a range query with the window. This will take time $O(\log^2 n)$. The structure uses $O(n \log n)$ storage.

So we only have to consider the second subproblem: find those line segments that intersect the boundary of the window. We will only look at the top boundary. The other boundaries follow in a similar way.

First we project all line segments on a vertical line. In this way each line segment becomes an interval. Of these intervals we construct a segment tree. All intervals stored at some internal node δ completely cover the interval I_δ associated to δ. I_δ corresponds to a horizontal slab in the plane. All the line segment stored at δ intersect the slab completely and, because they do not intersect each other, appear ordered in the slab. See figure 12. We store them in this order in the internal nodes of a balanced binary search tree T_δ. It is easy to see that the structure requires $O(n \log n)$ storage.

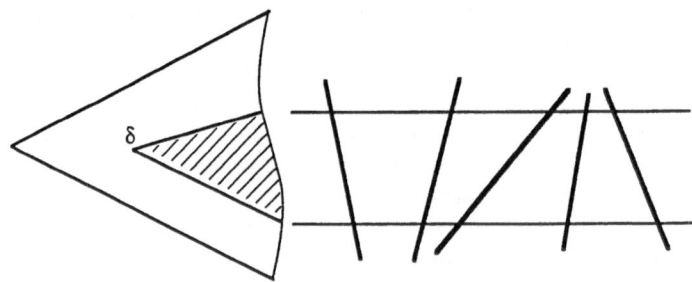

Figure 12: Line segments stored at δ.

To perform a query with the top boundary $\overline{(x_1, y)(x_2, y)}$ we search with y in the segment tree. Clearly, line segments intersecting the top boundary must be stored at one of the nodes on the search path. For each such node δ we search with x_1 and x_2 in T_δ, locating all the segments in between. It is easy to see that this can be done in time $O(\log n)$ plus the number of answers found. As we have to query $O(\log n)$ structures T_δ the total query time is bounded by $O(\log^2 n)$ plus the total number of answers. For details see [60]. It is also shown there that insertions and deletion can be performed in time $O(\log^2 n)$. Combining this with the result for range queries we obtain:

Theorem 4.8 *Given a set of n non-intersecting line segments in the plane, we can store them using $O(n \log n)$ storage such that those k segments visible in a given window can be determined in $O(k + \log^2 n)$ time. The structure is dynamic and can be updated in $O(\log^2 n)$ time.*

Using this method, some of the line segments might be reported more than once. This can easily be avoided by checking whether segments have already been reported before. This can be done in $O(1)$ time per reported segment.

4.4   General scenes

The restriction that the picture consists of line segments only can easily be dropped. The method of the previous section can simply be extended to more general objects. In fact, the only restriction is that they are orthogonal convex. (I.e., any horizontal or vertical line segment with both endpoints inside the object must lie completely inside the object.) And almost all objects can be decomposed in orthogonal convex objects. (Of course, the objects should not overlap or intersect but they are allowed to touch.)

The method now works completely the same. To find the objects that lie completely inside the window we choose a representation point inside each object and perform a windowing query on those points. To find the objects intersecting the top boundary we again project all objects on a vertical line, construct a segment tree on the projections and associate with each node δ a search tree T_δ storing the objects in the slab in their x-order. Queries are now performed in essentially the same way, yielding the same time bounds.

4.5   Further reading

Quad trees and k-d trees have been used in many different applications. For an overview of quad trees and their application see Samet [70]. See [69] for a bibliography of over 250 papers on quad trees and related structures. For dynamization techniques for ordinary quad and k-d trees see [64]. See [59] for an overview of general techniques for dynamizing data structures.

Other types of structures for windowing can be found in [5, 6, 25]. A very general (and tunable) technique can be found in [72]. An interesting related structure is the *priority search tree* introduced by McCreight [55] that is a combination of a search tree and a priority queue and can be used for many types of half-open range queries. In [20] this structure is used as a basis to obtain a very efficient and dynamic structure for range searching.

Many other applications of segments trees exist. See e.g. Edelsbrunner [21]. Here also a related structure, the *interval tree* is introduced. (See also [67].)

5   Intersection problems

Intersection problems form the basis of many types of applications. For example, hidden surface removal algorithms are often based on computing intersections (see the next section). In this section we will discuss some different intersection problems. First we consider the simple case in which all objects are axis-parallel line segments. Next we extend this result to arbitrarily oriented line segments. Finally we show how to treat more general types of objects as well.

5.1   Axis-parallel line segments

Let V be a set of horizontal and vertical line segments in the plane. We are interested in finding all intersections between segments. As the number of intersections can be as large as $(n/2)^2$ any algorithm for this problem will take time $\Omega(n^2)$ in the worst case. But in many applications the number of intersections will be much smaller. Hence, we would like to have an algorithm that runs fast when the number of intersections is small. Such an algorithm is called *output sensitive*.

We will use the scanline technique to solve this problem. We move a vertical scanline from left to right over the set of line segments. At any moment there will be a collection of horizontal line segments that intersect the scanline. These line segments we store, ordered by y-coordinate in a simple balanced search tree T (for example, an AVL-tree). Hence, T allows for insertions and deletions of line segments in time $O(\log n)$. The scanline will stop at each x-coordinate of an endpoint of a line segment. Hence, we first sort all endpoints by x-coordinate to obtain a list of halting points. Now each time the scanline halts there are three possible cases:

- A left endpoint of a horizontal line segment s. In this case we insert s in T.

- A right endpoint of a horizontal line segment s. In this case we delete s from T.

- A vertical line segment s. Let the endpoint be (x, y_1) and (x, y_2). We search with both y_1 and y_2 in T and report all horizontal segments that lie between them. In this way all horizontal segments intersecting s are found in time $O(k' + \log n)$ where k' is the number of answers found.

(When more than one event happens at the same moment some care has to be taken. We first have to perform the insertions, next the queries on T and finally the deletions.)

Theorem 5.1 *Given a set V of n horizontal and vertical line segments, all intersections in V can be determined in time $O(k + n \log n)$ where k is the number of intersections found.*

When we are only interested in the question whether there are intersections the method clearly takes time $O(n \log n)$ because we can stop after the first intersection found.

A similar technique can be used to determine intersections among axis-parallel rectangles in the same time bounds. Only some care has to be taken that rectangles that completely contain some other rectangle are also reported. (See e.g. [67] chapter 8 for details.)

5.2 Arbitrary line segments

We will now drop the restriction that line segments must be axis-parallel. Hence, we have a set of arbitrarily oriented line segments. Again we will try to obtain an output-sensitive method. This algorithm is due to Bentley and Ottmann [7].

The method is also based on the scanline technique. Again we move a scanline from left to right over the plane. At each moment the scanline is intersecting a number of line segments. These line segments we store in the order of intersection (from top to bottom) in a balanced binary search tree T. (Note that we do not store the actual intersection points. They change continuously when the scanline moves so they cannot be maintained.) The tree T changes whenever the scanline encounters an endpoint of a line segment. At a left endpoint the segment must be inserted and at a right endpoint the segment must be deleted. But T also changes at an intersection because two segments will change order in T at such a point. Hence, the scanline must stop at each endpoint and at each intersection. But we don't know the intersections!!

To avoid this problem note that, when the next halting point for the scanline is an intersection between segments s and s', then s and s' must be neighbors in T. Hence, it suffices to keep track of intersection points between neighbors in T. To this end we use a priority queue Q that stores all positions where the scanline must stop. We initialize Q to contain all endpoints of the line segments. T is initialized to be empty. The algorithm now is a simple loop that, as long as Q is not empty, takes the first element from Q and treats it according to the following cases:

- The point is a left endpoint of a segment s. Insert s in T. Let s_1 and s_2 be the two neighbors of s. If s and s_1 intersect to the right of the scanline, insert the intersection in Q. Similar for s and s_2. If s_1 and s_2 intersect to the right of the scanline, remove the intersection from Q. (They are no longer neighbors in T.)

- The point is a right endpoint of a segment s. Remove s from T. Let s_1 and s_2 be the two neighbors of s. If s_1 and s_2 intersect to the right of the scanline, insert the intersection in Q. They have become neighbors in T.

- The point is an intersection of s and s'. See figure 13 for the situation. Report the intersection. Let s_1 be the other neighbor of s and s_2 the other neighbor of s'. Switch s and s' in T. If s and s_2 intersect to the right of the scanline, insert the intersection in Q. Similar for s' and s_1. (These are the new neighbors.) If s and s_1 intersect to the right of the scanline, remove the intersection from Q. Similar for s' and s_2. (These are no longer neighbors.)

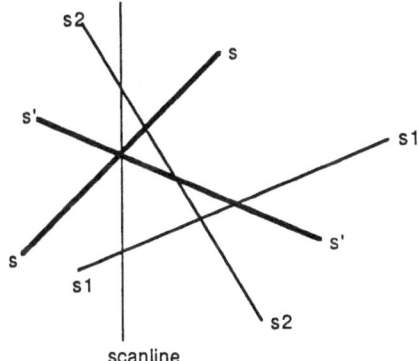

scanline

Figure 13: Treating an intersection.

So for each point passed by the scanline we have to do one insertion or deletion on T and at most 2 insertions and 2 deletions on Q. As all these operations take $O(\log n)$ time, each stop of the scanline takes time $O(\log n)$. The number of stops of the scanline is $2n + k$ where k is the number of intersections found. Hence, the total amount of time spend is $O((n + k) \log n)$. Note that the algorithm correctly maintains all intersections between neighbors in Q and, hence, correctly finds all answers. (Some care has to be taken when more points lie on a vertical line or segments are vertical. The second problem can be avoided by choosing a slightly different direction for the scanline to move. The first problem can be solved by first treating the left endpoints, next the intersections and finally the right endpoints, or the other way round if you don't want touching segments to be reported.)

Theorem 5.2 *Given a set V of n arbitrarily oriented line segments in the plane, all k intersections can be determined in time $O((n + k) \log n)$.*

5.3 Other objects

In some applications the objects between which one wants to compute intersection are no line segments. For example they are pieces of curves or triangles. When the objects are curves the method presented above can easily be adapted. The only restriction is that the intersection of the pieces with any vertical line (the scanline) consists of one point only and that intersections between two pieces can be calculated efficiently. If the curves do not satisfy the first requirement they can normally be cut up into smaller pieces that do satisfy the requirement. The method now works in exactly the same way, obtaining the same time bounds.

When the objects are solid, e.g. triangles or circles, some care has to be taken that objects that contain one another are also reported as intersecting. If we assume that the intersection between an object and a vertical line consists of one interval (i.e., the objects are convex with respect to the y-axis) again the same idea can be used. Only this time the tree T must store intervals. For this an *interval tree* can be used (see e.g. [67], section 8.8.1) and we again obtain the same time bounds.

We get a quite different type of problems when we ask for the intersection between two large objects, e.g. two polygons. When the polygons are convex this intersection can easily be computed in time $O(n)$ where n is the total number of vertices. (Note that the intersection will be a convex m-gon with $m \leq n$.) The idea is the following. Let P and P' be the two polygons. We sort all points by x-coordinate. (This can easy be done in time $O(n)$ by splitting the polygons in an upper and a lower half.) Now we move a scanline from left to right. At any moment the scanline will intersect both P and P' in one interval. Let s_1 be the top and s_2 be the bottom segment of P intersected by the scan line (if they exist). Similar s'_1 and s'_2 for P'. Clearly, the next position where the scanline should halt is either the next vertex in the x-order or the intersection of s_1 and s'_1 or the intersection of s_2 and s'_2 with the obvious modifications in the segments. (For details see e.g. [67] section 7.2.1.)

Theorem 5.3 *Given two convex polygons with n vertices, their intersection can be determined in time $O(n)$.*

Finding the intersection between two non-convex polygons is a lot harder. Note that the intersection can consist of $\Omega(n^2)$ parts. Hence, we again would like an output sensitive solution. One way of solving the problem is to simply compute all intersections between the boundaries using the technique in section 5.2 and using this information to compute the actual intersection. This would give an $O((n + k) \log n)$ solution for the problem. This can be improved to $O(k + n \log n)$ using so-called red-blue intersection. Mairson and Stolfi [54] show that, given one collection of blue line segments that do not intersect each other and another collection of red line segments that do not intersect each other, the intersections between the two sets can be computed in time $O(k + n \log n)$. Now we can colour the boundary of one polygon blue and of the other polygon red and we used this algorithm to compute the intersections.

Theorem 5.4 *Given two non-convex polygons with n vertices, their intersection can be determined in time $O(k + n \log n)$, where k is the complexity of the intersection.*

5.4 Further reading

For a large number of results on intersecting rectangles and similar object see Edelsbrunner [21]. Recently, Chazelle and Edelsbrunner [12] have improved the bound for finding intersections among arbitrarily oriented line segments to $O(k + n \log n)$.

6 Hidden surface removal

A fundamental problem in 3-dimensional graphics is the *hidden surface removal* problem. We are given a scene of objects in 3-dimensional space and a point or direction of view and want to know which parts of objects are visible. Many algorithms are known for this problem, e.g. the z-buffer algorithm, the depth sort algorithm, the area subdivision method, etc. See Sutherland et. al. [74] for an overview of many different techniques or any textbook on graphics. Unfortunately, all of these techniques are image space methods, i.e., they use the resolution of the screen and are unable to come up with a structural description of the visible scene.

In this chapter we will give two object space algorithms for the hidden surface removal problem. In both algorithms we assume that the objects consist of polygons and that the polygons are not penetrating each other. We assume that the point from which we are looking is along the z-axis at $-\infty$. In other words, the projection is a parallel projection on the xy-plane. Note that this does not impose restrictions because any type of projection and point of view can be reduced to this simple case by applying an appropriate transformation to the objects.

6.1 Projection method

The first method is by Schmitt [71]. It is based on the line segment intersection method presented in the preceeding section. As a first step we project all polygons on the xy-plane and compute all intersections between the boundaries. In this way we obtain a straight-line planar graph in which each node corresponds to an intersection or a vertex of a polygon. See figure 14 for an example. The thick lines form the graph. This graph might not be connected. To this end, and to be able to traverse the graph, we add one long edge *bot* below all the others and for each node that has only edges going to the right we add a so-called drain-edge that goes vertically down until it hits another edge. (These are the dotted lines in figure 14.)

We will only describe how to obtain the visible edges. Visible surfaces can be obtained in a similar way. We traverse the graph, starting at the left endpoint of *bot* and ending at the right endpoint of *bot*. At any moment we keep a tree T that contains all the polygons at the current position, sorted by relative depth. Moreover, we keep a value I that indicates the number of polygons that is covering the current edge. So the edge is visible when $I = 0$. In the beginning $I = 0$. Now we traverse the whole graph from left to right. Assume we follow an edge $e = \overline{pq}$. If $I = 0$ and e is not a drain edge and $e \neq bot$ then we report e as being visible. Now there are a few cases. (We assume for simplicity that no intersection point lies on a vertex or on another intersection point. Hence, every node has degree 2 for a vertex, degree 4 for an intersection and degree 3 when a drain-edge starts or ends here. The method can easily be adapted when this is not the case.)

- q is a vertex (has degree 2). If the other edge runs to the right simply continue along this edge. Don't change I or T. If the other edge runs to the left, stop here.

98

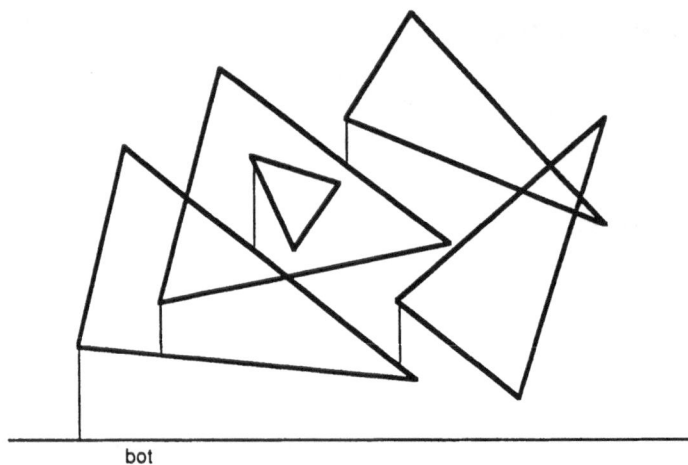

bot

Figure 14: The planar graph with drain-edges.

- q is an intersection (has degree 4). Let s be the edge of the polygon e is part of. Let s' be the edge that is intersecting s and P' be the polygon s' is a boundary of. We either enter P' or leave P'. If we enter P' insert it in T. If P' lies below the current edge, increase I. If we leave P', delete it from T. If P' lies below the current edge decrease I. Now continue along s.

- q is the bottom node of a drain edge. In this case we first continue along the drain edge. Next we continue along the normal edge. (I.e., we make two recursive calls of the procedure.) I and T are not changed.

- q is the top node of a drain edge. Let this node be a vertex of polygon P. We search with P in T to determine the number of polygons that lie below P at q. Set I to this number. Next we recursively call the procedure on both other edges starting at q.

See figure 15 for the four different cases. The arrows indicate the directions in which we continue. It is easy to see that the whole graph is traversed this way and that I and T are maintained correctly. At each node we have to do at most $O(\log n)$ work to insert, delete or search in T.

Theorem 6.1 *Given a set of non-penetrating polygons with a total of n edges in space, the hidden line removal problem can be solved in time $O((n + k) \log n)$ where k is the number of intersections between edges in the projection.*

6.2 Output-sensitive method

A disadvantage of the above method is that the time complexity can be very large even when the output size is small. For example, one big rectangle could be covering all the other objects. The method would still compute all intersections between the projections of all the invisible objects. Hence, again, we would like to have a true output-sensitive algorithm. We will now describe a recently designed algorithm by Overmars and Sharir

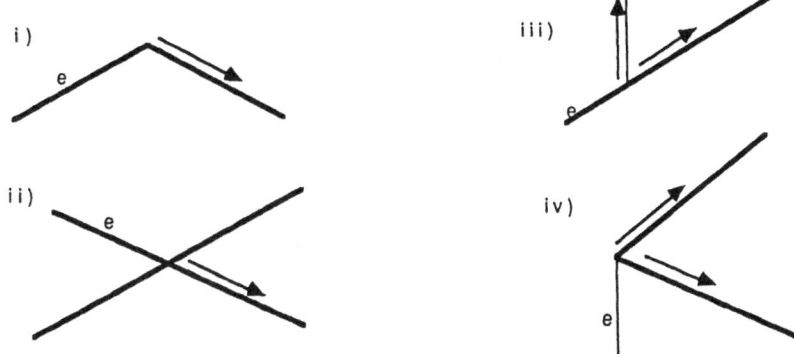

Figure 15: The four cases.

[66] that accomplishes this task. We make the restriction that all objects are triangles (remember that polygons can easily be triangulated), but the method can easily be extended to other polygons, as long as the number of vertices per polygon is limited. Moreover, we assume that the triangles can be ordered by depth, i.e., there is no cyclic overlap. If this is not the case, cyclic overlap has to be removed by cutting up some triangles.

The method is based on the following result:

Theorem 6.2 *Let A be a set of (non-overlapping) polygonal regions in the plane with a total of n_A bounding line segments. Let B be another such set with n_B bounding line segments. The parts of the polygons in A that do not lie inside polygons in B can be computed in time $O((n_A + n_B + k) \log(n_A + n_B))$ where k is the complexity of the resulting set of polygons.*

Proof. This can easily be done by computing all intersections between edges in A and in B and traversing the graph obtained. $\square$

This result can be viewed in the following way. Assume we have two subsets of triangles in space, one V_A lying completely behind the other V_B (in depth). Now assume we compute all visible parts of V_A (not looking at V_B) and all visible parts of V_B. Let A consist of the visible parts of V_A and B the visible parts of V_B. The theorem now says that the visible parts in $A \cup B$ can be computed in the time bound stated.

Let k_0 be some constant. Take the nearest $\sqrt{k_0}$ triangles and computed which parts are visible. This can be done in time $O(k_0 \log k_0)$ time in a trivial way. Let k_1 be the complexity of the resulting scene. Take the next $\sqrt{k_1}$ triangles. Compute the parts that are visible among them. This takes time $O(k_1 \log k_1)$. The complexity of the scene is at most $O(k_1)$. Merge this with the first part in the way described above in time $O((k_1 + k_2) \log k_1)$ where k_2 is the complexity of the new scene. Now take the next $\sqrt{k_2}$ triangles and repeat the process. In this way we continue until no triangles are left.

Theorem 6.3 *Given a set of n triangle in space. Their visible parts can be computed in time $O(n\sqrt{k} \log n)$ where k is the complexity of the visible scene.*

Proof. Note that the total amount of time spend in the above algorithm is bounded by $O(\sum k_i \log n)$ while $\sum \sqrt{k_i} = n$ and $k_i \leq k$ for all i. Now

$$\sum k_i = \sum (\sqrt{k_i}\sqrt{k_i}) \leq \sum (\sqrt{k_i})\sqrt{k} = n\sqrt{k}$$

from which the theorem follows. □

In fact the bound can be improved to $O(k + n\sqrt{c}\log n)$ where c is the maximal contour size during the execution of the algorithm.

6.3 Further reading

A number of other object space algorithms are known for hidden surface removal, e.g. Devai [19], Goodrich [32] and McKenna [56]. Also a number of algorithms exist that deal with restricted cases like e.g. polygonal terrains. See e.g. Reif and Sen [68].

An important special case occurs when the set of objects consists of axis-parallel rectangles, each at a particular depth. This situations occurs for example in applications where there is a large number of overlapping windows on the screen. The best solution for this problem known today is due to Bern [9] and runs in time $O(n \log n \log\log n + k \log n)$ where k is the complexity of the output scene. See also Güting and Ottmann [37].

7 Other research

In this section we give a number of other subjects treated in computational geometry and mention some results obtained.

7.1 Grids

In computer graphics coordinates of geometric objects often are not arbitrary reals but choosen from some bounded universe. For example, the screen coordinates. Although the general algorithms presented above can handle such cases as well, in a number of situations one can obtain more efficient or simpler algorithms when working in a bounded universe. Let us assume the coordinates are integers between 0 and $u - 1$ (i.e., u is the universe size). Hence, the plane has become a $u \times u$ grid. See Keil and Kirkpatrick [42], Karlsson [40] and Overmars [62] for overviews of such results. Most of them are based on the fact that one can use table look-up or perfect hashing techniques instead of searching. For example, in [62] (see also [41]) it is shown how to compute all intersections in a set of line segments with endpoints on a grid in time $O(k + u + n \log n)$ in a very simple way.

One of the basic tools used in algorithms is sorting. It is easy to see that, using bucket sort, a set of n values between 0 and $u - 1$ can be sorted in time $O(n + u)$. Using repeated bucket sort Kirkpatrick and Reisch [45] have improved this to $O(n \log\log_n u)$. Note that this is $O(n)$ as long as $u = O(n^c)$ for some constant c. Now consider the convex hull problem. Note that in the first method presented in section 2.1 the time consuming step was sorting. After sorting the method runs in $O(n)$ time. Hence, applying the efficient sorting method on a grid we obtain:

Theorem 7.1 *Given a set of n points on a $u \times u$ grid, the convex hull can be computed in time $O(n \log\log_n u)$,*

A second basic tool is searching. Van Emde Boas [27], see also [28], has shown that one can store n values between 0 and $u-1$ using $O(u)$ storage such that values can be inserted, deleted and searched for in time $O(\log\log u)$. Also 1-dimensional range queries can be answered this efficiently. Now reconsider the axis-parallel line segment intersection problem where we have a set of horizontal and vertical line segments and want to compute all intersection. In section 5.1 we have given a scanline algorithm to solve this problem. We moved a scanline from left to right and maintained the intersections with horizontal line segments in a balanced tree. When the line segments lie on a grid we can use a VanEmdeBoas tree for this purpose. Insertions and deletions now take time $O(\log\log u)$. When the scanline reaches a vertical line segment we perform a range query on this structure which also takes time $O(\log\log u)$. Sorting the halting points for the scanline can be done in time $O(n\log\log_n u)$ as stated above. We conclude:

Theorem 7.2 *Given a set of n horizontal and vertical line segments on a $u \times u$ grid, all intersections can be found in time $O(k+n\log\log u)$, where k is the number of intersections found.*

Many other problems can be solved more efficiently on a grid, including windowing, some proximity problems, etc.

7.2 Combinatorial geometry

Many result from combinatorial geometry are used in computational geometry. See the book of Edelsbrunner [22] for an overview of such techniques.

Let us just briefly mention one of these techniques, *duality*. Using dualization one can transform points into lines and lines into points maintaining the incidence relation. So a point p maps to a line $D(p)$ and a line l to a point $D(l)$ such that if p lies on l, $D(l)$ lies on $D(p)$. In fact not only incidence but vertical distance is maintained. (See [22] for details.) One can use dualization to turn problems into different problems. For example, the question whether in a set of points three points lie on a line dualizes to: given a set of lines are there three that pass through the same point. This problem can be solved in time $O(n^2)$ by traversing the subdivision of the plane induced by the lines (see [22] for details).

7.3 Partition trees

As we have seen in section 4 it is easy to store geometric objects in data structures as long as they are in some sense axis-parallel, or the query objects are axis-parallel. This is no longer the case when both objects and query objects are not axis-parallel. For example it is hard to store a set of line segments V such that for any other line segment s the elements in V intersecting s can be determined efficiently.

To solve such query problems so-called *partition trees* have been designed (see Willard [79], Edelbrunner and Welzl [26], Haussler and Welzl [38] and Welzl [77]). The easiest type of a partition tree is the so-called *conjungation tree* ([26]). Let V be a set of points in the plane. A conjungation tree is a binary tree in which each node corresponds to a part of the plane. The root corresponds to the whole plane. The leaves correspond to parts that contain just one point of V. Each node stores a line l that splits its part in the parts for its two sons such that each of the two parts contains the same number of points of V, i.e., l splits the subset of points in equal halves. Now the basic property of the conjungation tree is that the two sons of a node have the same splitting line. Such a line, that splits two subsets at the same moment in equal halves always exists and is called a *conjungate*. The points in the set V are stored in the leaves.

The conjungation tree requires $O(n)$ storage. Moreover, it can be constructed in time $O(n \log n)$. One can show that in a conjungation tree any line l will cut through at most $O(n^{.695})$ parts stored at nodes. Hence, the large majority of the parts lie on one side of the line.

One type of query that can be performed using partition trees is the so-called *halfplanar range query*. Given a halfplane H (i.e., the part of the plane on one side of a line l_H) determine all (or the number) of points in H.

Theorem 7.3 *In a conjungation tree, halfplanar range queries can be solved in time* $O(k + n^{.695})$ *where k is the number of answers found.*

Proof. We simply search with l_H in the tree. Assume we are at some node δ. If δ is a leaf we check whether the point stored lies in the halfplane H. Otherwise we look at the part of the plane corresponding to δ. If l_H intersects this part we continue the search in both sons. If the part lies completely inside H we report all points in it. If the part lies completely outside H we don't search any further (at this node).

It is easy to see that the number of nodes visited is bounded by the number of parts l_H is intersecting and, as stated above, this is at most $O(n^{.695})$. $\square$

Partition trees can also be used for storing line segments. Queries like: which line segments intersect a given query line segment, can then be answered in similar time bounds. (See e.g. Guibas et. al. [35].)

7.4 Random sampling

A technique that has recently received a lot of attention in computational geometry is *random sampling*. Algorithms using random sampling tend to be simple and have very good expected time bounds. The main difference with other expected-case algorithms (like the one for convex hulls presented in section 2.1) is that the time bounds depends on the random behaviour of the algorithm and not on some distribution of the set of objects.

The basic idea behind random sampling is that objects are added in a random order or that first a random subsets of the objects is taken. Such a random subset normally gives (at least in a probabilistic sense) a lot of information about the whole set. For example, if a small random subset V' of a set of points V is taken, the chance that another point in V falls inside the convex hull of V' is large. This information can be used to solve the problem more efficiently.

Many geometric problems can be solved using random sampling. See e.g. Clarkson [14, 15, 16], Haussler and Welzl [38] and Clarkson et. al. [17] for application of random sampling in proximity problems, point location, range searching, convex hulls, etc. For example, in [16] a simple method is given to compute all intersection in a set of line segments in expected time $O(k + n \log n)$ where k is the number of intersections.

7.5 Further reading

Many interesting papers on computational geometry have been published in the following journals (among others): Algoritmica, Computer Vision, Graphics and Image Processing, Information Processing Letters, Journal of Algorithms, Discrete and Computational

Geometry, SIAM J. of Computing, and ACM Transactions on Graphics. Another important source of publications form the proceedings of the ACM Symp. on Computational Geometry that is held yearly.

References

1. Aurenhammer, F., Voronoi diagrams – A survey. Techn. Rep. 263, Inst. f. Informationsverarbeitung, TU Graz, 1988

2. Bentley, J.L., Multidimensional binary search trees used for associated searching. C. ACM *18*, 509-517 (1975)

3. Bentley, J.L., Multidimensional binary search trees in database applications. IEEE Trans. Software Eng. *SE-5*, 333-340 (1979)

4. Bentley, J.L., Decomposable searching problems. Inform. Proc. Lett. *8*, 244-251 (1979)

5. Bentley, J.L., Friedman, J.H., Data structures for range searching. ACM Comput. Surveys *11*, 397-409 (1979)

6. Bentley, J.L., Maurer, H.A., Efficient worst-case data structures for range searching. Acta Inform. *13*, 155-168 (1980)

7. Bentley, J.L., Ottmann, T., Algorithms for reporting and counting geometric intersections. IEEE Trans. Comput. *C-28*, 643-647 (1979)

8. Bentley, J.L., Wood, D., An optimal algorithm for reporting intersections of rectangles. IEEE Trans. Comput. *C-29*, 571-577 (1980)

9. Bern, M., Hidden surface removal for rectangles. Proc. 4th ACM Symp. on Computational Geometry, 1988, pp. 183-192

10. Bykat, A., Convex hull of a finite set of points in two dimensions. Inform. Proc. Lett. *7*, 296-298 (1978)

11. Chazelle, B., Edelsbrunner, H., An improved algorithm for constructing k th-order Voronoi diagrams. IEEE Trans Comput. *C-36*, 1349-1354 (1987)

12. Chazelle, B., Edelsbrunner, H., An optimal algorithm for intersecting line segments in the plane. Proc. 29th IEEE Symp. on Foundations of Computer Science, 1988, pp. 590-600

13. Chew, L.P., Drysdale, R.L., Voronoi diagrams based on convex distance functions. Proc. 1st ACM Symp. on Computational Geometry, 1985, pp. 235-244

14. Clarkson, K.L., A probabilistic algorithm for the post office problem. Proc. 17th ACM Symp. on Theory of Computing, 1985, pp. 175-184

15. Clarkson, K.L., New applications of random sampling in computational geometry. Discrete Comput. Geom. *2*, 195-222 (1987)

16. Clarkson, K.L., Applications of random sampling in computational geometry II. Proc. 4th ACM Symp. on Computational Geometry, 1988, pp. 1-11

17. Clarkson, K.L., Tarjan, R.E., Van Wijk, C.J., A fast Las Vegas algorithm for triangulating a simple polygon. Proc. 4th ACM Symp. on Computational Geometry, 1988, pp. 18-22

18. Delaunay, B., Sur la sphère vide. Bull. Acad. Sci. USSR (VII), Classe Sci. Mat. Nat., 793-800 (1934)

19. Dévai, F., Quadratic bounds for hidden line elimination. Proc. 2nd ACM Symp. on Computational Geometry, 1986, pp. 269-275

20. Edelsbrunner, H., A note on dynamic range searching. Bull. of the EATCS *15*, 34-40 (1981)

21. Edelsbrunner, H., Intersection problems in computational geometry. Techn. Rep. F93, Inst. f. Information Processing, TU Graz, 1982

22. Edelsbrunner, H., Algorithms in combinatorial geometry. EATC Monographs on Theoretical Computer Science 10, Springer, Berlin 1987

23. Edelsbrunner, H., Guibas, L.J., Stolfi, J., Optimal point location in a monotone subdivision. SIAM J. Comput. *15*, 317-340 (1986)

24. Edelsbrunner, H., Kirkpatrick, D.G., Seidel, R., On the shape of a set of points in the plane. IEEE Trans. Information Theory *IT-29*, 551-559 (1983)

25. Edelsbrunner, H., Overmars, M.H., Seidel, R., Some methods of computational geometry applied to computer graphics. Comp. Vision, Graphics and Image Proc. *28*, 92-108 (1984)

26. Edelsbrunner, H., Welzl, E., Halfplanar range search in linear space and $O(n^{0.695})$ query time. Inform. Proc. Lett. *23*, 289-293 (1986)

27. van Emde Boas, P., Preserving order in a forest in less than logarithmic time and linear space. Inform. Proc. Lett. *6*, 80-82 (1977)

28. van Emde Boas, P., Kaas, R., Zijlstra, E., Design and implementation of an efficient priority queue. Math. Systems Theory *10*, 99-127 (1977)

29. Finkel, R.A., Bentley, J.L., Quad-trees; a data structure for retrieval on composite keys. Acta Inform. *4*, 1-9 (1974)

30. Fortune, S., A sweepline algorithm for Voronoi diagrams. Algorithmica *2*, 153-174 (1987)

31. Garey, M.R., Johnson, D.S., Preparata, F.P., Tarjan, R.E., Triangulating a simple polygon. Inform. Proc. Lett *7*, 175-180 (1978)

32. Goodrich, M.T., A polygonal approach to hidden line elimination. Proc. 25th Allerton Conf. on Communication, Control and Computing, 1987, pp. 849-858

33. Graham, R.L., An efficient algorithm for determining the convex hull of a finite planar set. Inform. Proc. Lett. *1*, 132-133 (1972)

34. Graham, R.L., Yao, F.F., Finding the convex hull of a simple polygon. J. Algorithms *4*, 324-331 (1983)

35. Guibas, L., Overmars, M.H., Sharir, M., Intersecting line segments, ray shooting, and other applications of geometric partitioning techniques. Proc. SWAT 1988, Lect. Notes in Comp. Science 318, Springer, Berlin 1988, pp. 64-73

36. Guibas, L., Stolfi, J., Primitives for the manipulation of general subdivisions and the computation of Voronoi diagrams. ACM Trans. Graphics *4*, 74-123 (1985)

37. Güting, R.H., Ottmann, T., New algorithms for special cases of the hidden line elimination problem. Comp. Vision, Graphics and Image Proc. *40*, 188-204 (1987)

38. Haussler, D., Welzl, E., ϵ-nets and simplex range queries. Discrete Comput. Geom. *2*, 127-151 (1987)

39. Jarvis, R.A., On the identification of the convex hull of a finite set of points in the plane. Inform. Proc. Lett. *2*, 18-21 (1973)

40. Karlsson, R.G., Algorithms in a restricted universe. PhD thesis, Techn. Rep. CS-84-50, Dept. of Computer Science, University of Waterloo, 1984

41. Karlsson, R.G., Overmars, M.H., Scanline algorithms on a grid. BIT *28*, 227-241 (1988)

42. Keil, J.M., Kirkpatrick, D.G., Computational geometry on integer grids. Proc. 19th Allerton Conf. on Communication, Control and Computing, 1981, pp. 41-50

43. Keil, J.M., Sack, J.R., Minimum decomposition of polygonal objects. in: G. Toussaint (ed.), Computational Geometry, North-Holland, Amsterdam 1985

44. Kirkpatrick, D.G., Optimal search in planar subdivisions. SIAM J. Comput. *12*, 28-35 (1983)

45. Kirkpatrick, D.G., Reisch, S., Upperbounds for sorting integers on random access machines. Theor. Comp. Science *28*, 263-276 (1984)

46. Kirkpatrick, D.G., Seidel, R., The ultimate planar convex hull algorithm? SIAM J. Comput. *15*, 287-299 (1986)

47. van Kreveld, M.J., Overmars, M.H., Divided k-d trees. Techn. Rep. RUU-CS-88-28, Dept. of Computer Science, University of Utrecht, 1988.

48. Lee, D.T., Two-dimensional Voronoi diagrams in the L_p metric. J. ACM *27*, 604-618 (1980)

49. Lee, D.T., On k-nearest neighbor Voronoi diagrams in the plane. IEEE Trans. Comput. *C-31*, 478-487 (1982)

50. Lee, D.T., On finding the convex hull of a simple polygon. J. Comput. Inform. Sciences *12*, 87-98 (1983)

51. Lee, D.T., Drysdale III, R.L., Generalisation of Voronoi diagrams in the plane. SIAM J. Comput. *10*, 73-87 (1981)

52. Lee, D.T., Wong, C.K., Voronoi diagrams in L_1 (L_∞) metrics with 2-dimensional storage applications. SIAM J. Comput. *9*, 200-211 (1980)

53. Lueker, G.S., A data structure for orthogonal range queries. Proc. 19th IEEE Symp. on Foundations of Computer Science, 1978, pp. 28-34

54. Mairson, H., Stolfi, J., Reporting and counting intersections between two sets of line segments. in: R. Earnshaw (ed.), Theoretical foundations for computer graphics and CAD, Springer, Berlin 1988, pp. 307-326

55. McCreight, E.M., Priority search trees. SIAM J. Comput. *14*, 257-276 (1985)

56. McKenna, M., Worst-case optimal hidden surface removal. ACM Trans. Graphics *6*, 19-28 (1987)

57. Mehlhorn, K., Data structures and algorithms 3: Multi-dimensional searching and computational geometry. EATCS Monographs on Theoretical Computer Science 3, Springer-Verlag, Berlin 1984

58. O'Rourke, J., Art gallery theorems and algorithms. Oxford Univ. Press, Oxford 1987

59. Overmars, M.H., The design of dynamic data structures. Lect. Notes in Computer Science 156, Springer, Berlin 1983

60. Overmars, M.H., Range searching in a set of line segments. Proc. 1st ACM Symp. on Computational Geometry, 1985, pp. 177-185

61. Overmars, M.H., Geometric data structures for computer graphics. in: R. Earnshaw (ed.), Fundamental algorithms for computer graphics, Springer, Berlin 1985, pp. 919-931

62. Overmars, M.H., Computational geometry on a grid: an overview. in: R. Earnshaw (ed.), Theoretical foundations for computer graphics and CAD, Springer, Berlin 1988, pp. 167-184

63. Overmars, M.H., van Leeuwen, J., Further comments on Bykat's convex hull algorithm, Inform. Proc. Lett. *10*, 209-212 (1980)

64. Overmars, M.H., van Leeuwen, J., Dynamic multi-dimensional data structures based on quad- and k-d trees. Acta Inform. *17*, 267-285 (1982)

65. Overmars, M.H., van Leeuwen, J., Maintenance of configurations in the plane. J. Comput. Syst. Sciences *23*, 166-204 (1981)

66. Overmars, M.H., Sharir, M., Output-sensitive hidden surface removal, Techn. Rep., Dept. of Computer Science, University of Utrecht, 1989, to appear

67. Preparata, F.P., Shamos, M.I. Computational geometry. Springer, New York 1985

68. Reif, J.H., Sen, S., An efficient output-sensitive hidden-surface removal algorithm and its parallelization. Proc. 4th ACM Symp. on Computational Geometry, 1988, pp. 193-200

69. Samet, H., Bibliography on quadtrees and related hierarchical data structures. in: L. Kessenaar, F. Peters and M. van Lierop (ed.), Data structures for raster graphics, Springer, Berlin 1986, pp. 181-201

70. Samet, H., An overview of quadtrees, octtrees, and related hierarchical data structures. in: R. Earnshaw (ed.), Theoretical foundations for computer graphics and CAD, Springer, Berlin 1988, pp. 51-68.

71. Schmitt, A., Time and space bounds for hidden line and hidden surface algorithms. Proc. Eurographics 1981, pp. 43-56

72. Scholten, H.W., Overmars, M.H., General methods for adding range restrictions to decomposable searching problems. J. Symbolic Computation *7*, 1-10 (1989)

73. Shamos, M.I., Hoey, D., Closest point problems. Proc. 16th IEEE Symp. on Foundations of Computer Science, 1975, pp. 151-162

74. Sutherland, I.E., Sproull, R.F., Schumacker, R.A., A characterization of ten hidden-surface algorithms. Computing Surveys *6*, 1-25 (1974)

75. Tarjan, R.E., Van Wijk, C.J., And $O(n \log \log n)$-time algorithm for triangulating a simple polygon. SIAM J. Comput. *17*, 143-178 (1988)

76. Voronoi, G., Nouvelles applications des parametres continus à la theorie des formes quadratiques. Deuxième Mémorie: Recherches sur les paralléloèdres primitifs, J. reine angew. Math. *134*, 198-287 (1908)

77. Welzl, E., Partition trees for triangle counting and other range searching problems. Proc. 4th ACM Symp. on Computational Geometry, 1988, pp. 23-33

78. Willard, D.E., Predicate-oriented database search algorithms. Garland Publishing Company, New York 1979

79. Willard, D.E., Polygon retrieval. SIAM J. Comput. *11*, 149-165 (1982)

80. Willard, D.E., Lueker, G.S., Adding range restriction capability to dynamic data structures. J. ACM *32*, 597-617 (1985)

81. Yao, A.C., A lowerbound to finding convex hulls. J. ACM *28*, 780-787 (1981)

82. Yap, C.K., An $O(n \log n)$ algorithm for the Voronoi diagram of a set of simple curve segments. Discrete Comput. Geom. *2*, 365-393 (1987)

Chapter 5
Object-Oriented Graphics

Edwin H. Blake, Peter Wisskirchen

Abstract

Any attempt to deal with the complexity of computer graphics should have a well founded and appropriate underlying abstraction. This tutorial introduces and critically examines the object-oriented paradigm as it applies to computer graphics. Regarding the parts of a model, interaction, or animation, as independent actors communicating via messages has an intuitive appeal. This initial appeal, elaborated to become object-oriented graphics, does seem to stand up to the closer scrutiny.

The object-oriented paradigm seems to be well suited to applications in dynamic graphics. Dynamic graphics comprises two broad areas: human-computer interaction and three- dimensional animation and simulation. The connection between the two is that in both cases users/modellers have intuitions which correspond closely to the notion of objects within the object-oriented paradigm.

We first introduce the concepts of object-oriented programming and pay special attention to those which are most relevant to computer graphics. Next object-oriented and classical approaches to providing usable abstractions for computer graphics are compared. The use of inheritance in a graphics kernel is treated. The concept of a multi-level graphics systems with group and part editing facilities is introduced.

To give a practical introduction to the use of object-oriented methods we present two examples: one of user interfaces and another of coordinate transformations. In paragraph 4 the concepts introduced earlier are brought together in the design of a simple animation system. It is clear that the design process is made much easier by the use of object-oriented methods.

Finally a brief survey of the field and references for further study are given on more advanced topics.

1. Introduction to Object-Oriented Concepts

In recent years the concept *object-oriented* has become one of the most frequently used slogans in the field of computer science. We should however differentiate between two different aspects of object orientation, the *object-oriented user interface* and the *object-oriented programming*.

By an object-oriented user interface we mean interfaces, which allow, as the the Apple Macintosh does, the direct manipulation of objects at the user interface using icons and mouse. The concept *object* is meant in a more intuitive sense here and refers to the representation of components of the entire on-on-screen information. The user views these components as belonging together. These components can be manipulated as such by user actions. They could, for instance, be mouse-clicked, moved, erased or have there representation changed. Examples of such objects are graphically visualized file folders which can be opened per mouse clicks, pop-up menus which can be positioned and activated as desired, windows which can be opened, enlarged, reduced, shifted, closed. The design of object-oriented interfaces does not require object-oriented programming languages.

By object-oriented programming we understand the use of an object-oriented programming language or, in more general terms, the use of an object-oriented programming environment in order to program as usual. Object-oriented programming languages are generally usable programming languages. Therefore, they are suitable for programming general (not necessarily object-oriented) interfaces.

Even though these two aspects differ substantially from one another, they nevertheless reveal a number of valuable cross-references when examined more closely; cross-connections we attempt to show in this tutorial. We believe that object-oriented programming provides a natural way of dealing with the concurrent actions of those entities that need to be modelled when dealing with interactive graphics and animation. All information is stored in terms of active objects having an internal state. This seems to appeal to a human having to program and use the systems interactively.

The purpose of this section is to review the basic ideas of the object-oriented abstraction and to see if they are an adequate and suitable foundation for building graphics systems. The aim of any abstraction is to provide a context within which problems can easily be solved.

1.1. Objects and Methods

Before explaining the basic concepts of object-oriented programming in detail by examples, we want to list them first.

- **Objects:** every entity in an object-oriented system is an object. An object can be regarded as a collection of its internal data, invisible from the outside, representing its present state. An object is addressed via one or several names. These names constitute the references to an object.
- **Messages:** objects are addressed via messages defined for the specific object. The object as a receiver of a message has different possibilities of reacting to a message. It can change its local state; it may send further messages to other objects (or to itself); it can return a value, i.e. another object, as a result.
- **Methods:** the reaction to the receipt of a message is by evaluating methods assigned to this object.
- **Classes:** every object is an instance of a class and behaves as specified in the class definition (i.e. the methods are defined here). The class therefore describes which messages an object can receive and how the corresponding messages are evaluated by methods.
- **Instance and class variables:** the internal states of an object are represented by instance and class variables. While instance variables contain individual information of an individual object, i.e. an instance, class variable are used for storing information common to all instances of a class.
- **Class methods:** in consistently object-oriented systems, classes are objects by themselves . Consequently, we can define methods for classes as well to set and modify the states of a class. These states, stored in class variables, can be accessed by all instances of a class.
- **Inheritance:** an important characteristic of object-oriented systems are the inheritance mechanisms they provide. When forming a new class, we can specify

the classes from which inheritance is to be permitted. Inheritance means that both variables and methods are inherited.

– **Hierarchical and multiple inheritance:** there are different inheritance mechanisms. With hierarchical inheritance, we can specify only one class from which an (direct) inheritance is possible. This produces an inheritance tree. With multiple inheritance, we can specify several classes from which inheritance is possible. In this case, we obtain a directed graph describing the inheritance relations.

As we review the concepts which belong to the object-oriented paradigm the following questions should be asked about these features for graphics:

– Are they desirable?
– How important are they for graphics?
– Are they sufficient for building graphical systems or are extensions needed?
– Are the features consistent?
– Are they orthogonal?

In the discussion which follows we shall be concerned with these questions. We shall first give some examples of objects and messages. Then we deal with a few of the object-oriented concepts which are particularly relevant for graphics: abstract data types, classes and inheritance, message passing and polymorphism.

In 1.6. we discuss the particular advantages of Smalltalk, an object-oriented language which we shall be using a great deal in this tutorial. Finally we consider programming environments.

1.2. Some Examples of Objects and Messages

Examples of objects are numbers, text strings or graphical objects, like lines, rectangles, etc.. An object can be regarded as a collection of its internal data representing its current state. A typical example is a rectangle with the diagonal corners (40,40) and (100,100)[1].

Objects are addressed via *messages* (which are sent by an object, the *sender*). An object has different possibilities of reacting to a message. It can change its internal state or it can send messages to other objects or even to itself. After the processing of a message, an object is returned to the sender as a *result.*.

Let us look to the example of a rectangle a. If we want to modify the coordinates of a rectangle, we can send the following message to the object a.

origin: 50@50 corner: 200@200

This message has the effect that the internal data of the rectangle is modified, namely the upper, left-hand coordinates are set to 50@50 and the lower left-hand ones to 200@200 The complete statement reads as follows:

b ← a origin: 50@50 corner: 200@200

This message consists of two parts, the name of the message, the so-called *message selector* origin:corner:, and the *arguments* of the message, 50@50 and 200@200. A message selector together with a set of argument names is called a *message pattern* .

---

[1]We use the syntax of Smalltalk-80 in the examples.

Thus origin: leftPoint corner: rightPoint[2] would be a message pattern. Parameters of a message "transport" information to the receiver. Following classical terminology they could therefore be viewed as input parameters. Output parameters such as found in Fortran do not exist. The result of a message is an object, in our above example referred to by variable b. The arrow is the *assignment* operator. It is used by the sender of the message to refer to the object returned by the receiver. With the above message, we have the simple case where only the internal state of the rectangle a is modified. Thus the returned object b is equal to the modified object a, and it suffices to write the following statement[3]:

>   a origin: 50@50 corner: 200@200 .

In Smalltalk-80, rectangles are instances of the class Rectangle. This class supplied by the Smalltalk-80 programming environment describes the messages instances are able to receive. The examples listed here come from this class. Note that objects of this class can receive a variety of other messages.

Let us present another example where an object returns another object as a reaction to a received message. We look at the statement

>   topLeftPoint ← a topLeft .

We first observe that we have sent a message of another type to a, a *unary* message. This message has no arguments. It consists only of the pattern topLeft. The result of the message topLeft consists of returning the top left corner of the rectangle a. topLeftPoint is a reference to a two-dimensional point with the coordinates 50@50 and 200@200. The assignment therefore represents an analogy to an output parameter of a procedure in conventional systems.

So far, we have specified examples of how to modify the internal state of an object and of how to generate and return to the sender a new object as a result of a message. So far we have not yet talked about how and where to program the methods which evaluate the messages sent to an object and which provide the corresponding services.

The *class* is used for describing the behaviour of objects. When we program in an object-oriented system, we generate or modify the programming code assigned to a class. As a rule, we start from available class descriptions of the given programming environment we intend to modify or to complete. Or we use the programming environment to form new classes.

Every object is an instance of a class and behaves as specified by the class definition. A class therefore describes which messages an object can receive and how these messages are interpreted. Thus the classes contain the actual programming code. The selector of a message determines the type of operations the receiver has to perform. A *method* is assigned to each selector. If a message is sent to an object, the method assigned to it is executed. A method has access to *instance variables* and *class variables*. Instance variables are used for representing the current state of each individual object. Class variables represent states common to all objects of a class.

---

[2]For increased legibility, the first character of each word is capitalized. In this case, the first character must be a lower case one for syntactic reasons since upper case characters at the beginning are reserved for class names.

[3]Communication is however always two-sided. The receiver of a message always returns a result. Therefore, only the reference to this result has been omitted. For messages which modify only the internal state of an object, the empty object 'nil' is frequently returned in addition to the object itself. We frequently use a double arrow in the figures to point to the returned value of the result.

It is very important to note that communication with objects is done via messages and that a direct access to the internal object states is not feasible. That means, from an outside viewpoint, we can do with an object only what has been defined by the available methods. We call this *information hiding*. It has the advantage that the programmer who uses the facilities of an object from the outside can do that only via a well-defined interface. For the programmer who has implemented the methods, it has the advantage that s/he is totally free in how to program in detail the service to be rendered by a method[4]. Each class has a unique name which begins with an upper case character in the SM-80 syntax. In our example, it is the name Rectangle. The class Rectangle has the instance variables topLeftPoint and buttomRightPoint (class variables are possibly not required for the class Rectangle).

It is worth mentioning that two objects of a class or even different classes can (using the applicable methods) be programmed such that they can mutually call each other. We thus have a much greater flexibility in our communications compared to a subroutine call in Fortran. This flexibility is, for instance, used in the architecture of a graphical application-system (see MVC concept in paragraph3.1).

In addition to instance methods sent to instances of a class, we find messages which can be sent directly to a class. They are defined by means of *class methods*. These methods are often used to generate new objects of the corresponding class. A predefined standard message, the unary message *new*, is frequently used in this context. The effect of this message is the generation of a new object of this class not provided with internal values as yet.

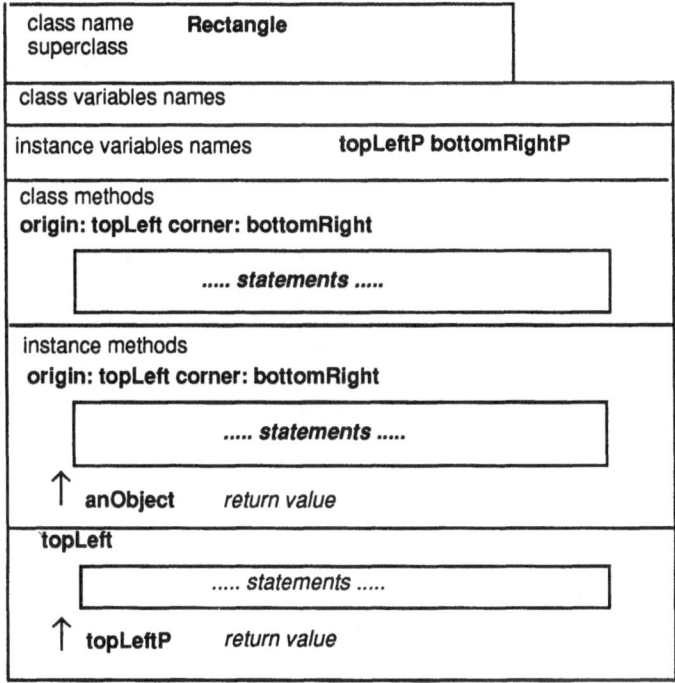

Fig. 1.1: Structure of a class

---

[4]Information hiding also applies to languages supporting abstract data types.

Thus with

a ← Rectangle new

we generate a new rectangle not provided with special coordinates as yet.

For a message of the pattern origin:corner: we can also define a class method. It does not matter that this pattern is identical with that of an instance message. Such a message can be used as follows:

aRectangle ← Rectangle origin: 200@200 corner: 300@300

With this class message, a new rectangle is generated. It is directly provided with the coordinates described in the arguments. Figure 1.1 illustrates the structure of a class.

1.3. Abstract Data Types

In object-oriented programming the computing process is factored into objects. Each object is comprised of data elements and procedure elements. Objects are typically instances of some class, or, equivalently, objects belong to a type. The programmer is free to define new types and their associated operations: their protocol.

Procedural abstraction means that procedures can be invoked by naming them without regard to their internals, that is, without regard to how the particular part of the algorithm was implemented. This forms the basis of structured, modularized, procedure oriented programming.

Data abstraction is used for similar reasons in object-oriented programming. The state and implementation of an object is hidden from other objects. Instead an object possesses a protocol of messages which form its only interface with the outside. In order to use an object one need only know the protocol, or equivalently, its class or type.

1.4. Classes and Inheritance

In most object-oriented languages objects belong to classes (these classes being objects in their own right). Objects which are instances of the same class are similar in that they share the same interface and have the same structure. Class and inheritance are based on an analogy with both taxonomy and genetics.

Classes in object-oriented languages form a hierarchy. Subclasses are specializations of their superclasses, and they inherit all the characteristics of the superclasses. Simple abstract classes characterize the higher levels of the hierarchy while more complex behaviours, in concretely useful classes, are found at lower levels.

The simple hierarchy of inheritance relationships can be extended to a network of relationships. This is referred to as multiple inheritance. In some systems a class need not inherit all the features of a particular super class. This is even closer to the situation in biology where traits are distributed amongst individuals in a gene pool and can be inherited separately.

1.4.1. Hierarchical Inheritance.

Hierarchical inheritance means that classes can be organized in a tree structure, i.e. for each class (except for the root of the tree, the class Object which is predefined in the environment) exactly one directly superordinated class, the superclass, is defined.

1.4.2. What is the Semantics of Inheritance?

The semantics of inheritance means that methods and variables of the superclass (including what the superclass itself has inherited from above) are valid for the subclass. In particular, all messages for which inherited methods are exist can be sent to an object of a class.

Since inheritance can extend over several levels, the inheritance tree is searched for the uniquely defined superclass till the appropriate method is found if a message is sent to an object, This is shown by the following figure.

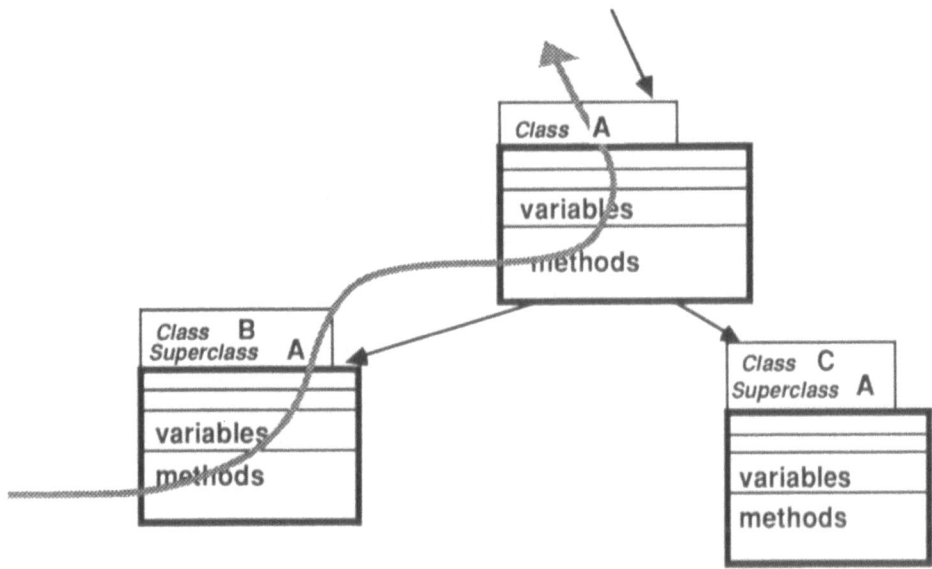

Fig. 1.2: Searching for inherited messages

The figure also illustrates that several classes, in this example B and C, can inherit methods and variables from a common superclass. This means that the code needs be realized only once for the methods inherited by A and those inherited by B. Instead of occurring in the classes B and C each, the method m1 common to both is occurs only once. In this case, we also speak of factorization. If we set up the "right" class hierarchy by creativity and appropriate programming, we can succeed in factorizing out everything in common, i.e., to combine it in an appropriate superclass. This means for the classes A and C that only those methods must be realized which apply in a very special manner to this class. Therefore, the generation of subclasses is also called specialization. Inheritance can be used in many contexts. Its advantages for computer graphics will be demonstrated below.

1.4.3. Overriding Inherited Methods.

As mentioned already, the search for appropriate methods begins bottom-up. When we consider the case represented in the next figure, we will see that the method myMessage: is realized both for A and B. Therefore, B is responsible for evaluating myMessage. In this case, we say that the method normally inherited from A to B has been overridden.

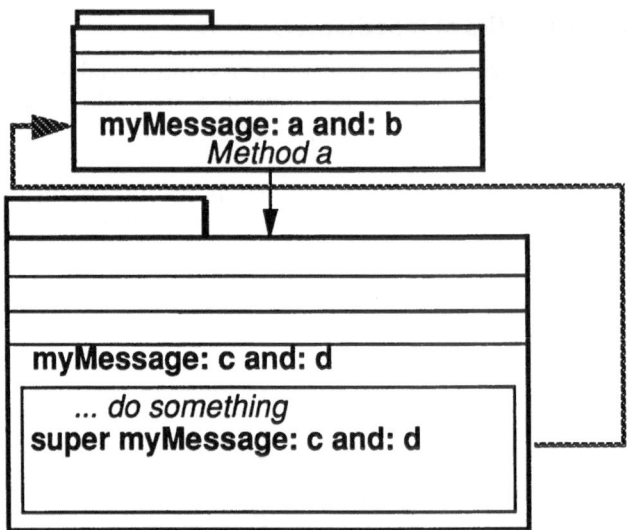

Fig. 1.3: Message to super.

From a merely content-oriented viewpoint, it often occurs that the method realized in A is to be used by a method of B. This is possible by introducing the pseudo-variable super. If we send a message to super, the object addresses itself. In contrast to self, however, the search for the appropriate method is started at the superclass.

1.4.4. Multiple Inheritance

In case of the hierarchical inheritance described in the last section, behaviour is inherited from an uniquely defined inheritance chain.

More flexibility is provided by multiple inheritance where a subclass may inherit from several superclasses resulting in an inheritance *graph*. Therefore, it is possible to inherit, apart from specialized methods realized in the corresponding methods of the subclass, methods from various superordinated superclasses. We also speak of a method mix which can be inherited into a class to be generated. We will later show the possibilities resulting from the hierarchical inheritance for computer graphics, but also which limitations the hierarchical inheritance imposes on system construction. These limitations can be overcome almost completely by means of multiple inheritance.

It should be noted that various Smalltalk-80 implementations also allow multiple inheritance.

1.5. Message Passing and Polymorphism.

Polymorphism can be used in a number of senses; the meaning is usually that a single external operation can be applied to a variety of underlying types. For example: conventional typed programming languages allow the parameters of functions to have only one type. If this idea was strictly applied then addition would require a different function for each type of number and generalized routines would be impossible. Examples of simple polymorphic arithmetic messages are:

2 + 3.   "Send the message '+' to the SmallInteger 2 with the parameter 3"

5 * 3.5.   "Send '*' to the SmallInteger 5 with the Float parameter 3.5"

2.7 + (1/3) "Send '+' to the Float 2.7 with the Fraction parameter (1/3)"

Polymorphic languages allow for the same functions to accept many different parameter types. In object-oriented languages the same messages can be sent to a number of different classes and the messages can have any type of argument. Unlike procedure calls, messages sending allows polymorphism without the requiring constant checking of parameter types (Ingalls, 1986). The existence of class hierarchies must entail a certain polymorphism if related but distinct classes are to understand the same messages.

The conceptual power of inheritance hierarchies derives, at least partly, from the way in which they allow automatic but controlled polymorphism for all subclasses. One largely knows the behaviour of an object if one knows the behaviour of its superclass.

An example: in graphical systems one normally has a large number of different representations, or models, being used together. Each of these representations has to be rendered. The standard solution is to ensure that all models have the same kind of primitive. However with polymorphic messages we can use different methods for the representations provided that the same message, like "render", is understood by all the representations.

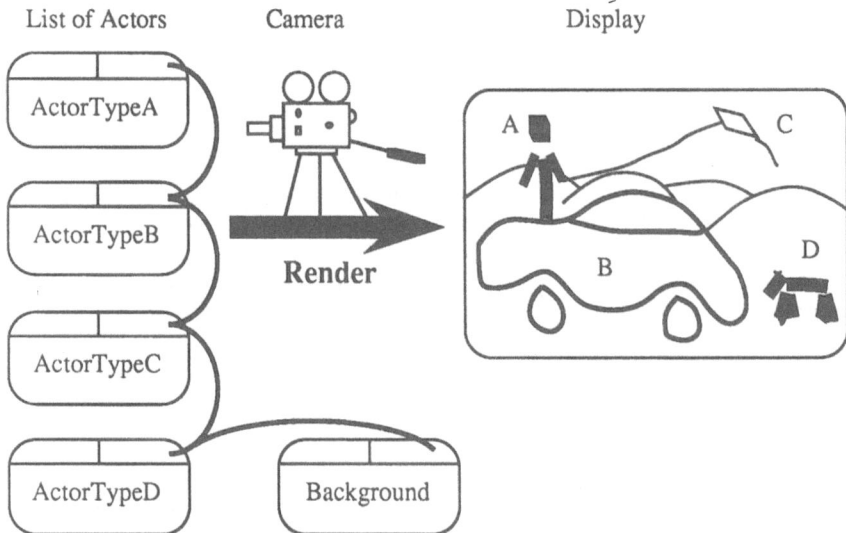

Fig. 1.4: Polymorphic message 'render' being sent by the Camera to render different kinds of Actors.

The different Actors all have different internal representations, but all have to be drawn on the display. Thus the Camera merely has to send the message 'render' to all the Actors on the display list and the mechanisms of the object-oriented language will ensure that the right methods are invoked.

Having polymorphic messages makes it possible to program by extending the language with new types. For example, it was very easy to add a new class of number, namely quaternions, to Smalltalk. These quaternions understand exactly the same messages, for multiplication, addition, square root, and so forth, as other numbers. Smalltalk can be said to exhibit "true" polymorphism because all objects are uniformly represented and can exhibit uniform behaviour without coercion or explicit type checking.

C++ does not use message lookup for procedure calls and is statically typed, but it does allow operator overloading, i.e., the same operator can have a number of different, but predetermined, types of arguments. Quaternions can be implemented just as elegantly as with Smalltalk.

1.6. Why Smalltalk?

Smalltalk (Goldberg and Robson, 1983) is an object-oriented language that makes a very attractive prototyping tool. A great deal of effort has gone into designing its programmer and user interface. When the application is a graphical simulation there is seems to be little to beat it.

The following are key features of Smalltalk:

– Consistent use of Objects. In Smalltalk everything is an object. There are no inconsistencies in the application of the object-oriented paradigm.
– Graphical user interface. The user interface already provides the basic data types for graphical bitmap display and mouse interaction.
– Powerful development tools. Programming in Smalltalk is designed to be an incremental activity. The whole library of existing programs can be examined with ease. Powerful interactive debugging is provided. Since binding is dynamic there is no need to link new methods.
– Smalltalk is easily modifiable. All system classes (including, for example, the compiler) are accessible and can be modified or, preferably, extended by adding sub-classes.

A disadvantage of Smalltalk is that a number of new concepts and approaches to programming have to be learned. Smalltalk programming consists in defining data types or classes, or rather refining existing classes. Although the language itself is small, one has to have a good grasp of existing system classes. Once these classes are understood however, they assist greatly in writing new programs.

Other restrictions of existing Smalltalk implementations, such as restricted object memory, lack of colour primitives, slow speed and poor support for parallel processes have been, or are being, alleviated (Miranda, 1987).

1.7. Object-Oriented Programming Environments

It is very important to say that object-oriented languages are not provided nakedly, as a rule, but rather together with an object-oriented programming environment. Object-oriented programming environments like the Smalltalk system consist of a set of prefabricated classes and method definitions. In addition, important tools (editor, browser, debugger) for program development are provided in form of an interactive graphical user interface. In the Smalltalk 80 system these tools are realized in an object-oriented way as well. This means that even elementary editing operations can be regarded as messages to objects.

Object-oriented programming in such an environment consists of the specification of class descriptions, the generation of instances of a class and the compilation of messages to the instances. This process is supported by the programming environment in such a way that an incremental program development is feasible. The supply of prefabricated classes is by far greater than, for example, the availability of elementary data types in classical programming languages.

In contrast to classical programming languages (coding, compiling, test), programming in object-oriented environments is based on the heavy use, modification and frequent re-use of available parts.

It is to be noted that many kernel functions (classes, objects) for programming graphical interfaces are among the prefabricated aids which will be discussed in more detail below.

2. Object-Oriented and Classical Graphics Systems

The new facilities provided by object-oriented graphics systems can be illustrated by a comparison with classical graphics systems. A comparison enables us to recognize differences more clearly and to better identify the advantages and disadvantages of the various approaches. On the basis of such an analysis we wish to present GEO++ as a concept attempting to combine the best of both worlds.

A comparison between the two different types of kernel systems is not entirely unproblematic. Object-oriented systems have not been standardized as yet and there is no de facto standard either. The object-oriented graphics kernels of the various systems differ considerably in the power of the graphical programming aids. For this reason we orient ourselves at the Smalltalk-80 graphics kernel and concentrate on those aspects valid for other object-oriented graphics kernels as well.

By *object-oriented graphics kernels* we understand tools for the construction of graphical interfaces as they are offered in object-oriented programming environments. Apart from the Smalltalk-80 graphics kernel the rich kernel of the Lisp-machine (Weinreb et. al. 1987) deserves special mention.

It is important to point out that apart from the object-oriented systems in the true meaning of the word there are several development tools incorporating most of the criteria listed in 2.2.. The QuickDraw™ graphics kernel of the Apple Macintosh™ (Chernicoff 1987) well as corresponding graphics tools in the X-Windows system belong into this category. Even though these systems do not posses an inheritance mechanism, they have nevertheless been heavily influenced by the object-oriented philosophy.

Under *classical systems* we understand both systems which either have already been standardized or are being standardized as well as systems or specifications which have influenced standardization. Graphics kernels implemented in Fortran, as they are used in the field of computer aided design, reveal similar properties. Systems of this type reflect a long-term experience in the programming of graphical systems. Examples of such systems are

- *Siggraph Core*, the first attempt to define the functionality of graphical systems by making it available in form of a standardized core (Michener and Foley 78).
- the *Graphical Kernel System* (GKS) which has been defined as an ISO standard (ISO 7942 1985, Enderle et. al. 1987).
- the proposed standard *Programmer's Hierarchical Interactive Graphics System* (PHIGS) (ISO 9582 1988, Brown 1985).

2.1. Characteristics of Classical Graphics Systems

We begin with a brief presentation of the features of classical graphics kernels, limiting ourselves to GKS and PHIGS.

2.1.1. Graphical Data Structure

A major characteristic of classical systems is the definition of a *welldefined graphical datastructure*. In GKS and PHIGS, the way in which higher level constructs (segments, groups) may be generated out of graphical primitives is defined, just as how these may be represented and modified on an output media. By this we mean those operations permitting the construction and change of an on-screen representation.

GKS permits the generation of a *segment* from output primitives, where a segment may be viewed as a collection of such primitives[5]. The entire GKS-datastructure consists of a set of segments. Combining segments to even higher aggregates is not permitted. The GKS-functionality for building segments is frequently called *one-level segmenting*. A segment receives a name through a segment identifier. Segments and only segments are addressible through a name.(*one-level naming*). A segment is generated through a sequence of steps: (1) through a corresponding statement the kernel is put into the state *Create-Segment*. In this state any later operations for the construction of output primitives (and the assignment of attributes) are interpreted in such a way that these are assigned to the currently open segment. Only one segment may be open at any time. Only after the open segment has been closed (2) is the opening of a new segment permitted(3).

(1)   CREATE SEGMENT(NAME1)

      (insertion of graphic primitives for NAME1)

(2)   CLOSE SEGMENT

(3)   CREATE SEGMENT(NAME2)

      (insertion of graphic primitives for NAME2)

PHIGS permits the construction of multi-level hierarchies. In PHIGS a so-called *structure* corresponds to what is called a segment in GKS. A structure is defined as a linear list containing output primitives, attributes, transformations, and references to other structures. Multiple references to other structure are allowed, cycles are not permitted, resulting in an acyclic directed graph.

The following figure shows the basic elements of a PHIGS structure.

---

[5]GKS primitives outside segments are not mentioned here, becaue they are not important in connection with our comparison.

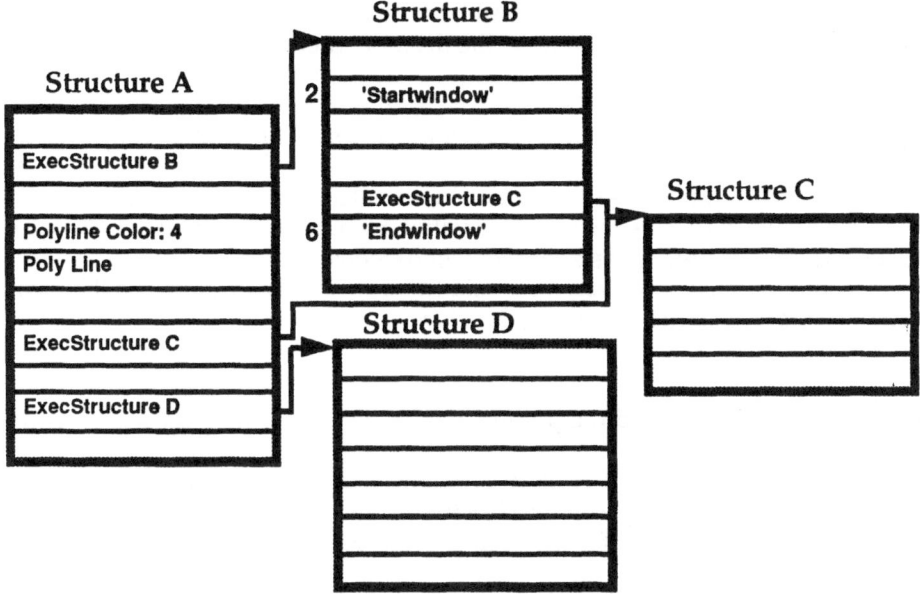

Fig. 2.1: The PHIGS model

2.1.2. Output Primitives

In order to display the differences to object-oriented systems more clearly, we shall distinguish between *geometrical primitives* and *output primitives*. Viewing a polygon or a rectangle as a geometrical primitive, we interpret this as an object in two- or three-dimensional space, suitable for several purposes (geometry, construction and display). In contrast, under an output primitive we understand an object suitable for display only.

It is important that GKS and PHIGS merely offer objects directly related to the representation of graphical objects. GKS and PHIGS have no geometrical objects corresponding to output primitives. The only geometric information in GKS and PHIGS are coordinates or sequences of coordinates. It is from these that, by way of an atomic action, a component of a segment or a structure is constructed. Thus by

(4)   CALL POLYLINE(N,XA,XB)

a polygon is inserted into a segment or a structure, and he may now be used by the kernel system (and only the kernel system).

2.1.3. Modification of the Data Structure

GKS permits a change in the graphical datastructure only through either deleting a segment or generating a new segment. An existing segment may not be changed.

In PHIGS structures can be edited. Elements of a structure may be deleted or changed and new elements can be generated. In this way the content of a structure or the construction of the directed acyclic graph can be changed at will.

The linear list of a structure is accessible in PHIGS via an element pointer of the type Integer. This permits, for example, the deletion of elements 2 to 6 of a structure using

DELETE-ELEMENT-FROM-TO(2,6)

This modifies the element pointer of the following structure elements by the value -5.

In addition PHIGS permits the insertion of so-called *label elements* into a structure. Thus, it is possible to execute the above operation by means of a statement of the form

DELETE-BETWEEN-LABELS('startwindow','endwindow')

Before this we must, however, insert 'startwindow' and 'endwindow' as the second and sixth element respectively into the structure.

2.1.4. Posting

Under *posting* we understand the presentation of the generated datastructure on an output device.

In GKS, an output device is always associated with the generation of a segment, which is immediately displayed. In PHIGS the construction (of one or several acyclic graphs) and the presentation of a graph are viewed separately.

2.1.5. Transformation and Coordinates

We do not wish to treat the transformation of coordinates in detail. Regarding GKS it is worth mentioning that, after having defined a window/viewport-transformation, a transformation from world- to normalized device-coordinates takes place. This transformation applies to every output primitive generated later. With a segment-transformation applied to a single segment, this segment can be used in other segments.

PHIGS always inserts transformations into structures as elements, and this transformation has effect only upon the subgraph spanned by this structure (and not further up upon the calling structure). Strictly speaking PHIGS has no transformations which can be associated to a structure as an object, but this effect can be achieved by inserting the transformation as the first element into a structure.

Neither GKS nor PHIGS feature a direct assignment of a transformation to an output primitive.

2.1.6. Assignment of Attributs

In GKS and PHIGS the assignment of attributes with a direct effect on an output primitive is achieved in a way similar to the transformations. There is no direct assignment.

Apart from these attributes GKS features segment-attributes (for highlighting, visibility, detectability). These attributes are given by using the segment name and may thus be interpreted as an object-oriented assignment.

2.1.7. Graphical Input

The most important function for us is the pick-operator. In GKS it produces the name of a segment (as well as a group identifier) picked with the aid of a graphical input device (mouse, lightpen). In PHIGS it yields, apart from a pick-id, a pickpath (e.g. a sequence of element pointers through the graph hierarchy).

Important to note is that classical graphics systems offer the applications programmer the possibility to return an identifier for the interactively chosen object within an object hierarchy into the application.

2.1.8. Control Structure

The control structure of classical systems is characterized by the functions of the graphical kernel being called as procedures. The flow of control is defined solely by the application layer.

2.2. Characteristics of Object-Oriented Graphics Kernels

As mentioned, we use the graphics kernel of Smalltalk-80.

2.2.1. Graphical Data Structures

Object-oriented graphics kernels offer no higher graphical data structures. On the whole merely the handling of output primitives is supported in the programming environment The construction of a graphical datastructure must be performed by the applications programmer. The construction of such a model is, however, simplified somewhat by the good mechanisms Smalltalk-80 contains for building complex object structures.

2.2.2. Output Primitives

Smalltalk-80 offers a wealth of output-primitives. More precisely it has classes of *geometric* primitives which may also be used for graphical output. The geometric objects which are suitable for graphical output are gathered in a class hierarchy. Thus Smalltalk-80 has in class **Path** the subclasses Circle, Arc, Quadrangle, Line, LinearFit. Every output primitive is regarded as a rectangular picture. The rectangular area surrounding the primitive (the *bounding box*) can be queried, assigned values or modified.

Output primitives are thus instances of a class and have numerous methods. Subclasses of a class may be constructed, further enhancing their functionality. (see 2.3.2).

2.2.3. Modification of the Graphical Data Structure

Since the construction of a graphical data structure is the responsibility of the applications programmer, this naturally holds for all changes to this structure as well.

2.2.4. Posting

The representation on the screen is achieved by directing *directing every output primitive explicitly onto an area of presentation*. This implies sending every output primitive a message containing information about the device, the presentation area in which clipping occurs, the transformation and the attribute of representation. By specifying default methods, however, having to specify all of the above information can be avoided.

2.2.5. Transformation and Coordinates

Smalltalk-80 does not differ between world coordinates and device-coordinates. Instead, this model must be interpreted as working with a single coordinate system, possibly larger than that of the screen. The left upper corner of the screen is Zero, the x-direction is counted right, the y-coordinate is counted down. In such a coordinate system output primitives are defined. When generating a primitive, the left upper screen coordinate (0,0) is default definition for the left upper corner of the bounding box.

For an output primitive to be displayed correctly, it has to receive a message giving it a transformation and a clipping area. The corresponding transformation is applied individually to every output primitive. This causes a primitive to change its own coordinates, so the coordinates used by its generation are no longer known to it.

2.2.6. Assignment of Attributes

In Smalltalk-80 representational attributes are assigned to an object directly via message.

2.2.7. Graphical Input

Generally all that is offered for graphical input is is a locator. A pick function needs to be realized by the applications programmer himself.

2.2.8. Control Structures

Object-oriented systems permit the definition of control structures of a far greater flexibility than is possible within a classic procedure-oriented system. These possibilities are used in Smalltalk-80 to elegantly structure the flow of control between an application and the graphical input- and output-functions. This is generally referred to as the model-view-controller concept, described in 3.1. in greater detail.

2.3. An Object-Oriented Modification of GKS

In the following we wish to discuss the pros and cons of a one-to-one binding of GKS to Smalltalk-80 as well as discuss some modifications to GKS in the light of the object-oriented philosophy.

2.3.1. Segment Naming

In GKS names for segments are defined as input parameters. Thus the application must give the segment-names (as integer values).

In order to rigorously follow the above rules, a Smalltalk-80 interface should look like the following:

    GKS createSegment: aName

The disadvantage here lies in the fact that the application (resp. the programmer) has to take care that each name is unique. Generally, if segments are generated in a main- and a sub-program, then segment numbers must be used as parameters in the sub-programs, if naming clashes are to be avoided, as the following example shows.

We assume that we wish to construct a module in which several graphical segments for representing a house are to be generated. We intend to repeatedly use this module in an application (under different transformations and after the modification of attributes not to be discussed here). We intend to obtain a graphical representation which may be manipulated interactively.

In classical systems, modules are realized as procedures. Therefore, it is self-suggesting to proceed as follows: construct a procedure HOUSE and call this procedure repeatedly. Within the procedure, generate the "house segments" (door, window, roof).

(1) IBHOUSE1=LASTSEGNR+1
(2) CALL HOUSE(IBHOUSE1,IEHOUSE1,.........)
(3) LASTSEGNR=IEHOUSE1

....

(4) IBHOUSE2=LASTSEGNR+1
(5) CALL HOUSE(IBHOUSE2,IEHOUSE2,.........)
(6) LASTSEGNR=IEHOUSE

Within the procedure:

(7) PROCEDURE HOUSE(IB,IE,...........)
(8) IDOOR=IB
(9) CREATE SEGMENT(IDOOR)

Output primitives for IDOOR

(10) CREATE SEGMENT(IWINDOW))

.... Output primitives for IWINDOW

(11) IE=IWINDOW
RETURN

Comment: Note that in GKS the names must be initialized as input parameters. To avoid name clashes, we must count up the segment names upon each call. Therefore, in (1)(2), the next free segment number must be determined and transmitted. After executing the procedure, the available segment number must be incremented in (3). Then, the operation is repeated. Within the procedure, the current segment number must also be taken over (8) and finally delivered to the outside (11).

2.3.2. Segments as Objects

It corresponds to the object-oriented programming style to provide the application programmer with segments as objects. This is possible if we provide segments as instances of a class Segment and if we make them referenceable via an assignment. Thus we obtain the following specification of segment operations:

```
aSegment <-- Segment create
aSegment setVisibility: vis
Segment delete: aSegment
listOfSegments <-- Segment listSegments
```

The above example shows that Segment (as a component of the kernel system) generates the segments as instances so that they can be accessed directly. The benefits are as follows:

- The user defines symbolic identifiers for a segment, the kernel assigns this name a reference to the new segment. This way name clashes are avoided. For future kernels (including the classic programming languages) we generally recommend using names as output parameters.
- The second benefit is more noticeable in object-oriented systems. Since we have a class Segment, we are able to construct subclasses and thus specialize our graphics kernel. To illustrate this point we give an example.

Example: Specialization of a graphical kernel

Among the many possibilities of using inheritance, we consider the following very attractive: use of inheritance to enrich segments by functions of geometric modeling.

In many applications of graphical data processing, it is required to apply complex geometrical functions to objects (*modeling function*) before they can be displayed. As an example, let us consider a cylinder. From the application point of view, it is to be described by its normally used parameters (radius, height). The results of the modeling functions are then the primitives for a graphics system such as GKS or PHIGS. In GKS and PHIGS, these operations are regarded as an "application-dependent" layer "between" application and kernel.

In object-oriented systems, we can do without the intermediate layer. We use the facilities of inheritance for the specialization of graphical segments. For this purpose, we create subclasses of the class Segment for the various types of geometric objects. A subclass of Segment is then addressable via messages from the "application world". Its internal methods convert these messages to the graphic primitives of the kernel system.

We create a subclass of Segment in which we perform the corresponding geometric operations. The cylinder then sends the results which are normal output primitives to super, for display by the graphical kernel system. Since Cylinder inherits the usual methods from Segment, the usual segment operations such as assignment of attributes, deleting, transformation are still applicable.

2.3.3. Output Primitives as Objects

A closer adaptation of GKS to object-oriented systems leads to the suggestion of defining a class for output primitives as well.

Instead of inserting a polyline into a segment with a single operation, this modification will look as follows.

With

> myPoly ← PolyLine new: vertices

we create an instance, which can be inserted into a segment with

> mySegment insert: myPoly

The main aspect of the definition of graphic primitives as objects of a class is the facility of creating subclasses. We wish to explain this by an example of an application from cartography. If we wish to generate contour lines, which, in addition to the graphic definition, are to be described by objects of the class PolyLine, we define a subclass ContourLine of PolyLine and then realize methods for assigning and inquiring application data, specification of height etc, for this subclass. In this way, we can mix the inherited methods with the special carthographic ones.

2.4. GEO++ – An Object-Oriented Multi-Level Graphics System

We wish to suggest GEO++ (Graphics System with Editable Objects) as an alternative to PHIGS. In (Wisskirchen 1988, 1989) this system is described more extensively. Prior versions and first concepts have been published by (Wisskirchen 1986a, 1986b). Just as PHIGS, GEO++ is a multi-level system. It contains the following basic constructs, for which predefined classes exist:

- *Output Primitives*, which we handle in the way they are handled in Smalltalk-80 and 2.3.3.
- *Groups*, taking the place of segments in GKS and structures in PHIGS. Groups may interpreted as *sets* . By way of an insert operation output primitives and other groups are inserted into a group. Together, output primitives and groups are called *building patterns*. Groups differ from the structures in PHIGS, since they are not sequences and only contain visible objects.
- An important new idea is the concept of *Parts*. A part corresponds to one and only one displayed object (in contrast to a building pattern, whose "visualization" will occur several times on a screen).

We wish to demonstrate the most important functions of GEO++ by an example, showing the schematic object hierarchy of a car radio's frontpanel.

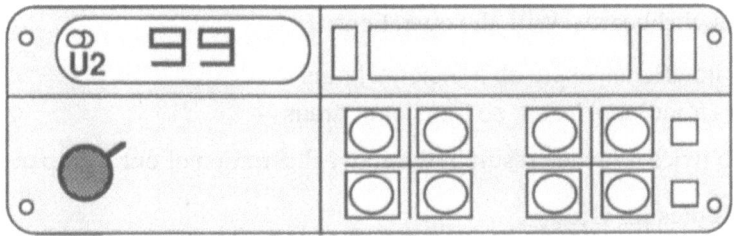

Fig. 2.2: The frontpanel of a car radio as an example for a multi-level data structure

2.4.1. Output Primitives and Groups

First we show the construction of the switchboard sb with four buttons which occurs twice in the above illustration. First the construction of the group button. The button uses two output primitives. With

    sq ← PolyLine points: sqPoints
    circle ← Circle center: cPoint radius: r

we construct the output primitives for the square and circle of the button.

    button ← Group new

gives us a new (empty) group button. In this we insert the output primitives with

    sqButton ← button insert: sq
    cButton ← button insert: circle

The result of the insert-operation, sqButton and cButton, becomes an *immediate part* (or: level 1 part) of button. An immediate part such as cButton may informally be interpreted as an "element" of the "set" button, with the semantics: "A new element of the set button with the name cButton has been constructed through the insert-operation."

We now begin with the description of the switchboard sb with its four buttons. We construct a group, in which first poly1 and poly2 describe the horizontal and vertical part of the cross, around which the buttons are grouped. We then insert the prepared button four times.

```
sb ← Group new
c1 ← sb insert: poly1
c2 ← sb insert: poly2
tl ← sb insert: button transform: tr1
tr ← sb insert: button transform: tr2
bl ← sb insert: button transform: tr3
br ← sb insert: button transform: tr4
```

Here we have used a transformation as an extended insert-operation. Thus purpose of such a transformation is to correctly position the four buttons. It thus has influence upon sb. However, the operation is defined so that the transformation will not change the status of button.

We assume that we have modelled the front panel frontPanel of our radio except for the two switchboards. With the operations:

```
left ← frontPanel insert: sb transform: ltrans
right ← frontPanel insert: sb transform: rtrans
```

we insert sb twice. We then result in the above illustration of our frontpanel.

2.4.2. Attributes for Groups

Besides the attributes for graphical output primitives we introduce attributes for a group. In addition to the segment attributes offered by GKS (detectable, highlighting, visible), we permit the attributes defined for output primitives as well. These attributes are inherited by all elements within the group. Thus, if a group attribute is set for the group sb, then all successor nodes will be effected by this operation. Thus setting sb to:

```
button polyLineStyle: bold
```

makes this Linestyle valid for all objects of class PolyLine used for the construction of button. Therefore, all eight squares of the buttons are set to bold.

2.4.3. Editing of Groups

Up to now we have only dealt with the extension of groups by way of the insert operation and the assignment of attributes to groups. To edit a group it is necessary to insert further elements, to change existing elements, or to delete an immediate part. With

```
left changeBy: aNewElement
```

we assign to a part a new element. With

```
left delete
```

we delete an immediate part.

2.4.4. Parts of Higher Level

When constructing a display generation, the posted graph is expanded into a tree. Each individual pointing to an inserted element leads to a subtree (node plus subnodes) within the tree. The parts arising through a pointing to the same building pattern are called *equivalent*.. Every operation addressed to a building pattern has an effect to all "its" equivalent nodes in the tree. This is exactly the same as in PHIGS.

As an extension to the PHIGS functionality, we are able to access parts of a group with a level higher than one, allowing us to modify every individual node in the tree. For achieving this we use pathnames which can be constructed through a sequence of existing parts. We shall describe the sequence of indicators through an array. In our example, the path #(right tl) yields the upper left button in the right switchboard of the radio.

myButton ← frontPanel part: #(right tl)

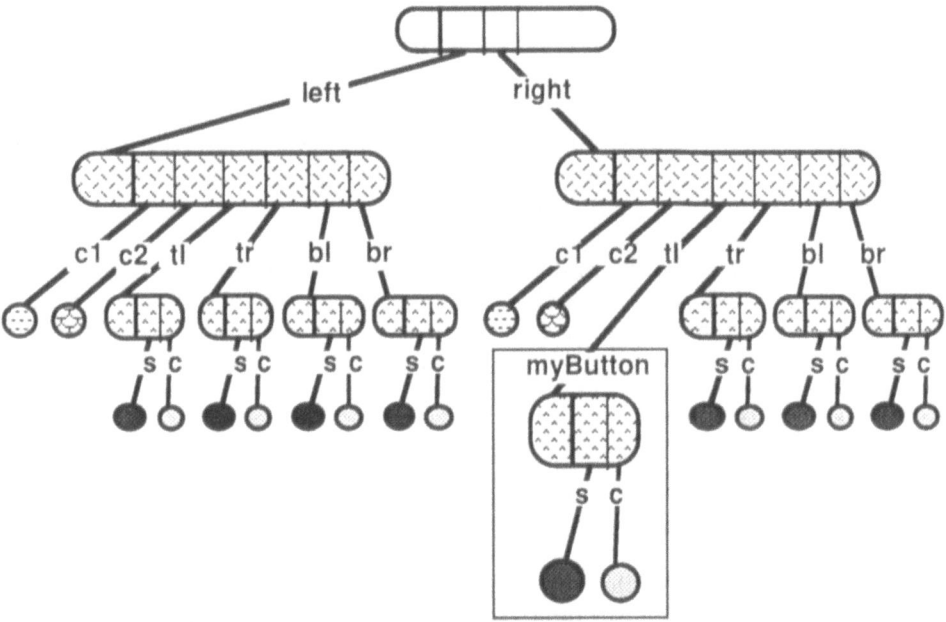

Fig. 2.3: Tree with equivalent nodes, and the part myButton.
Equivalent nodes have the same hatch style, different equivalence classes have different styles. We use no hatching (white) for individual nodes with no equivalent partners in the tree. The names of the direct parts of the different groups are drawn at the edges of the tree.

It should be noted that the way how we implement the access to the part is invisible from the outside (principle of information hiding). Especially, there is nothing said about using the group switchboard during the access to the specified button! With our way to access parts we avoid a dilemma which has been articulated by (Blake and Cook 1987).

2.4.5. Attributes for Parts

Apart from the attributes for building patterns we can assign *part-attributes* to myButton with myButton polyLineStyle: bold .

The semantics of this assignment is as follows: during posting, i. e. when constructing the tree, every component of myButton which is a primitive of class PolyLine (in our button the square) has this attribute assigned. An attribute (including transformations) will not change the equivalence relation.

With this concept of addressing individual parts, we support in addition to attribute assingment also "real" editing of parts (insertions and deletions). This leads to a modification of the equivalence relations in the sense that the part has been "individualized". Such a part is no more affected by operations on the building block of its former equivalent partners.

3. New Concepts in Object-Oriented Programming for Graphics

3.1. The Model-View-Controller-Triad – A New System Architecture

The Model-View-Controller concept (MVC concept) is the most important concept in Smalltalk-80 for interface design. Unfortunately this model is not discussed in the otherwise outstanding publications (Goldberg and Robson 1983, Goldberg 1984) since a special book was planned for the design of user interfaces which however has not yet been published. One of the objectives pursued by the MVC concept is the stronger modularization of interfaces. The MVC concept is more than a concept. Because of its many prefabricated classes, it can also be regarded as a toolbox for interface design. We wish to list the main construction steps for an user interface and will explain them shortly. A more extended presentation, together with a complete programming example can be found in (Rome and Wisskirchen 1988).

3.1.1. What is the Problem?

State-of-the-art software ergonomics have not yet reached a point where it is possible to construct an entirely satisfactory user interface in a single step. Instead, a prototype is constructed first, this prototype is then evaluated and revised. The Model-View-Controller concept (MVC concept) supports this revisioning by guaranteeing that interface revisions are possible with minimal effort. This is mainly achieved by the MVC facility to modify the user interface without having to modify the code of the application. MVC thus offers a *separation facility*. (Szekely 1987).

The layer-concept in GKS and PHIGS sets the application on top of the graphical kernel. It thus modularizes the functionality produced by the application and the kernel. However, the *calls* of the graphical procedures (both for output and input) and everything concerned with the preparation of these calls (construction of the drawing) belong to the code of the application program. We wish to call those portions of code dealing with the preparation of graphical information and the calling of the kernel *mapping*. If a change of the user interface is desired in such a system, substantial changes in the application code are unavoidable.

3.1.2. Separation Facilities of the MVC Concept

We wish to anticipate the result of the MVC concept. It provides a separation facility which works as follows:

– Representation of data and operations of the application by an instance of a class Model, a class which is defined by the application programmer.

- One instance of a subclass of the predefined class View, the *view*, as a mapping object for output.
- One instance of a subclass of the predefined class Controller, the *controller*, as a mapping object for input.

The following figure shows six communication paths which can be established between the components. Not every application requires every communication direction.

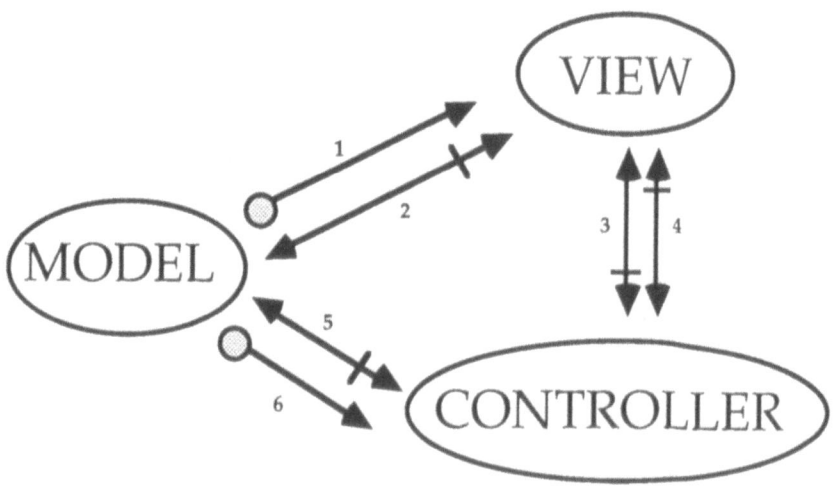

Fig. 3.1: Communication paths in the MVC concept

Ad 1: If the model changes, and a modification of presentation is required, a corresponding method can be activated.

Ad 2: In this direction, a view can inquire information required for a representation.

Ad 3: A controller can effect the modification of a presentation (without having to use paths 5 and 1) due to an input. This can be useful if only a representation is to be modified without any change of the model.

Ad 4: A view can activate an input device dependant upon states in the presentation.

Ad 5: A controller can effect a modification of the model due to an input.

Ad 6: It is again a dependency structure. In this case, a controller can be influenced due to a modification of the model. For example, the sequence of menu labels could be permuted.[6]

It must be noted that communication streams (1) and (6) are not realized through the conventional message passing, but rather through a trigger concept. The model merely calls a *change-message* with a code (integer)as parameter. The effect of this trigger is to start an update-message in view or model, which will react to the

---

[6]This type of communication is not prefabricated in the programming environment. It can however be realized easily.

transmitted code, prepare operations for the graphics kernel and call functions of the kernel. In this way we avoid having any code dependent upon the user interface in the model.

3.1.3. Prefabricated Classes

To avoid any confusion: Smalltalk-80 does not provide any prefabricated class of the name Model!

The class View is a prefabricated class with many useful subclasses. These classes in particular provide everything required for constructing windows, even in form of window hierarchies (i.e., windows divided into subwindows).

The class Controller is also a prefabricated class with many useful subclasses. These subclasses support, for example, all input devices such as mouse, keyboard, menus etc.

Many of the prefabricated subclasses of View and Controller correlate to one another for usage in the MVC concept. For example, there are the classes TextView and TextController (with corresponding subclasses) which support text editing.

3.1.4. Establishing Communication

After having given some examples of the different communication flows we should describe how to establish these flows.

We proceed as follows:

We define three classes called MyView, MyModel, MyController with their associated methods. Then, we show how to generate triangles of the types myModel, myView, myController as instances of these classes.

We do all this in such a way that the components of these triangles "know" each other so well that all six directions of message passing are supported.

Constructing a Model Class

We have already seen that there is no prefabricated class Model and there is also no obligation to name such a class in this way. Therefore, we are free to construct any class. We want to call it MyModel. The following recommendations should be noted accordingly:

- We model our application without defining the user interface concretely. We therefore avoid any call of a function for output on the screen or of any input tool.
- If our model shows a situation which requires a modification of representation, we insert a change message into our code.
- The mapping objects, in our example MyView and MyController, have to inquire all information required for presentation (i.e., objects of the view domain in the MVC model) from an object of the class MyModel, so we should not forget to "release" this data. MyModel must therefore provide methods for inquiring every internal information required for constructing a representation (of any con-creteness).
- As a result of the user interaction, the state of the model can be modified. Mapping objects for the input (i.e., objects of the Controller domain) regulate this by sending messages to the model. Therefore, the class MyModel must provide such methods for the acceptance of desired modifications.

Constructing a Controller Class

The construction of a Controller class, i.e., the class MyController in our example, is always done as a direct or an indirect subclass of the prefabricated class Controller. Through insertion into the inheritance chain, MyController can be specialized for its own specific needs and the inherited potential of Controller can be used as well.

The essential way of specialization consists in mediating between the input on the lower level of the kernel functions and the modification of the model. Due to the useful prefabricated subclasses of Controller, it is quite simple to accept the user action, for example, a selected menu option or a pressed mouse button. The conversion of messages to the model requires knowledge of the model semantics and can therefore not be predefined. Rather, the application programmer who will generally have programmed the model as well must take care that the corresponding messages are sent to the model.

For addressing the model, an inherited inquiry method (unary message model) is available. myController can send this method to itself and obtains the current model as a value, i.e., myModel in our case. It is also possible, via a unary message view, to obtain the current View, i.e., MyView in our case.

Constructing a View Class

The View class is of special importance to the whole MVC model. Apart from defining an instance, in our example myView, the class View introduces all components of the triangle to each other. How this can be done will be shown in the following.

First, we wish to characterize the class MyView. MyView is defined as a subclass of View (or of a subclass of View). An instance myView of View has a method update: aParameter at its disposal. The method is triggered by a change of the model (change:). This method must, as a rule, inquire data from the model. For the addressing, the inherited method model is provided and the methods available for MyModel. View use the functions of the (graphical) kernel system for presentation. It is therefore the primary task of the programmer to convert the internal model data to visible representations.

We now explain how to instantiate the whole triangle after we have created the classes MyModel, MyView and MyController, i.e., after we have generated almost the complete programming code (except for the class methods of MyView). In a class method of MyView, we create the instances myModel, myView and myController as usual (by the message new). Then, we send the message with the selector model:controller:

myView model: myModel controller: myController

to myView. This message is inherited from View and establishes the whole communication. The programmer does not need to know the individual actions in every detail. The service rendered by View includes among other things the following individual steps:

- establishment of the dependency of myView and myController[7] on myModel.
- information of myController about myModel and myView. They can be questioned by the messages model and view from myController.

---

[7]The Controller was not included in the dependence list of our environment. This is however very simple, i.e., by overriding model:controller:.

– information of myView about myModel and myController. They can be questioned by model or controller from myView.

Now we have finally finished, and the communication in the triangle can start.

3.2. Coordinate Transformations in Animation

We first discuss the importance of coordinate transformations in animation (below). We briefly introduce some of the essential features of quaternions in paragraph 3.2.2. We illustrate the implementation of quaternions with some examples in Smalltalk (paragraph 3.2.3) and C++ (paragraph 3.2.4)

3.2.1. Coordinate Transformations

Coordinate transformations play a vital role in computer graphics and animation. Scene composition, rendering and motion would be impossible without them.

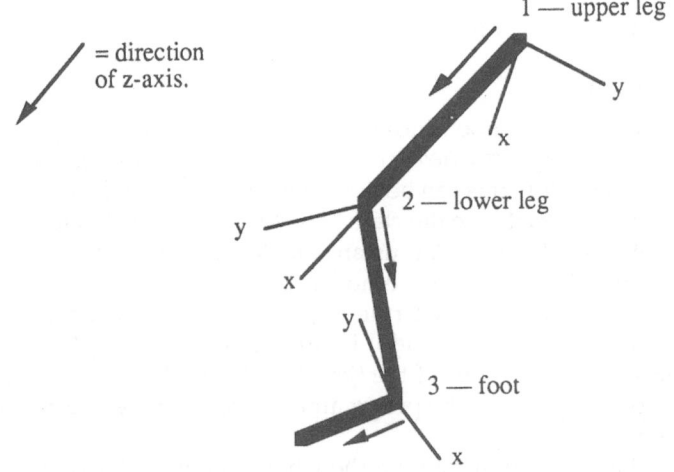

Fig. 3.2: The Hierarchy of Local Coordinate Systems.
This particular hierarchy arises when modelling the left leg of a stick figure. Each limb has its own local coordinate system.

Each object is modelled in its own coordinate space and is placed in its correct position relative to other objects in the environment by means of its own coordinate transformation. The camera is similarly positioned in the modelled environment. To render three-dimensional models of objects on the display they have to be transformed into the camera coordinate space and then projected by a perspective transformation. The movement of rigid objects is achieved by altering their coordinate transformations.

Each part of the hierarchical representation of an object has its own changing local coordinate system. In animation and rendering these coordinate systems have to be related to one another and to the world coordinate system.

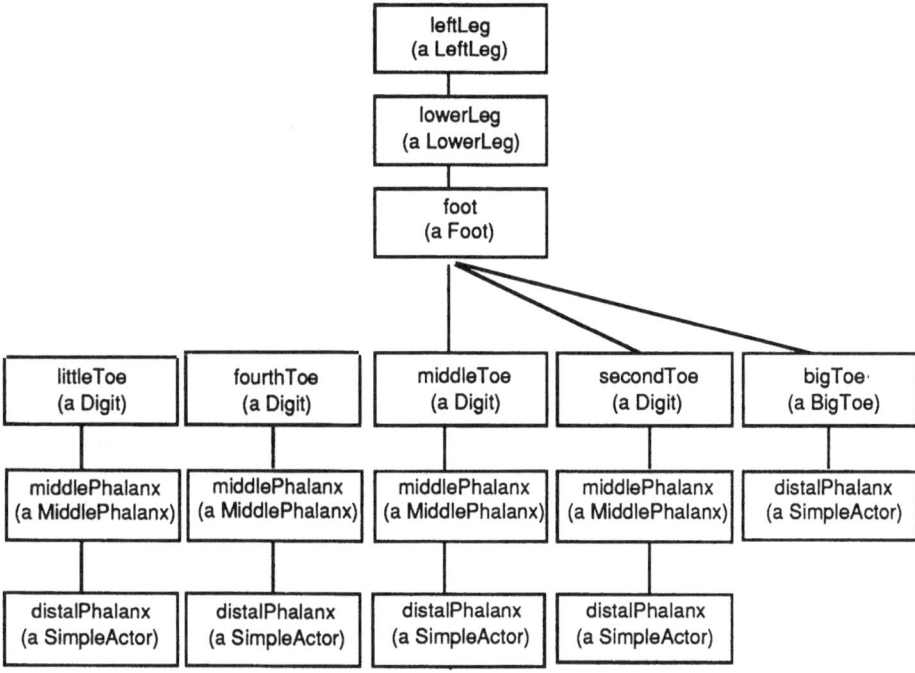

Fig. 3.3: The Part Hierarchy of the Left Leg of a Stick Figure.
The top name in each box is the part name and the bottom name (in parentheses) is the
class to which the part belongs. All the classes are a kind of (i.e., subclass of) Actor.

The most general motion of a rigid body in the world coordinate system can be
described as the combination of a translation of a fixed point in the object combined
with a rotation about that point. The most general motion if one point is fixed is just
rotation. Rotations are thus the most important transformation when implementing a
system of localized coordinates for an animal's limbs (or robot's for that matter).

The standard formalism for 3-D computer graphics has tended to be
homogeneous coordinates (Newman and Sproull, 1979). Hamilton's quaternions,
although rather neglected since the turn of the century (Goldstein, 1980: "musty
mathematics"), make a computationally efficient formalism which is also easy to
understand. Compared to homogeneous transformation matrices quaternions have
fewer redundant terms (Shoemake, 1985)..

Each limb of the modelled figure has a local transformation quaternion (actually
unit quaternion) which specifies its rotation with respect to the coordinate system of
the limb to which it is attached. It also has a quaternion (actually a vector) which
specifies its position relative to the origin of that coordinate system. This vector does
not change for most limbs, only those which form the root of the hierarchy of
coordinates reflect the changing translation of the actor as a whole. The synthetic
camera requires a similar pair of quaternions. Perspective projection is achieved by
bringing all objects into the camera coordinate system and then dividing by the
distance along the viewing direction (invariably the z-axis coordinate).

3.2.2. Quaternions

Hamilton's quaternions were introduced above as a way of representing coordinate transformations. Quaternions consist of a scalar part and a three-dimensional vector part (Hamilton, 1969, Pervin and Webb, 1982). Those with the same unit vector part are isomorphic to complex numbers. Quaternion multiplication combines scalar and vector multiplication and is non-commutative in general. The famous formula discovered by Hamilton in 1843 shows the scalar result of multiplying the unit vectors:

$$i^2 = j^2 = k^2 = -1$$

Quaternions represent rotations in terms of the axis of rotation and the angle about that axis. The effect of applying a quaternion is far easier to visualize than the more common Euler angles. Quaternions represent both the operands (vectors) and operators (rotations and translations) uniformly. Rotations can be combined by multiplying the quaternion representations. Quaternions provide a uniform representation of operators and operands; a vector can simply be regarded (and implemented) as a quaternion with a zero scalar term.

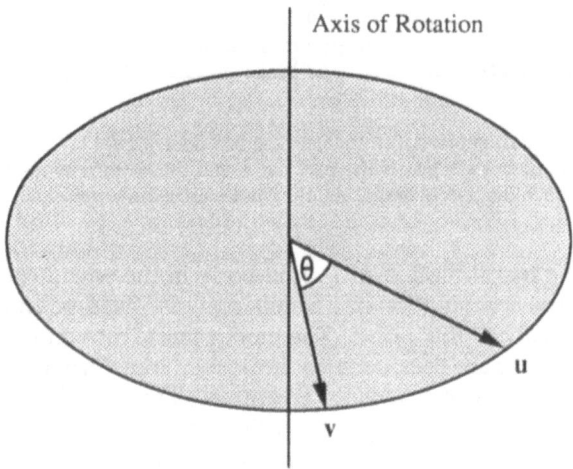

Fig. 3.4: Two unit vectors **u** and **v** with a common origin.

The shaded ellipse indicates their common plane, with the axis of rotation perpendicular to the plane. The angle between them is θ.

In order to illustrate the use of quaternions for rotation consider two unit vectors (**u** and **v**) with a common origin (see Figure 3.3). Let Q be the quaternion which represents the rotation from **u** to **v**. Then we can write:

$$Q = \sqrt{-\mathbf{v}\,\mathbf{u}}$$

$$Q = \cos\frac{\theta}{2} + \sin\frac{\theta}{2}\cdot\mathbf{n}$$

where **n** is the axis of rotation. The result of applying the rotation Q to the vector **u** is then **v**. That is:

$$v = Q \, u \, Q^{-1}$$
$$= Q \text{ appliedTo: } u$$

The details of these manipulations can be found in the references given for those who are interested.

3.2.3. Adding Quaternions to Smalltalk

The inherent polymorphism of messages (or overloading of operators) in Smalltalk allows easy and elegant implementation.

The normal arithmetic messages can be implemented for quaternions; combined with a few coercion messages that is really all that is required to add quaternions as a subclass of numbers (Figure 3.7 shows multiplication). Quaternions then become fully integrated in an extended system-wide concept of Number.

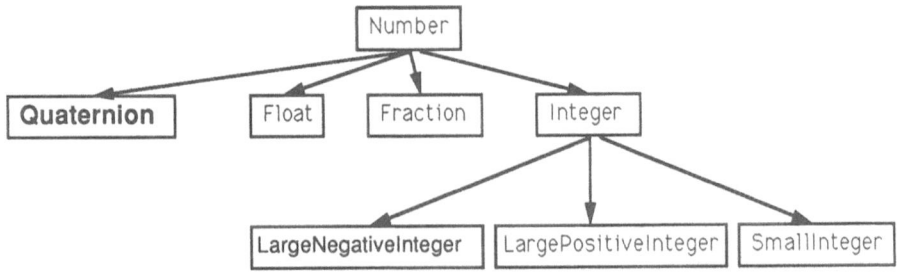

Fig. 3.5: The Numerical Classes of Smalltalk showing the addition of the new class "Quaternion" in the hierarchy.

We define Quaternions to have four instance variables, called "alpha" for the scalar part and "beta, gamma, delta" for the vector part. We provide all the required messages. Now if we implement Quaternions as a subclass of Number then we first implement the normal arithmetic messages. We also need specific methods, for example, to access the various instance variables.

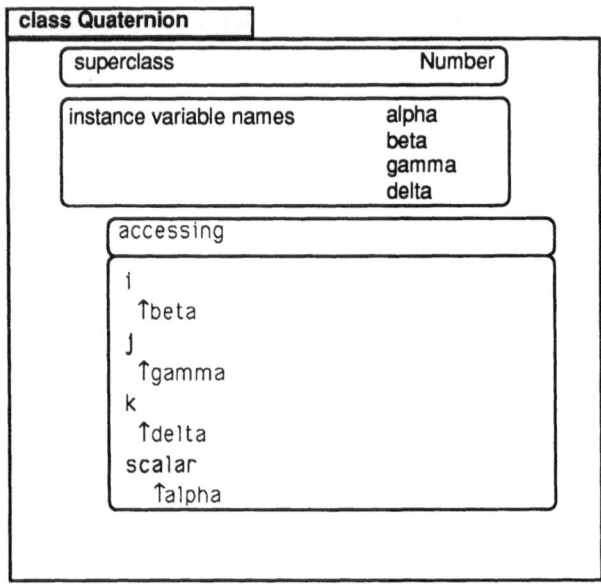

Fig. 3.6: Class definition of Quaternion.

We also need methods to implement the arithmetic messages which all subclasses of Number have to understand. Here are some examples:

Quaternion methodsFor: *'arithmetic'*

* aQuat

> *"The multiplication rule, where the quaternions Q1 and Q2 are written as (s1, v1) and (s2, v2) in terms of scalar and vector parts, is Q1 o Q2 = (s1s2 - v1.v2 + s1v2 + s2v1 + v1 x v2)"*

> | a tempI tempJ tempK|

> a ← aQuat scalar.
> tempI ← aQuat i.
> tempJ ← aQuat j.
> tempK ← aQuat k.
> ↑Quaternion
> > new: alpha * a - (beta * tempI) - (gamma * tempJ) - (delta * tempK)
> > i: alpha * tempI + (a * beta) + (gamma * tempK) - (delta * tempJ)
> > j: alpha * tempJ + (a * gamma) - (beta * tempK) + (delta * tempI)
> > k: alpha * tempK + (a * delta) + (beta * tempJ) - (gamma * tempI)

\+ aQuat

> ↑Quaternion
> > new: alpha + aQuat scalar
> > i: beta + aQuat i
> > j: gamma + aQuat j
> > k: delta + aQuat k

Naturally many more methods have to be defined. The above are just examples.

A minor complication is having to represent translation and rotation as separate transformations. Once again one can simply define a new class which incorporates both and the rest of the system need never know of the true implementation.

For greater efficiency, unit quaternions, which are used for rotation transformations, are given special treatment. This is quite easy in Smalltalk and is transparent to the user. It is analogous to the way small integers are treated in the standard system. Unit quaternions are declared as a subclass of quaternions.

The general messages are then handled by the superclass but specialized messages and more efficient implementations are dealt with by the subclass. For example, the inverse of a unit quaternion can be found without recourse to division and so this message is re-implemented in the subclass.

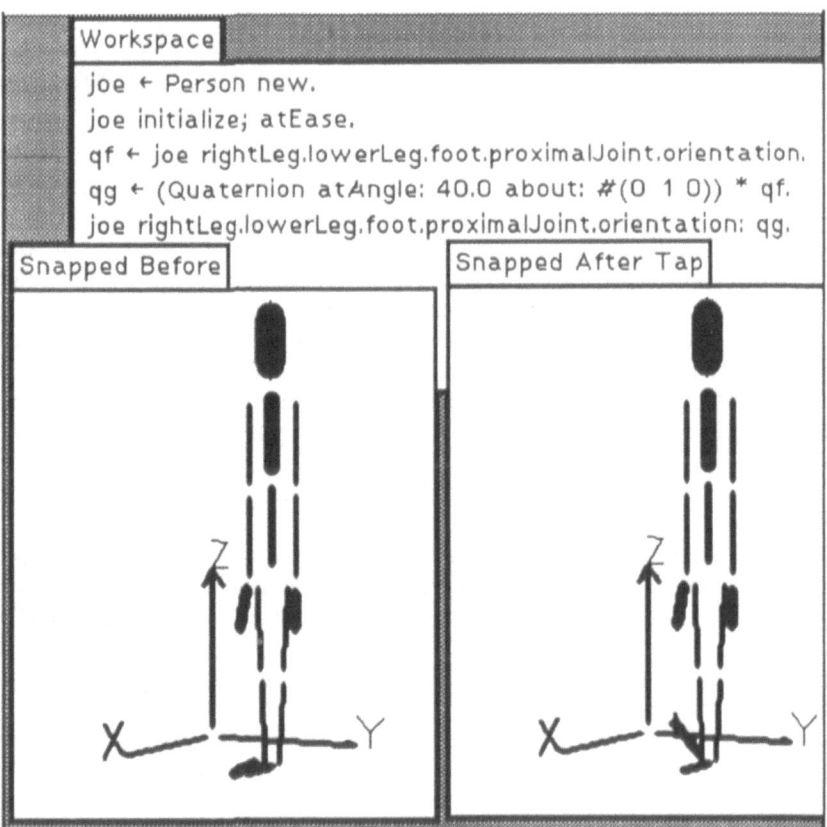

Fig. 3.7: Moving a Foot.
The new instance of Person is assigned to the variable 'joe'. The part-whole hierarchy is accessed with a compound message. Joe is asked to forward messages to its right foot. The request is to replace the orientation Quaternion by one which has been rotated by 40 degrees about a vector along the y-axis. Notice that the familiar multiplication message "*" is also understood by Quaternions.

3.2.4. Adding Quaternions to C++

This section is intended for programmers who are familiar with C or Pascal. C++ is an object-oriented extension of C (Stroustrup, 1986). In many practical situations C++ is used because it offers advantages of computational efficiency over Smalltalk. Like Smalltalk classes and inheritance hierarchies can be defined. Compared to C type checking is improved, and inline functions can be defined for greater efficiency.

In general the polymorphism of Smalltalk is provided via three mechanisms in C++:

- *Operator Overloading.* This means that the same message with different types (or classes) of parameters can be sent to an object provided that all the type information is known at compile time.
- *Overriding the methods* defined by the superclass in the subclass. This mechanism can be used whenever all the types can be determined at compile time.
- *Virtual Functions.* At run-time a message may be sent to a pointer to an object whose class is unknown, provided that the unknown object belongs to a class for which the particular message has been declared "virtual". Such classes must all belong to the same inheritance tree.

Except for virtual functions then, C++ lacks dynamic binding. In the case of quaternions the lack of dynamic binding does not matter greatly. Dynamic binding obviates the need for re-linking when the underlying representation of a type is changed. It is in the nature of a number system like quaternions that the implementation and messages understood does not change very often, although new optimizations may occasionally be introduced.

Dynamic binding also allows a particular place holder (variable name) to contain a number of different types of objects. The binding is made at run time when the variable has been instantiated. Quaternions can reasonably be interchanged only with scalars and vectors and for such a limited set of possibilities coercion rules can be drawn up which the C++ compiler will then invoke automatically. It has generally been the case that the types of objects used in arithmetic can be determined at compile time.

The use of automatic coercion does have some hidden snags. Unless one is careful a lot of conversion can happen from unit quaternions to quaternions (this is cheap) and then back again (which is expensive since it involves division and square root calculation).

For a comparison with Smalltalk we give some examples of code for implementing Quaternions in C++.

Classes are defined almost like structures in C (or records in Pascal). Except that now both data and functions are included in the class. Unlike Smalltalk C++ is much stricter in enforcing data encapsulation: if a method or variable is not declared 'public' then it may be accessed from the outside. Generally one first declares the instance variables and the message protocol and then defines the methods separately.

```
/*
 * Quaternion Class Definition
 */
class Quaternion
{
/** 'protected' = only accessed by me or my subclasses **/
protected:
    float   alpha;
```

```
      float   beta;
      float   gamma;
      float   delta;
/** 'public' = methods can be accessed by anyone         **/
public:
      /**  Creation messages ('constructors') have the same
      **   name as the class.                              **/
      Quaternion( float a = 0);            // Scalar, default 0
      Quaternion( float b, float c, float d);     // Vector
      Quaternion( float a, float b, float c, float d);
      /** accessing **/
      float i()    { return( beta);};  // Short methods can be
      float j()    { return( gamma);};// declared and defined
      float k()    { return( delta);};//  in one.
      float scalar()       { return( alpha);};
      /** functions **/
      /** 'friend' is used for functions (rather than
      ** messages).  A friend function can access protected
      ** and private data. The suffix '&' is used to indicate
      ** an argument passed by reference rather than by
      ** value.                                            **/
      friend float   norm( Quaternion& );
      friend float   arg( Quaternion& );   // etc ...
      friend Quaternion operator+( Quaternion&, Quaternion& );
      friend Quaternion operator-( Quaternion& );
      friend Quaternion operator-( Quaternion&, Quaternion& );
      friend Quaternion operator*( Quaternion&, Quaternion& );
      friend Quaternion operator/( Quaternion&, Quaternion& );
      friend int      operator==( Quaternion&, Quaternion& );
      /** The (typical C) operator `+=' is implemented as a
      **message (so-called member function).              **/
      void operator+=( Quaternion& ); // etc ...
};
```

Having declared our class we can now define the methods. Some methods are made 'inline' for greater speed. First then some inline methods:

```
      /** arithmetic **/
inline Quaternion operator+(  Quaternion& x, Quaternion& y)
{
      return Quaternion( x.alpha + y.alpha,
            x.beta + y.beta,
            x.gamma + y.gamma,
            x.delta + y.delta);
};
/** Unary Minus **/
inline Quaternion operator-( Quaternion& a)
{
      return Quaternion( -a.alpha,-a.beta,-a.gamma,-a.delta);
};
```

Multiplication is better declared as an ordinary function. The parameters are declared to be unchanging references (i.e., automatically dereferenced pointers).

```
Quaternion operator*(  register const Quaternion& x,
                  register const Quaternion& y)
{
      return Quaternion( x.alpha*y.alpha
```

```
        - x.beta*y.beta - x.gamma*y.gamma - x.delta*y.delta,
    x.alpha*y.beta
        + x.beta*y.alpha + x.gamma*y.delta - x.delta*y.gamma,
    x.alpha*y.gamma
        + x.gamma*y.alpha - x.beta*y.delta + x.delta*y.beta,
    x.alpha*y.delta
        + x.delta*y.alpha + x.beta*y.gamma - x.gamma*y.beta);
};
```

4. A Simple Animation System

There are a number of aspects to computer animation and simulation. We have to model various objects in three dimensions. We have to make them move. We have to organize all the objects in a system which repeatedly produces the frames of the animation on the screen.

In paragraph 3.2 we used coordinate transformations as our example of object-oriented programming. That example was chosen because of its relevance to computer graphics in general and animation in particular.

4.1. Animating Jointed Figures

There are two aspects to modelling animated figures: producing computer representations which allow movement and controlling that movement. The problem of controlling figure movements so that they appear realistic is an area of active research to which answers are only now appearing (Badler, 1987). In developing our chosen representation we shall be very concerned with providing an underlying mechanism which allows constraints on movement to be handled elegantly.

At the simplest level we can regard people and animals as being composed of limbs connected by revolute joints. Each part of the hierarchical representation of an object has its own changing local coordinate system. In animation and rendering these coordinate systems have to be related to one another and to the world coordinate system.

Animated figures and robots (Nicol, 1984) are governed by constraints on their allowed movements. Computer animators note the need for abstraction as a way of dealing with their rather difficult problem. Zeltzer points out how a human figure can be modelled as a tree structure of joints and parts. The parts are embedded in a generalization lattice of attributes, this lattice being supplied by some sort of multiple class inheritance hierarchy (in the object-oriented sense) (Zeltzer, 1985). He emphasizes that the complex modelled environment of an animated object has to be structured in some way which allows rapid testing for the proximity of objects. The description of objects in terms of a hierarchy of parts which also reflect levels of detail should go a long way towards meeting this need.

4.2. A Simple Priority Based Animation System

The basic specification for the animation system presented here is to illustrate and provide a simple testbed for the hierarchical object-oriented methods. The main requirement of the user interface was that experimental parameters could be altered quickly and easily. To get maximum performance the programming language would probably be C++ rather than Smalltalk.

We shall here simply give an outline of the classes which have to be implemented. Code fragments will be dispensed with in favour of an outline description. It should be noted that we make extensive use of concepts introduced earlier, for example, part hierarchies and polymorphism.

The following sections show how the object-oriented approach simplifies the task of designing complex systems. When we design the system we consider the classes and design the class and part hierarchies. During the design we are frequently content with producing so-called "abstract" superclasses, these classes are intended to have the general protocol of messages but perhaps not the specific functionality. The full functionality being provided by subclasses which are specified at a later stage.

4.3. The Parts of the Animation System

The animation system is thus split between the user interface part and the animation production system proper (see Figure 4.1). The animated world consists of three basic types of objects and numerous supporting objects (class names are indicated by capital letters):

- *Stage.* The global object which contains all other objects as parts or sub-parts. An important part of the Stage is the Clock. There is only one Stage per animation. The Clock owns a list of all active objects, the list of Frenetics.
- *Actor.* An actor is the basic unit of animation. The actors have a Script which is the sequence of actions which they execute. They have an Appearance which determines how they will look on a display. There can be any number of Actors in the world. Appearances exist for every Camera.
- *Camera.* The camera takes the Appearance of an Actor and renders it on a Segment. The Segments are submitted to a Window to be displayed. Although there can be a number of Cameras the current user interface only allows one to be set up. The Camera owns a number of renderers, Quick and Perfect, corresponding to such different algorithms as might be required.

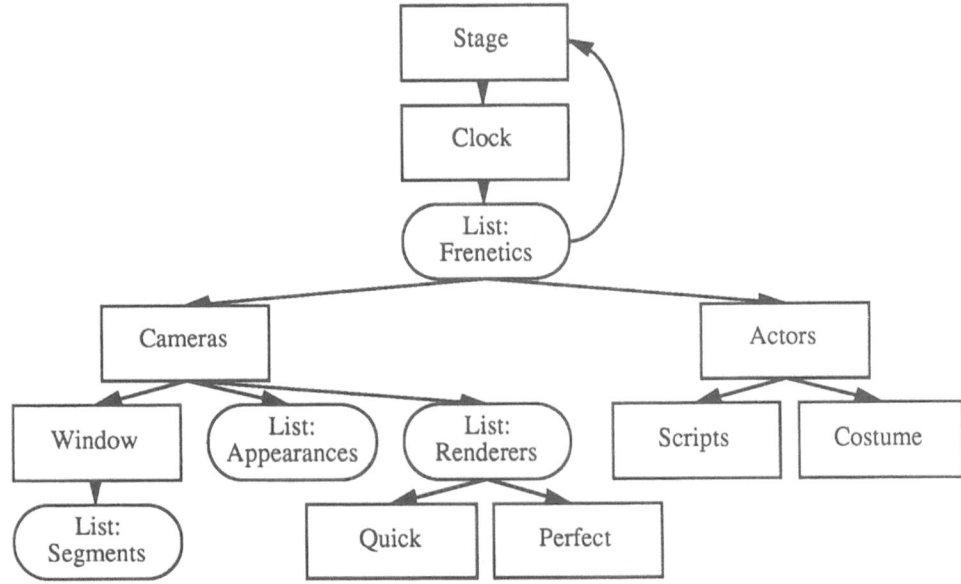

Fig. 4.1:The part hierarchy of selected classes in the animation system.

These objects are linked by a number of lists. The three most important ones are:

- Appearance List. The Appearances are really delayed messages from an Actor to Camera telling how an actor should be rendered. An instance of this list is owned by each Camera.
- Segment List. Each Window has a list of Segments ordered according to their display priority (depth priority).
- Frenetic or Kinetic Object List. Every object which can move is placed on a list owned by the Clock. These objects are updated once for each frame that is rendered.

4.4. The Animation Classes

Up to now we have been talking in terms of the part hierarchy, that is, which object owns which, how the parts fit together to form the whole. The other side of an object-oriented implementation is the class inheritance hierarchy (Figure 4.2). All objects which can change over time are subclasses of the abstract superclass KineticObject. So the Stage, Actors and Cameras are all subclasses of KineticObject.

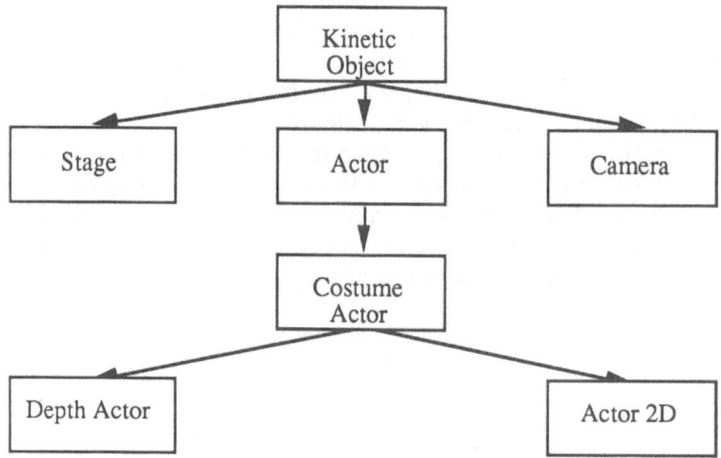

Fig. 4.2.: Part of the class hierarchy of the animation system

We have emphasized that we need to be able to use many underlying representations together in a single animation sequence. However we can reduce the full load of rendering an Actor by only passing relevant information about its appearance at a particular instant in time. This relevant information is encapsulated in the class Appearance (see the Figure below). The Appearance is a very important kind of object since it is part of the mechanism which frees us from having to rely on a single common primitive for all our representations. An Appearance is an abstract superclass, the real task of interpreting the way an Actor looks to a Segment is performed by its subclasses.

The full importance of these class hierarchies will become apparent once we have considered the processing steps which take place during animation.

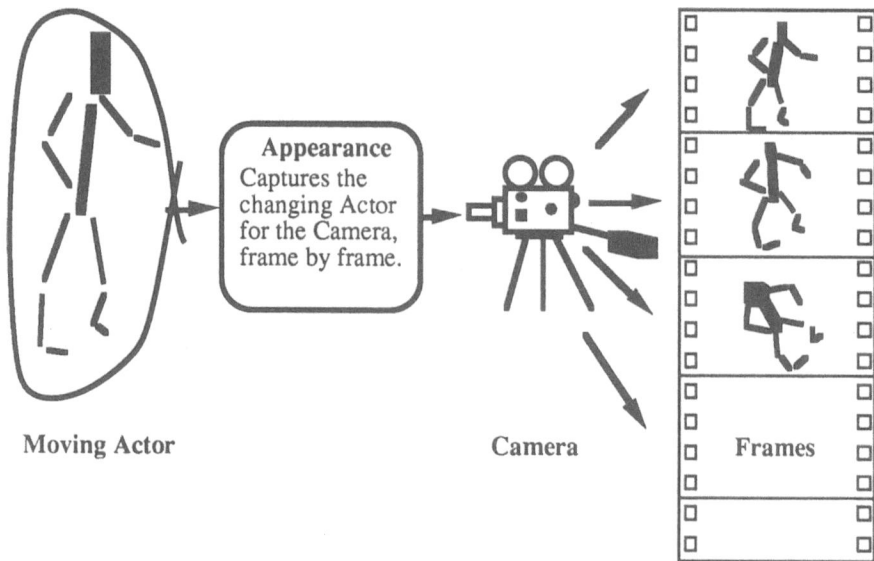

Fig. 4.3: The Appearance of an Actor mediates between the Camera and the Actor.

4.5. The Animation Processing Cycle

Animation processing is centered around the cycle of operations which produce the output frames. At the center of this processing cycle is a clock object which distributes a tick to all objects and which notices when a cycle is complete. Since this system is implemented on a single processor machine synchronization is achieved by distributing the 'tick' in some correct predetermined order, but the idea is extensible to multi-processor systems. This order is determined by the order in which objects appear in the KineticObject list mentioned above.

The first objects to receive 'tick' are the Cameras. They then proceed to render the Appearances received in the previous cycle. Then they update their own positions. This has to be done before the Actor's are activated because temporal priority depends on the relative positions and speeds of Camera and Actor.

Next the Stage receives 'tick'. Actually the very first object to be created is the Stage, it owns and sets up the Clock and is informed when the Clock has completed processing. During processing the stage maintains a subsidiary list of suspended but not deleted Actors, but the main purpose of sending a tick to Stage is to allow it to function as a kind of background actor.

Finally the Actors receive a 'tick', in no particular order. In response they update their position by asking their Script for the next action to be performed. Once updated their temporal priority is calculated w.r.t. each Camera. The Stage supplies an iterator object which will answer with each Camera in turn, when it is interrogated by the Actor.

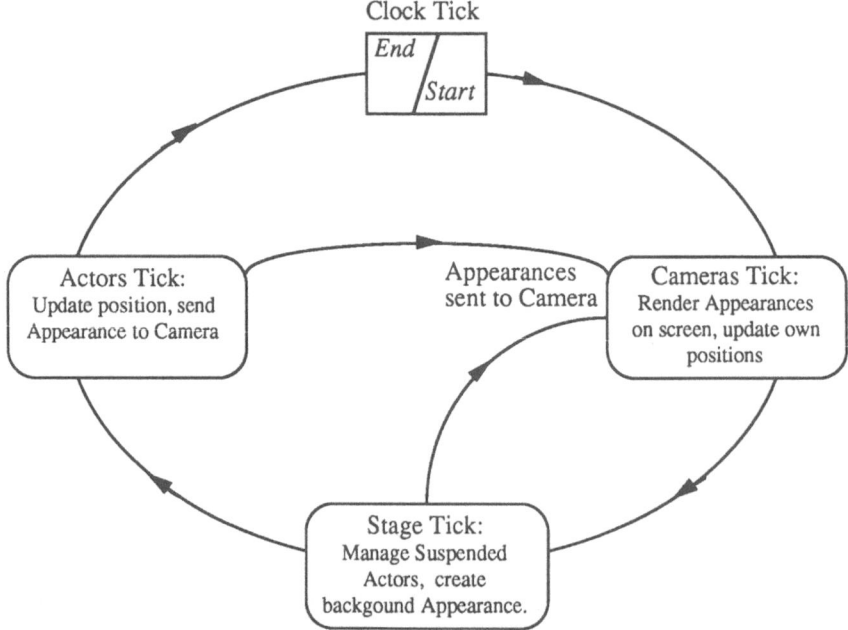

Fig. 4.4: The Animation Clock Cycle.

For each Camera a new Appearance is created if needed. The Actor's 3-D state is transformed and stored in the Appearance as a 2-D state relative to the Camera. Each Appearance is then submitted to the Camera by placing it on the appropriate list. This list can reflect the relative importance of the Appearances by the order they are kept in.

There can be numerous kinds of Actors. These depend on the specific application.

The Camera takes the Appearances from its appearance list and has them rendered by a Renderer. These renderers can come in many classes depending on their speed and the degree of realism they yield.

The Renderer returns a Segment which has a screen position and depth priority. A bounding box is also provided to indicate the area of the segment actually used by the image. These Segments are maintained in a depth priority list. This list provides a simple method of hidden surface removal. Segments are rendered depth first.

The processing cycle for one frame is now complete and a new one can begin. The Stage is informed of this. Certain housekeeping such as image recording or user interaction takes place at this stage of the cycle.

4.6. Generic Lists and Dynamic Binding

In the discussion of the Appearance and KineticObject list we have glossed over a crucial point: these lists can contain many different kinds of object. When a particular object is taken from the list we do not know its type beyond the fact that it is either a kind of KineticObject (on the Clock's list) or a kind of Appearance (on the Camera's list). Clearly this will be a feature of any animation system with many kinds of active objects or any implementation of a priority measure which must apply to different kinds of objects.

It is here that dynamic binding provides the most elegant solution. We send the same message to all objects in the clock queue (i.e. 'tick') and the same message to all objects in the Camera queue (i.e. 'scanConvert'). Then at run-time the system binds the correct function corresponding to the type of the object encountered.

This is an application of polymorphism which was introduced in the introduction.

In C++ these functions are known as virtual functions. In general at least two more virtual functions are needed: 'printOn' to print a description of the object on some output stream, for debugging and general enquiries. And a virtual destructor which will clean up behind the object if it is deleted.

A less elegant feature of the generic lists which are used to implement these queues is the way they are declared: they are generated by a rather baroque collection of C preprocessor macros. Their virtue is that creating a new kind of list is simply a question of naming it.

4.7. Conclusion

We have given the practical details of how a simple animation system may be set up. An interesting feature was the use of polymorphic messages (virtual functions in C++) for generic lists. These lists allow us to render objects with different internal representations and so we avoid the requirement for a common primitive representation for all our objects.

Another feature of note was that the moment by moment appearance of an object was abstracted as a kind of Appearance. This Appearance helped to mediate between the Actors and the synthetic Cameras.

The object-oriented approach is also extensible to the more complex computer animation problems which include feedback and constraints between concurrent Actors. Some of these features will be discussed in paragraph 5.

5. For Further Study - An Annotated Bibliography

5.1. Historical Aspects of the Object-Oriented Paradigm

"Object orientation" has sometimes been used rather loosely in graphics to mean nothing more than using 3-D object models instead of doing 2-D images. This is not what is meant by the term here. We adopt the more conventional "definition" (Cardelli and Wegner 1985; Rensch 1982; Stefik and Bobrow 1985) where object-orientation is some combination of:

- *Data abstraction* (named interfaces and hidden local state) plus *object types* (or classes) plus *type inheritance* (attributes inherited from superclasses).
- Processing is done by objects sending and replying to *messages*.

Languages need not conform to all these characteristics to be called "object-oriented". Computer abstractions are expressed in languages. We can illustrate the various object- oriented approaches by looking at languages that have realized them. This has the benefit that it also introduces a concrete way of implementing the ideas.

Object-oriented languages descend from Simula (Dahl and Hoare, 1973) and are exemplified by Smalltalk (Goldberg and Robson, 1983). Some established languages have also been given object-oriented features (e.g. C++ (Stroustrup, 1986), Objective-C (Cox, 1984; 1986)). In Hewitt's actor formalism (Agha, 1986; Agha and Hewitt, 1987) greater emphasis is placed on concurrency and message passing. The NeWS windowing system has shown how naturally PostScript supports object-oriented programming for user interfaces (Adobe Systems, 1985; NeWS, 1987; Densmore and Rosenthal, 1987). Meyer (1988) discusses general features of object-oriented programming as well as the language Eiffel.

To summarize the constellation of features which comprise object-oriented programming, we have (Wegner, 1987):

- Objects.
- Message Passing.
- Classes or Prototypes.
- Inheritance or Delegation.
- Information Hiding.
- Strong Typing or Run-Time type checking.
- Concurrency.

Languages can be classified according to these features. For example one might call all languages with objects "Object Based": e.g. Ada and Modula. Languages with objects and classes can be called "Class Based": e.g. CLU. "Object-Oriented" under this scheme would be reserved for languages which also supported inheritance: e.g. Smalltalk. Some object-oriented languages do not support information hiding: e.g. Simula and Flavors.

Actor languages do not have a particular mechanism for inheritance. They do support delegation. Thus one can have actors for an object, the prototype of that object, and even the class of that object. Readers requiring a fuller introduction to object-oriented programming can consult some of the more general texts on the subject (e.g., Cox, 1986; Meyer, 1988).

5.2. ThingLab

ThingLab (Borning 1979; 1981; 1986a; Borning et al. 1987) is a system for simulating physical objects (e.g., geometric shapes, bridges, electrical circuits, documents, calculators). In ThingLab, objects consist of parts. Multiple class inheritance hierarchies, and part-whole hierarchies are used to describe the objects and their interrelations. Parts are referred to symbolically by means of paths that name the nodes to be visited in proceeding down the part hierarchy.

In ThingLab the superclasses of an object are a part of the object: an object contains an instance of its superclass (in the type theoretic sense) as sub-part (in the sense of part versus whole objects). The class which describes such a superclass part is a subclass of the normal part description class. Apart from this notion of multiple superclasses ThingLab also employs prototypes to provide initialized instances of objects.

The major contribution of ThingLab is a system for representing and satisfying constraints which exist between the parts. However, when it comes to providing a tool for modelling complex objects confusion can arise. In particular we should draw a clearer distinction between class hierarchies and part hierarchies. When classes are available it is also possible to dispense with prototypes, not that classes are necessarily preferable to prototypes.

5.3. Constraints

Constraints specify relations between objects which must be maintained. When a change occurs in the system it has to adjust all affected objects such that all the constraints remain satisfied. There are therefore two aspects to constraints:

- *Descriptions*. Constraints specify the relations which obtain between objects, particularly between parts and sub-parts. This is the declarative aspect of a constraint, it is a rule.
- *Methods*. In order to satisfy the constraints methods of constraint satisfaction have to be given. This is the procedural aspect of constraints.

Once the methods for satisfying constraints have been defined constraint based programming acquires a declarative feel, that is, the programs become largely static specifications of the relations which have to obtain between objects (Duisberg, 1986).

Unfortunately satisfying constraints is far from simple, it also needs to be fairly rapid in interactive graphics. Other problems can arise from contradictory or incomplete constraints. It seems therefore that programmers will have to specify both the constraints and the constraint satisfaction techniques.

The basis for object-oriented constraint satisfaction was laid by ThingLab (paragraph 5.2). It is argued that the locality of reference afforded by data encapsulation is vital in reducing the scope of an alteration to the system. This reduces the number of objects which have to be involved in satisfying a constraint. Furthermore the generality of methods allowed in object-oriented programming allows many constraint satisfaction techniques to be employed (including, for example, those found in logic programming).

Constraints based programming has not been seen as an integral part of object-oriented programming. However it must be viewed as an integral part of interactive computer graphics and of computer animation. Constraint satisfaction techniques often have a pleasing generality, however domain specific knowledge will also be required. Thus the technique cannot be provided independently of the intended application.

5.3.1. Coordination between Model and View via Constraints

In the MVC model presented above, the communication between Model, View and Controller was done via methods. The case of an interaction of a changing representation and a changing model which is quite common in practice had to be programmed for each direction separately. The approach of the filter paradigm in (Ege et. al. 87) establishes constraints for formulating the interaction of model and application. Depending on the modification source, the other partner is then automatically kept consistent within the constraint definition.

5.4. Representing Physical Objects: The Part Hierarchy

Things are often described in terms of parts and wholes; the way the division into parts is made depends on the purpose of the analysis. A part is a part by virtue of its being included in a larger whole. A part can become a whole in itself, which can then be split into further parts. In this way we build up a hierarchy of parts and wholes, which we have called the *part hierarchy*. We present a series of illustrative examples:

We distinguish between a mere *collection*, or additive whole, or heap, (e.g., a bag of marbles, a pile of electronic components) and a more *structured whole* (e.g., an animal, a wired-up electronic circuit). To the former we apply set theory, to the latter a part hierarchy.

Part-whole analysis is crucial in engineering and technology. Objects are often described as a hierarchy of assemblies and subassemblies. Parts are also met in those branches of computation where physical objects are represented, for example, *model-based computer vision* and *computer graphics*. Model-based vision draws upon the work on knowledge representation in artificial intelligence (Brooks, 1981). *Frame-based* representation (Winston 1984) has similarities to the object-oriented approach. Frames describe parts and attributes by means of *slots*.

One of the standard texts on computer graphics (Foley and van Dam, 1982) devotes a chapter to "Modelling and the Object Hierarchy". PHIGS (Programmer's Hierarchical Interactive Graphics System) and GEO++ organize objects in a structure or in a group hierarchy (see paragraph 2). Both *structure hierarchy* and *object hierarchy*, as used above, are instruments for managing a part hierarchy.

PHIGS also has the concept of *inheritance* on a part hierarchy where attributes of the whole are inherited by the parts. E.g., the legs of the table could inherit the colour of the whole. The requirement is not quite as general as it at first appears. This "inheritance" is only used when the whole structure is traversed from the root down in order to display it. Thus the wholes are always accessed before the parts and the attributes can therefore be stacked.

We should adopt the policy that information is stored in the part hierarchy at its corresponding logical level. Information about the whole is not stored in the parts, information about the parts which is not modified by the whole remains with the parts. Ideally the whole knows the parts but the parts do not know of the whole.

But, Smalltalk and many other object-oriented languages fail to provide the facility to describe objects in terms of their parts. Or more accurately, when we want to model objects consisting of parts in Smalltalk, and many other object-oriented languages, we are confronted with a dilemma: either sacrifice the data encapsulation properties of the language or utterly flatten the part-whole hierarchy (Blake and Cook, 1987). This problem has been solved by Blake and Cook by a modification of the Smalltalk-80 system; addressing parts in GEO++ is also an attempt to avoid unvealing of the intermediate parts when accessing parts which are deep in the hierarchy.

Composite objects are provided in Loops (Stefik and Bobrow, 1985). The emphasis seems to be on providing a uniform method for instantiation. For this purpose a simple type system is developed where classes are specified for each part. Using these classes the parts can then be correctly generated when a new instance of the whole is required.

In the examples in the sections which follow we shall indicate some of the uses of parts in object-oriented graphics. These include the limbs of a stick figure and the parts (Actors, Cameras, Stage, Clock, etc.) of an animation system.

5.5. Actors and Animation

Actors of a different type are met in object-oriented animation systems. Early examples are DIRECTOR (Kahn 1976) and ASAS (Reynolds 1982). A succession of animation systems based to a greater or lesser extent on the actor formalism have been developed by Magnenat- Thalmann and Thalmann (1985).

Message passing actors have proved to be very appropriate for modelling 3-D animation. Object-oriented animation has its origins with Smalltalk and this aspect of Smalltalk was influenced by Logo (Kay, 1977). Logo is not object-oriented: in Kay's terms Logo is a data-procedure language. Whereas in Smalltalk the data and procedures are replaced by the single idea of "activities" which belong to families. New families are created by combining and enriching properties which are inherited as traits. This message-activity system is inherently parallel. The kinds of animation produced nevertheless still have a distinct Logo-like flavour.

A similar strong influence of Logo is apparent in Kahn's (Kahn, 1976; Magnenat-Thalmann and Thalmann, 1985) Director language. Like Kay he emphasizes that a computer language should reflect both the structure of its applications and the intuitions of its users. For animation this means that each entity should be a "little person" who communicates with others by means of messages. An animation as a whole is then produced by a number of parallel cooperating processes.

Kahn's animation system is a practical approximation to this ideal. There is a Universe which holds the actors. Each actor remembers its own actions and the Universe (the scheduler) merely sends a 'tick' message to them. At each tick an actor performs its actions and interactions for that time increment. The display messages are sent to a screen actor and these messages can also be remembered to make a movie.

Kahn mentions the need for better primitives for dealing with composite objects and for constructing objects out of parts.

Both Kay and Kahn produced rather simple two-dimensional images. In ASAS (Reynolds, 1982) we get much more realistic three-dimensional graphics. An object-oriented language for video game design has been developed (Larrabee and Mitchell 1984). Other object-oriented approaches to animation include (Uchiki et al. 1983, Blake 1987, Breen et al. 1987, Fiume et al. 1987 and Reynolds 1987). A physical simulation system based on actors has been described by Haumann and Parent (1988).

5.5.1. Controlling Figure Animation

There are two aspects to modelling animated figures: producing computer representations which allow movement and controlling that movement. The first problem has already been addressed in the sections on modelling. The problem of controlling figure movements is related to the problem of modelling motion subject to various constraints.

There are two principal ways of controlling three-dimensional animated figures:

- Firstly, we can choose to drive the animation from an external script which specifies every movement explicitly.
- Secondly, we can indicate constraints which apply to the objects and the provide a broad outline of the configurations required and then depend on the system to provide the complete configuration.

With the first approach the animator has complete control and freedom at the expense of having to be concerned with every detail of the animation. The essential feature from the programming point of view is that there is no feedback between elements of the modelled environment: control is strictly top down. The central task of such an animation system is to provide access to all parts of the environment and to determine when all the processes in the simulation have completed there tasks. This access is used to distribute instructions to the objects and to inform them of clock ticks. The objects are also asked to return their relative positions when the rendering process traverses the modelled environment and when the user attempts to pick a displayed object for some input operation.

In the second approach we are conducting a much more realistic simulation of some imaginary world. The animator is freed from having to concentrate on mundane tasks at the expense of having to learn about a somewhat more complicated system and not having the same total freedom to manipulate objects. From the programming point of view there is mutual feedback between objects in the environment. In addition to the operations specified above, some mechanism must exist to detect interactions between objects (collisions or relatively constrained movements). As a result of such an interaction objects may need to communicate with other objects in order to adjust their configurations. Since any object can set off a new spurt of activity in the system it is somewhat more difficult to detect termination of a frame generation cycle.

6. Conclusion

We hope that we have shown that the concepts of object-oriented programming are the right paradigm to model what is intuitively felt to be "object-oriented" in the field of computer graphics and animation. The object-oriented paradigm will sooner or later have an influence on the thinking of the majority of application programmers, and we are optimistic that it will have significant impacts on the future work in computer graphics standardization.

Acknowledgements

We would like to thank our colleagues at CWI and GMD for practical assistance in preparing this paper.

References

Adobe Systems (1985) PostScript Language Reference Manual. Addison-Wesley, Reading, MA.

Agha, G. (1986) An overview of actor languages. SIGPLAN Notices 21, 10, 58-67.

Agha, G. and Hewitt, C. (1987) Actors: a conceptual foundation for concurrent object-oriented programming. In Shriver, B. and Wegner, P. (ed) Research Directions in Object-Oriented Programming. The MIT Press, Cambridge, Massachusetts. pp. 49-74

Badler, N.I. (1987) Articulated figure animation: Guest editor's introduction. IEEE Computer Graphics and Applications 7, 6 10-11.

Blake, E.H. (1987) A metric for computing adaptive detail in animated scenes using object-oriented programming.Eurographics '87. Elsevier, Amsterdam. 295-307.

Blake, E., Cook, S. (1987) On including part hierarchies in object-oriented languages, with an implementation in Smalltalk. In Proceedings of the European Conference on Object-Oriented Programming ECOOP '87, pp. 41-50, LNCS no. 276, Springer Verlag, Heidelberg.

Borning, A.H. (1979) ThingLab: A constraint-oriented simulation laboratory. Xerox Palo Alto Research Center report SSL-79-3 (a revised version of: Stanford University PhD. thesis, Stanford Computer Science Department Report STAN-CS-79-746).

Borning, A.H. (1981) The programming language aspects of ThingLab, a constraint-oriented simulation laboratory. ACM Trans.Programming Languages and Systems 3, 4 353-387.

Borning, A.H. (1986) Classes versus prototypes in object-oriented languages. IEEE/ACM Fall Joint Computer Conf. 36-40 Dallas, Texas, Nov 1986.

Borning, A.H., Duisberg, R.A., Freeman-Benson, B., Kramer, A., Woolf, M. Constraint hierarchies (1987) OOPSLA'87: SIGPLAN Notices 22, 12 48-60

Breen, D.E., Getto, P.H., Apodaca, A.A., Schmidt, D.G., Sarachan, B.D. (1987) The Clockworks: An object-oriented computer animation system. Eurographics'87. Elsevier, Amsterdam. 275-282

Brown, M.,D. (1985) Understanding PHIGS.. Megatek, San Diego, Cal., USA.

Cardelli, L., Wegner, P. (1985) On understanding types, data abstraction, and polymorphism. Computing Surveys 17, 4 471-522

Chernicoff, St. (1987) Macintosh™ Revealed – Unlocking the Toolbox. Hayden Books, Indianapolis.

Cox, B.J. (1984) Message/Object programming: an evolutionary change in programming technology. IEEE Software 1, 1 50-61

Cox, B.J. (1986) Object-Oriented Programming: An Evolutionary Approach. Addison-Wesley., Reading, Massachusetts.

Dahl, O.-J. and Hoare, C.A.R. (1973) Hierarchical program structures. In: Dahl, O.-J., Dijkstra, E.W. and Hoare, C.A.R. (ed) Structured Programming. Academic Press, London. 175-220

Densmore, O.M. and Rosenthal, D.S.H. (1987) A user-interface toolkit in object-oriented PostScript. Computer Graphics Forum 6, 3 171-180

Duisberg, R.A. (1986) Animated graphical interfaces using temporal constraints. ACM CHI'86 Proceedings 131-136.

Ege, R.K., Maier, D., Borning, A. (1987) The filter browser: defining interfaces graphically. In Proceedings of the European Conference on Object-Oriented Programming,, pp. 155-165.

Enderle, G., Kansy, K., Pfaff, G. (1987) Computer Graphics Programming. GKS – The Graphics Standard (2. Ed.). Springer-Verlag, Berlin .

Fiume, E., Tsichritzis, D. and Dami, L. (1987) A temporal scripting language for object-oriented animation. Eurographics'87. Elsevier, Amsterdam 283-294

Foley, J.D., van Dam, A. (1982) Fundamental of Interactive Computer Graphics. Addison-Wesley, Reading, Mass.

Goldberg, A. and Robson, D. (1983) Smalltalk-80: the language and its implementation. Addison-Wesley, Reading, Massachusetts.

Goldberg, A. (1984) Smalltalk-80: The Interactive Programming Environment. Addison-Wesley, Reading, Massachusetts.

Goldstein, H. (1980) Classical Mechanics. Addison-Wesley, Reading, MA (2nd edition)

Hamilton, W.R. (1969) Elements of Quaternions, Vol. 1 . Chelsea Publishing Co, New York (3rd edition).

Haumann, D.R. and Parent, R.E. (1988) The behavioral test-bed: obtaining complex behavior from simple rules. The Visual Computer 4, 332-347

Ingalls, D.H.H. (1986) A simple technique for handling multiple polymorphism. OOPSLA'86: SIGPLAN Notices 21, 11 347-349

ISO International Standard 7942, Information Processing Systems – Computer Graphics – Graphical Kernel System (GKS), Functional Description, Aug. 1985.

ISO International Standard 9592, Information Processing Systems – Computer Graphics – Programmer's Hierarchical Interactive Graphics Standard (PHIGS),1988.

Kahn, K.M. (1976) An actor-based computer animation language. User-oriented design of interactive graphics systems (ACM/SIGGRAPH workshop). 37-43.

Kay, A.C. (1977) Microelectronics and the personal computer. Scientific American 237, September 230-244.

Larrabee, T. and Mitchell, C.L. (1984) Gambit: A protyping approach to video game design. IEEE Software 1, 4 28-36.

Magnenat-Thalmann, N. and Thalmann, D. (1985) Computer Animation: Theory and Practice. Springer-Verlag, Tokyo.

Meyer, B. (1988) Object-oriented software construction. Prentice-Hall, London.

Michener, J.C., Foley, J.D. (1978) Some major issues in the design of the Core Graphics System. Computing Surveys 10,4 , 445-463.

Miranda, E. (1987) BrouHaHa - A portable Smalltalk Interpreter. OOPSLA'87: SIGPLAN Notices 22, 12 354-365.

Newman, W.M. and Sproull, R.F. (1979) Principles of interactive computer graphics. McGraw-Hill (2nd edition).

NeWS (1987) NeWS Technical Overview. Part No: 800-1498-05. Sun Microsystems, Inc, Mountain View, CA.

Nicol, C.J. (1984) Modelling solids in four dimensions. PhD thesis, University of Glasgow (see also Computer Graphics Forum 4 239-244 (1985))

Pervin, E. and Webb, J.A. (1982) Quaternions in computer vision and robotics. Research Report CMU-CS-82-150 15pp Carnegie-Mellon Univ.

Rensch, T. (1982) Object oriented programming.SIGPLAN Notices 17 51-57

Reynolds, C.W. (1982) Computer animation with scripts and actors. SIGGRAPH'82: Computer Graphics 16, 3 289-296.

Reynolds, C.W. (1987) Flocks, herds and schools: A distributed behavioral model. SIGGRAPH'87: Computer Graphics 21, 4 25-34

Rome, E., Wisskirchen P. (1988) Object-Oriented Graphics. SIGGRAPH '88 Tutorial Notes (obtainable from the second author).

Shoemake, K. (1985) Animating rotation with quaternion curves.SIGGRAPH'85: Computer Graphics 19, 3 245-254

Stefik, M. and Bobrow, D.G. (1985) Object-oriented programming: Themes and variations.The AI Magazine VI, 4 40-62

Stroustrup, B. (1986) An Overview of C++.SIGPLAN Notices 21, 10 7-18

Szekely, P. (1987) Modular implementation of presentations. Proc. CHI+GI (Toronto, April 5-9). ACM, New York, pp. 235-240.

Uchiki, T., Ohashi, T. and Tokoro, M. (1983) Collision detection in motion simulation. Computers and Graphics 7, 3and4 285-293.

Weinreb, D. L., Moon, D. A. et. al 1987 Programming The User Interface. The Lisp Machine Manual, Vol. 7 a, b, Cambridge, Mass., 1897.

Wegner, P. (1987) Dimensions of object-based language design. OOPSLA'87: SIGPLAN Notices 22, 12 168-182.

Winston, P.H. (1984) Artificial Intelligence. Addison Wesley, Reading (MA), 2nd Edition.

Wisskirchen, P. (1986a) Towards object-oriented graphics standards. Computers & Graphics 10, 2, 1986, 183-187.

Wisskirchen, P. (1986b) GEO – Graphics system with editable objects. In Advanced Computer Graphics. T. L. Kunii Ed. Springer Verlag, Tokyo, 172-179.

Wisskirchen, P. (1988) Editing groups and parts in a multi-level graphics system. Internal Report GMD-F3.

Wisskirchen, P. (1989) GEO++ – A system for both modelling and display. Conference Proceedings of Eurographics '89, Hamburg, September 4-9, 1989. Elsevier Publ. Amsterdam (to appear).

Zeltzer, D. (1985) Towards an integrated view of 3-D computer animation. The Visual Computer 1, 249-259.

Chapter 6
Page Description Languages (PDLs)

Jürgen Schönhut

Abstract

About a decade ago laser printers were first used to print images. In the mean time laser printers have become a standard component not only in desk top publishing (DTP) systems. The advent of the page description language PostScript (tm Adobe) was a major milestone in this development. Today PDLs offer a high quality output road ranging from 300 dots per inch non impact printers to 3000 dots per inch laser image setters. PostScript and its predecessor Interpress (tm Xerox) will be discussed and used as examples. The underlying concepts of PDLs, their advantages and drawbacks are discussed together with PDL applications. Performance considerations with respect to functionality are also dealt with. An outlook to developments in standardization of PDLs is given, which is based on the status and latest version of SPDL, the Standard Page Description Language worked on in ISO.

1. Introduction

Page description languages have become famous over the last few years mainly by the market success of the Apple Laserwriter. This has lead to the de facto industry standard PostScript which was developped by Adobe Systems. The wide availability of PostScript on printers and high resolution laser image setters and the advent of clones on the market characterize the current scene. Recently several color PostScript devices (both with Adobe PostScript and PostScript clones) have appeared on the market featuring mostly thermo transfer color printing technology. Given the market position of PostScript we will use this language as source of examples throughout these notes. Remarks are given when there are significant differences to other important page description languages.

From a historic point of view page description languages have a history of quite some years. The most important predecessor of PostScript is clearly Interpress developped at the Xerox Palo Alto Research Center. The problem with Interpress was that it has not been available publicly, outside of Xerox systems for quite some time. PostScript however from the beginning set its direction to be a component of an open system. Adobe PostScript interpreters and many clones are now available in a large variety of printers from low to medium resolution as well as in laser image setters with extremely high resolution - and the claim is that a PostScript output file generated from some application will produce equivalent results across all devices.

We will discuss this point in more detail later. This device independence however is one of the most important properties of modern page description languages.

1.1 PostScript as a Language

PostScript is a stack oriented language with postfix notation of operators, i.e. the operands precede the associated operation. We will give one simple example to illustrate this. The addition of two numbers 37 and 24 formulated in PostScript language looks like this:

    37 24 add

The result of this operation is 61 and is returned on the operand stack. PostScript is an interpreted language; compared to a compiled language, its source is interpreted during execution time, rather than compiled into a machine language and executed as machine language program.

At this point we introduce a convention - which is also used throughout the PostScript literature (Adobe Systems Inc. 1985a,b) - to specifiy the effect of operators: to the left of the operator name we specifiy the required operands (on the stack), to the right of the operator name we specify the results (to be left on the stack). For the above example of the operand add this would look like:

    number number add number

The processing of PostScript language constructs by the interpreter is done using several stacks; the most important is the operand stack; it is used very heavily by most operators. The interpreter reads so called tokens from the input stream. If the token is an operand, i.e. a number, a string, etc. (we will talk about other operands later), it will be placed on top of the operand stack. If the token is the name of an operator, the associated operation is executed using the required operands off the operand stack.

PostScript allows for the definition and execution of procedures. The definition of a procedure shall be shown by an example for computing the arithmetic mean of two values; the name of the procedure shall be "arithmean"; the following sequence of code defines the procedure:

    /arithmean { add 2 div } def

This procedure expects two numeric operands on the operand stack and returns the result on the stack. So the invocation

    10 20 arithmean

would push the numbers 10 and 20 onto the operand stack, would execute the body of the procedure definition, thereby popping the two topmost elements 10 and 20 from the stack, adding them, and leaving the result 15 on the stack.

1.2 PostScript as a Page Description

PostScript is not only a programming language, it is also a means for specifying exactly where to put ink on a page. This is done in a device independent way (or almost device independent) way. The underlying imaging concept, on which this device independence is built, will be dealt with in more detail in a special section.

Another important aspect is also the handling of text using high quality fonts. Font handling together with handling of raster images is one of the most critical areas for a page description language interpreter; the quality of the rendering of text and images is to a large extent a quality measure for the whole implementation.

The underlying imaging model is based on a raster device that allows placing of opaque ink only; the color of the ink may be identical to the background color, but there is no combination of ink and already placed image parts; the raster frame buffer may be set only.

The PostScript language among others has also operators to transfer the image built up in the frame buffer to a printing device in order to produce the output required. Specialities of the printing device are dealt with in the interpreter and are (mostly) shielded from the PostScript generating application.

2. Basic Concepts of Page Description Languages

This section is to give an overview over the basic underlying concepts used in modern page description languages. These concepts already have a tradition over several years and differ to some extent from the concepts typically used in graphics systems. The common goal of device independence is achieved by different means. The most elementary concepts in PDLs are the path concept, the operations on paths and the concept of raster images; fonts are integrated into those basic concepts, however special treatment of fonts mainly for performance reasons can be widely found.

2.1 Path Concept

The path concept is the basic underlying data structure concept in a PDL. It is build up from elementary entities. The set of these entities is depending on which PDL we are looking at, but in general one can say that paths are constructed from line and curve segments; the different PDLs can be distinguished by the kind of curve primitives allowed in paths. Paths can be closed or open, and there need not be a single connected sequence of entities, there may be multiple connected sequences in one path.

The following example gives a definition of a simple path in PostScript (Adobe Systems Inc. 1985a,b). It describes a closed square of size 100 units, with its lower left corner at position (200,100); this square is the only object on the path:

```
newpath
200 100 moveto
300 100 lineto
300 200 lineto
200 200 lineto
200 100 lineto
```

The token newpath empties or clears the current path data structure of anything that may have been there before; after that the current point is set by a moveto command to point (200,100); the following lineto commands supply the data for the square; every lineto command also sets the current point. The concept of current point that was abandoned in computer graphics during the definition phase of GKS in the early seventies is still present in todays PDLs; however there is a silvery shine at the horizon; the latest version of the Standard Page Description Language SPDL will also abandon that concept and thereby make it consistent with what has been a basic principle in computer graphics for more than a decade now. The above example will be used later when we talk about operations on paths.

We have not discussed the coordinate system used in these examples. This will be done in detail under "Coordinate Systems and Transformations". Only so much for now that PostScript provides a default coordinate system that gives coordinates approximately in typographic point units (1/72 inch), and if there is nothing done to transformation this unit is in effect, and the origin is the lower left corner of the page.

Another version of our square example could use relative coordinates instead of absolute. The lineto command for relative coordinates is rlineto. The example could look like this:

```
newpath
200 100 moveto
100 0 rlineto
0 100 rlineto
-100 0 rlineto
0 -100 rlineto
```

This example gives exactly the same square path as the example above.

Besides linear path elements like lineto and rlineto there exist also curved path elements; here PostScript has a limited set of curves, namely circular arcs (arc, arcn, arcto) and Bezier curves (curveto); Interpress has a richer set of curves available for path construction, including general conic curves. PostScript circular arcs can be used to generate elliptical arcs by non-uniform scaling transformation. All operators in this section are called path construction operators, as they all serve the purpose of constructing a path in a data structure, called the current path.

2.2 Operations on Paths

Basically three operations can be performed on paths. The most elementary is stroking a path, i.e. drawing a line along the sequence of connected path entities. Certain attributes control the appearance of the line. Typical attibutes are line width, line join and line cap. The next operation is the filling of paths with a specified color, gray value or pattern. In addition the use of a path as a specification of clipping regions leads to a very powerful clipping operation. All these operations on paths belong to the class of painting operators.

2.2.1 Stroking of Paths

An elementary operation on paths is to draw the path. Drawing a path (the current path) is performed by the operator stroke. When the path is drawn, several attributes are used to specify the appearance of the path. These attributes are kept in the graphics state of a PostScript interpreter. Line width, line cap or line join are examples of such attributes; they are modal attributes that are set by the operators setlinewidth, setlinecap and setlinejoin respectively. The following example contains a setlinewidth operation. The command showpage copies the page memory to the actual output device medium.

```
newpath
200 100 moveto
300 100 lineto
300 200 lineto
200 200 lineto
200 100 lineto
10 setlinewidth
stroke
showpage
```

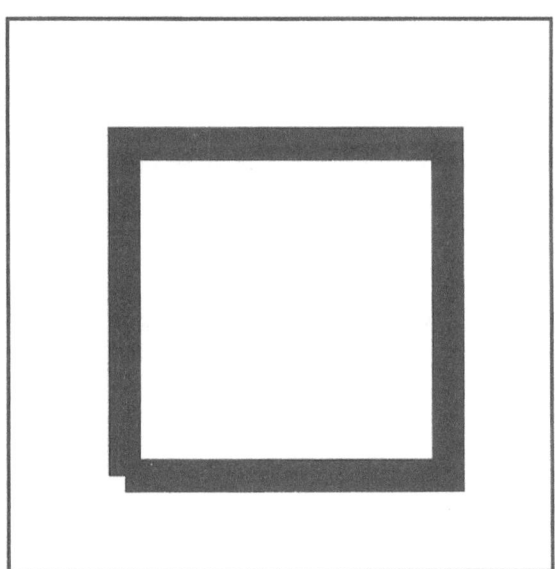

Fig. 1: A square defined as a PostScript path.

The above example shows an unexpected effect at the starting and ending point of the square. The rendering of line ends does not behave the same as the rendering of line joins. To correct this effect the path has to be closed or an appropriate setlinecap operation has to be performed. The following example show the solution using the closepath operator.

```
newpath
200 100 moveto
300 100 lineto
300 200 lineto
200 200 lineto
200 100 lineto
10 setlinewidth
closepath
stroke
```

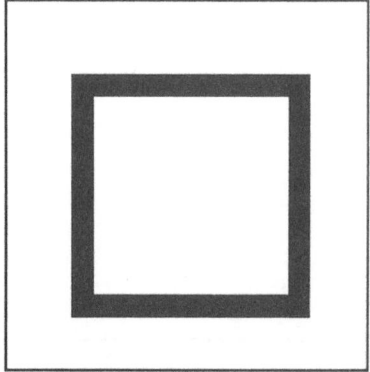

Fig. 2: A square with the closepath operator.

Line ends for the stroke operation can take one of three forms; the respective command is:

int setlinecap

The values for int are 0, 1 or 2, meaning butt, round or square ends of lines.

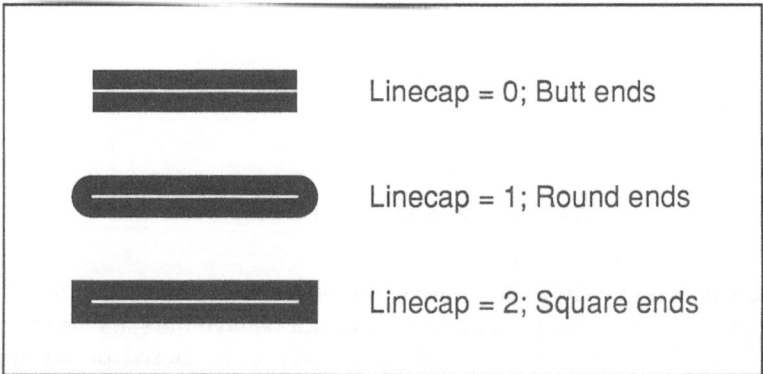

Fig. 3: Types of line caps.

Line joins for stroke operations can also take one of three forms; the respective command is:

int setlinejoin

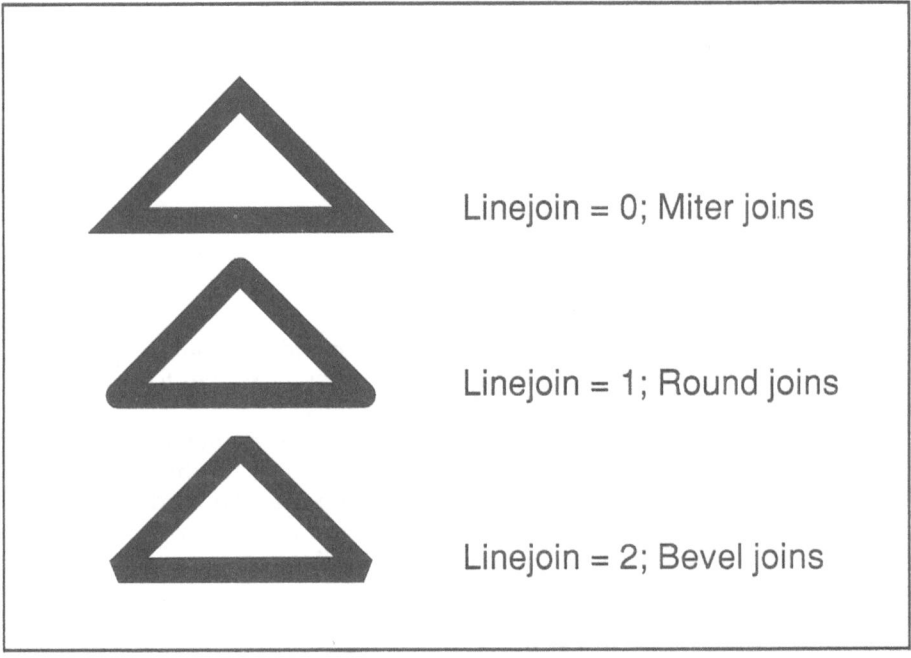

Fig. 4: Types of line joins.

The values for int again are 0, 1 or 2, standing for mitered, round and beveled line joins.

One other important attribute is the dash pattern for stroking of paths. It is possible to control even complex dash patterns using the operator setdash. This operator uses the values of an array on the stack to give the lengths of the on/off dashes in the pattern and an offset to control the start of the pattern at the beginning of a new subpath. The command has the form:

array offset setdash

An array in PostScript is constructed by enclosing the values in brackets. The following example gives a dash pattern starting at a new subpath of 2 on, 3 off, 6 on, 3 off, 6 on, 3 off, etc.:

[6 3] 4 setdash

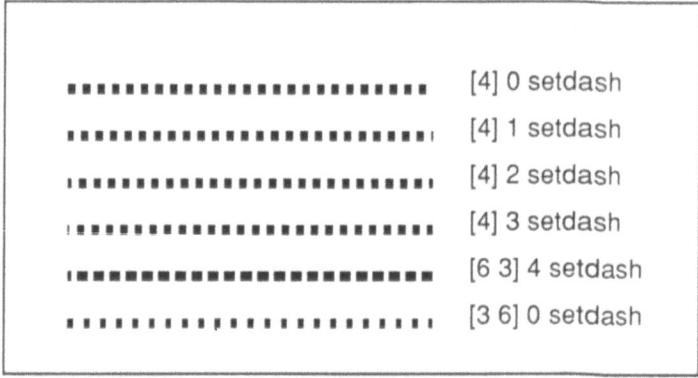

Fig. 5: Dash patterns.

2.2.2 Filling of Paths

Paths can not only be stroked, they can be used as boundary of an area to be filled with ink. This is similar to fill areas in graphics systems. The rules for what is to be considered inside an area are similar to graphics systems.

Two inside rules exist in PDLs: one called the non zero winding number rule, the other called the even/odd filling rule; the latter is identical to the fill area inside definition in graphics standards; the winding rule specifies the inside of a path by counting the borders going counterclockwise against the borders going clockwise around the point to be tested. If the number of borders going clockwise and the number of borders going counterclockwise is not identical, the point to be tested is inside the area.

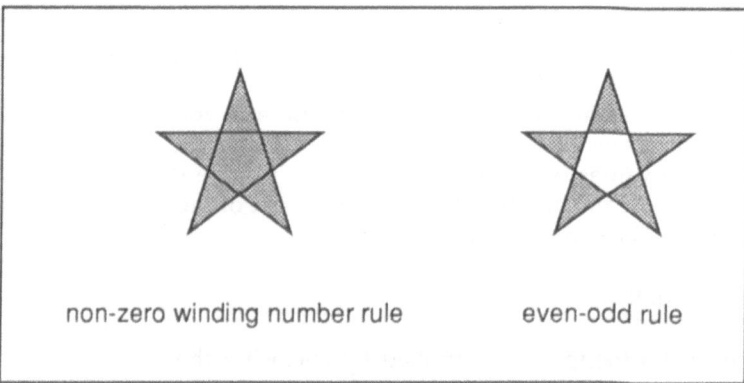

Fig. 6: Inside rules.

The following example shows a simple filled square, using the square path defined in earlier examples. The square is filled with solid black ink.

```
newpath
200 100 moveto
300 100 lineto
300 200 lineto
200 200 lineto
200 100 lineto
closepath
fill
showpage
```

Fig. 7: A square filled with black.

Another important area in relation to filling are screens. Screens allow for filling of paths with a shade of gray. The operator used to specify is the setgray operator; it takes the gray value (a value between 0 and 1) from the top of stack; this value specifies the amount of black to be output for filling. The value 0.3 in our example below specifies a gray produced by painting 70 percent of the area in black.

```
newpath
200 100 moveto
300 100 lineto
300 200 lineto
200 200 lineto
200 100 lineto
```

```
closepath
0.3 setgray
fill
showpage
```

Fig. 8: A square filled with gray.

The gray values are produced using a screening function; there is a default screening function available that is tuned to the device characteristics. Besides the screening function itself the angle of the screen and the screen frequency can also be specified. This is important especially for color applications when producing color separations for printing.

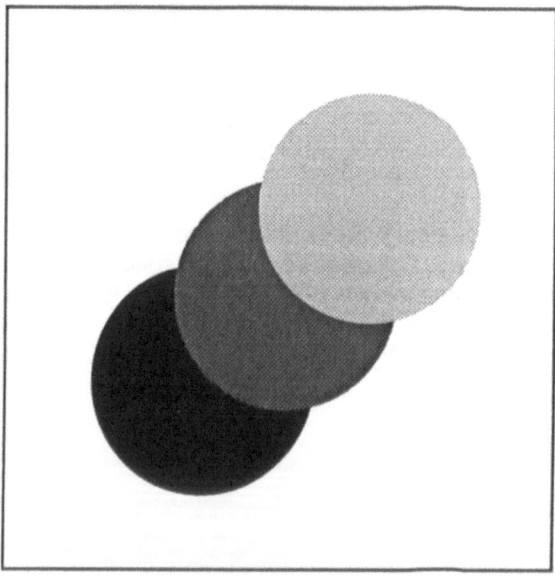

Fig. 9: Overlapping circles with different gray values.

The following code creates the previous figure (for the definition of the gsave and grestore operators see section Coordinate Systems and Transformations):

```
/circle {
  /gray-value exch def
  gray-value setgray
  newpath
  0 0 moveto
  0 0 1 0 360 arc closepath
  fill
  } def

gsave
100 100 translate
40 40 scale
0.0 circle
grestore

gsave
130 130 translate
40 40 scale
0.3 circle
grestore

160 160 translate
40 40 scale
0.8 circle

showpage
```

2.2.3 Clipping Paths

Clipping in PDLs is not the restricted clipping well known from computer graphics using axis parallel rectangular clipping regions! Clipping can be performed at arbitrary paths. This includes curved and possibly overlapping paths used as clipping boundaries. There may be even multiple disjoint regions specified. This gives very interesting functionality, however at the expense of being very time consuming. Clipping is one of the performance killers of current PDL implementations. This is illustrated by an example given under the section on applications and performance problems showing a page using character outlines as clip paths; one page of that type needs 40 (forty) minutes on an Apple Laserwriter, and still eight minutes on a Laserwriter Plus.

The following example gives an idea of the power inherent in that clipping mechanism.

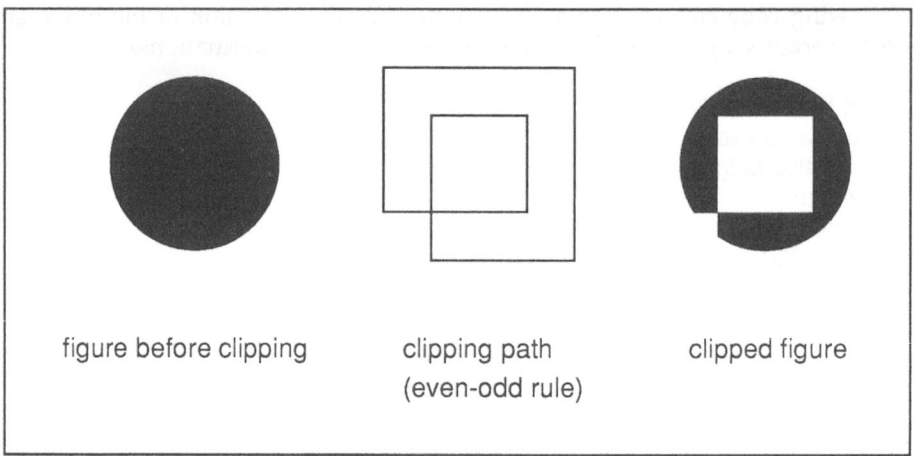

Fig. 10: Clipping mechanism.

The following code creates the clipped figure in the previous picture:

```
/Helvetica findfont 14 scalefont setfont

/figure          % define figure to be clipped
{ newpath
   0 0 45 0 360 arc
   fill
} def

/clippath        % define clipping path
{ -50 -25 moveto
  -50 50 lineto
   50 50 lineto
   50 -50 lineto
  -25 -50 lineto
  -25 25 lineto
   25 25 lineto
   25 -25 lineto
   closepath
} def


% ----- Begin Program ----
```

```
400 300 translate     % move origin
-40 -100 moveto
clippath eoclip     % set the current clipping path
newpath
figure          % draw figure again

showpage
```

2.2.4 Font Handling

Text is a very important entity for PDLs. One criteria for a good PDL is the availability of high quality fonts for the outputting of text. Font scaling is the very difficult issue in this context. Intelligent font scaling is required, since normal geometric transformation of glyphs leads to very poor quality results. This is especially true for small sizes where the device raster plays an important role.

As PDLs build on a raster device model, all characters finally have to be converted to raster information. The source information typically is contained in three different forms. Font definitions are available as raster fonts, as stroke fonts and as outline definitions of fonts. All three forms normally are supported.

Raster fonts are fonts normally available only in the tuned raster sizes; scaling of raster fonts leads mostly to a degradation of quality.

Stroke fonts are defined by specifying the strokes usually in form of straight line segments, circular arcs, conic sections, and Bezier curves, or any combination of these. They can be scaled by simple geometric transformations and drawn using stroke operations with an appropriate line width.

Today high quality fonts in most instances are produced from outline definitions of their glyphs; these outline definitions are constructed again using straight line segments, circular arcs, conic sections, and Bezier curves, or any combination of these to form a path. These paths then can be stroked to produce outlines of glyphs, or they can be filled to produce a glyph in a solid color, black or gray.

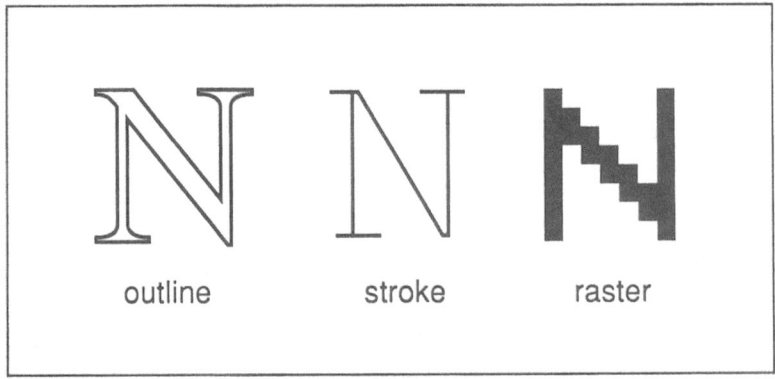

outline   stroke   raster

Fig. 11: A character as outline, stroke and raster.

Intelligent font scaling has to take the device raster into consideration in order to avoid awkward effects from truncation occuring in geometric computations when performing the mapping to raster. The other important typographic rule is that simple geometric scaling does not work properly with fonts; a linear magnification of a character does not always imply a linear magnification of the width of character stems (vertical or horizontal strokes).

The complete font machinery e.g. in PostScript is a rather complex mechanism. It is based on the elementary concepts outlined with paths and operations on paths; for performance reasons however there has been introduced some special treatment for painting of characters.

If a lot of text is produced, the scaling of the characters does not change very often. Natural languages also tend to use some letters more frequently than others. This lead to the implementation of font cache mechanisms, where the scan conversion from the outline path to the raster representation is made once only for a specific transformation. The raster information is stored in a cache for later use. This raster representation is reused whenever the character is needed, and as long as the transformation does not change. The speed improvement is especially significant for those letters that are used very frequently in a language.

The organisation of fonts in PostScript is done with dictionaries; they contain all necessary information about the font and links to the set of glyphs defined. The mapping between a character code and the actual glyph is done by an encoding table. This encoding table maps a special code to the name of the PostScript procedure that defines the path for the associated glyph.

An additional dictionary contains the information about all fonts available. This leads to one of the serious problems, if you try to use the same PostScript output on different PostScript devices, supporting different sets of fonts. Besides the problem of distinct fonts, there is the problem of very similar, or even the same fonts, available under different names. This is critical if PostScript is used to transmit documents to other locations where special fonts might not be available. Currently this leads to a reduction of fonts used to Times Roman and Helvetica, but even there due to copyright problems some clone implementations substitute for these very similar fonts with different names, e.g. Swiss for Helvetica. If the font metrics are not identical however results produced e.g. by a formatter may be scrambled.

Font naming and specification is a problem currently also under consideration in the international standards arena, but it probably will take some time to come up with an agreed solution that really solves the problem.

2.2.5 Image Handling

A sampled image is stored as a rectangular array of cells of sampled data. The image is subdivided into rectangular cells by the use of a grid, each containing either one, two, four or eight bits of gray information. One bit per cell gives only black and white images with zero being black, and one being white. With eight bits per cell 256 shades of gray are representable.

These sampled images can be transformed by normal 2 by 3 transformation and painted by the operator image or imagemask. The operator image paints the specified image, the imagemask operator uses the image (of one bits per cell) to apply the current gray value in places where the image contains ones.

We want to demonstrate this in the following example. The sampled image that is going to be generated is a rectangular array of 16x6 sample values, each of which consists of 1 bit of data per sample. The image operator is used:

width height bits/sample matrix proc image

The image exists in its own coordinate system and has its lower left corner at (0,0) and its upper right corner at (width,height).

Therefore a matrix that specifies a transformation from user space to the image coordinate system is necessary. The procedure proc contains the actual image data. The sample values are assumed to be received in a fixed order: left-to-right, bottom-to-top. First The image is printed in a 2 inch square, then a non-uniform scaling is used in order to proportion the image properly (the image is printed in a 2 by 1 inch square).

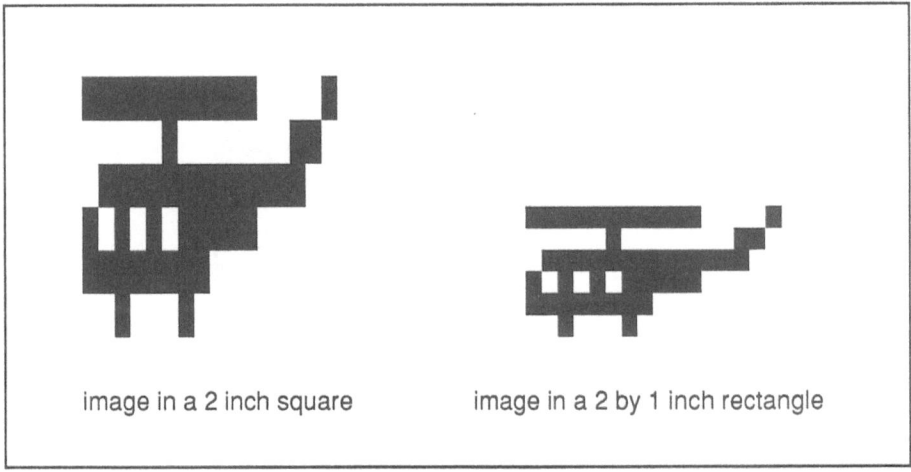

image in a 2 inch square   image in a 2 by 1 inch rectangle

Fig. 12: A bitmap image.

2.3 Coordinate Systems and Transformations

As outlined at the beginning PostScript provides a default coordinate system with its origin being the lower left corner of the page, and units being 1/72 inch, which is approximately equivalent to a typographic point.

This default coordinate system can be changed by the scale, rotate, and translate operators. The syntax for these operators is as follows:

tx ty translate
angle rotate
sx sy scale

By execution of these operations the current transformation matrix (CTM) is modified; this matrix is used to transform all geometric information that is executed. It also contains the device dependent transformation to the device raster.

Since PostScript concatenates transformations, it is usually difficult to reset the transformations to a previous one. For that purpose PostScript provides operators to save and restore the whole graphics state. These operators are:

gsave
grestore

Upon execution of a gsave operator the current graphics state is pushed onto the graphics state stack. The execution of the corresponding grestore pops that state off the graphics state stack and restores the values in the graphics state. Among other values also the current path and the clip path is part of the graphics state.

This save/restore mechanism allows local modifications of the graphics state without side effects. The content of the current page is not effected.

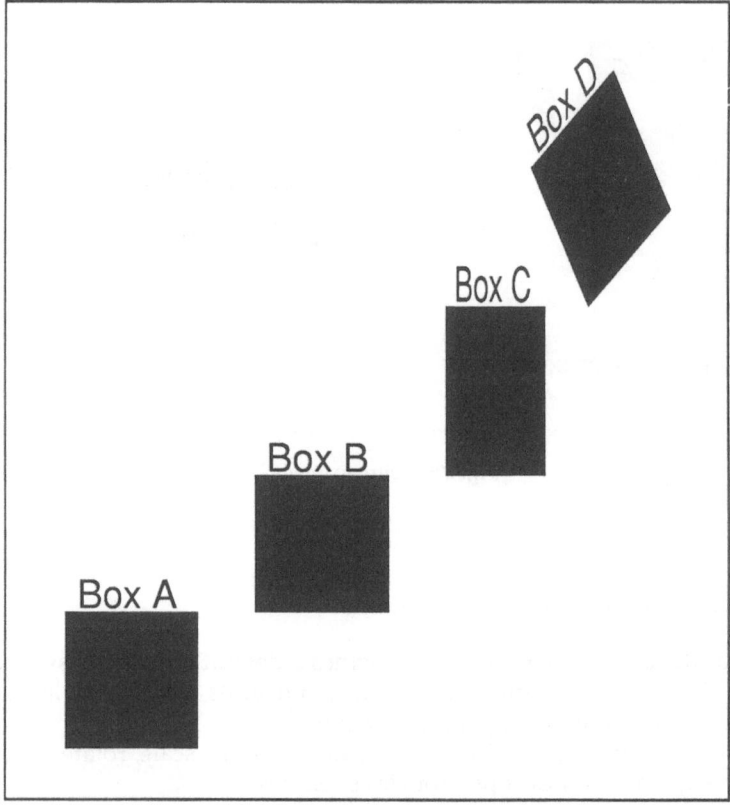

Fig. 13: Translation, scaling and rotation of a box.

The CTM is a 2*3 transformation matrix only; this implies that perspective transformations cannot be performed. It is not possible to emulate perspective transformation either for text or for image. For that purpose a 3*3 transformation matrix would be required.

This is a clear handicap for using PostScript as an output device for high quality 3D output, but it should be kept in mind as a requirement also for 3D to be able to use high quality fonts and to use the same fonts that occur also in the text part of a document.

2.4 Imaging Models and Device Independence

The imaging model underlying PostScript is that of a device independent raster device. This means that no PostScript program needs to refer to device specific information; this information is hidden in the PostScript interpreter not affecting the PostScript file. This is true for almost all of PostScript. There are some small details however that allow access to device specifics; a typical example for that is the possibility to define screening functions (besides the always available default screening function) which operate in device raster.

The device model contains a device frame buffer. Its pixels can only be set by PostScript painting operations. There is no pixel readback capability and no combinatorial operation on pixels. The paint is applied through a stencil, and a mask is available to perform clipping. This is the simple device model for PostScript. Halftoning is available in a device independent way that is normally well adjusted to the device.

The data structures implementing this device model are the current page, the current path and the clip path. These data structures represent the frame buffer, the stencil and the clip mask; the ink is applied by using the current gray value together with the (default or user defined) screening function.

2.5 Color Extensions

The initial versions of PostScript were mainly addressing black and white devices. Color was supported initially only very rudimentary. The color support was derived from the known requirements from computer graphics; the publishing and graphics industry were practically left out and only later got included. This was also reflected in the supported color models.

The color models supported werde RGB and HSB only. Later additional support came for the CMY and CMYK color models. The currently selected color is kept in the graphics state. Similar to the black and white screens, transfer functions and images the new operators setcolorscreen, setcolortransfer and colorimage were added to the PostScript language. In addition to the operators setrgbcolor and sethsbcolor the new operator setcmykcolor was defined to cope with the printing color process.

The definition of the color related operators is given in the following with the color values in the range of zero to one:

```
red green blue setrgbcolor
hue saturation brightness sethsbcolor
cyan magenta yellow black setcmykcolor
```

The PostScript language color models support one, three and four color output devices (Adobe Systems Inc. 1988a). The devices may be one bit per pixel per color component or multiple bits per pixel giving gray scale or multiple intensities of each color. Three-color devices may be either red-green-blue (RGB) or cyan-magenta-yellow (CMY) devices; four-color devices are cyan-magenta-yellow-black (CMYK).

The different color models can be converted. The basis for the conversion are the following simple equations:

```
cyan = 1.0 - red
magenta = 1.0 - green
yellow = 1.0 - blue
```

These conversion formulas only give results for CMY, not for CMYK. For color printing processes it may be desirable to generate also black; this is done using the setblackgeneration operator; in addition undercolor removal can be used to compensate for the addition of black by removing some of the CMY parts instead; this is controlled by the operator setundercolorremoval.

Binary devices use halftoning techniques, devices with eight bits per pixel are called full gray-scale devices using no halftoning. Devices with less than eight bits per pixel but more than one bit per pixel use a combination of halftoning and device intensities to produce the full color (and gray scale) images.

All these color processes are highly device and printing process dependent, however they are needed if PostScript is to be used in color printing industry.

2.6 Structuring Conventions

Structuring conventions are the formal specification of guidelines for PostScript languages programs.

They are very important with regards to the merging of PostScript files: the well-defined structure of a program facilitates the interchange of PostScript files with print spoolers, page reversal programs, font servers and other application programs.

The PostScript language comments in a program file, showing the program structure, are the way in which the structuring conventions can be expressed.

They are not thought to be used by humans, but they are useful for some parsing software, that can collect the information about the program structure.

PostScript files containing these comments and following the structuring rules are called "conforming" files.

A PostScript program can be structured into several levels. The structuring convenctions suggest that a program has to consist of three different parts: a prologue, a script and a trail.

The prologue may consist of many procedure sets, handling different specific tasks. It should contain just procedure definitons and constants and not modify the graphics state.

The script consists of pages, divided into page elements and it is usually generated by software.

The trailer section restores the original state at the end of a file and can be also empty.

Even if the PostScript interpreter works also without the previous described structure, this is very important for pre- and post-processing of PostScript files.

The following example shows the use of the structure comments (starting with %%), indicating also the version number of the PostScript Document Structuring Conventions, to which the program is conforming (Adobe Systems Inc. 1988c):

```
%!PS-Adobe_2.0
%%Title: example
%%Pages: 1
%%BeginProcSet: TextProcs 1.0 0
/F{
   findfont exch scalefont setfont
}bind def
%%EndProcSet
%%EndProlog
%%Page: one 1
12/Optima-Oblique F
100 100 moveto
(Fairly Oblique) show
showpage
%%Trailer
```

Some applications make use of Encapsulated PostScript files (EPS).

These files are standard files with a bitmap screen dump optionally included in the format. They are used as illustrations for other document makeup systems.

Their structure and structuring comments are a subset of the rules contained in the PostScript Document Structuring Conventions.

2.6 Error Handling

PostScript offers an error handling mechanism, which is able to identify about twenty five different error conditions. It provides specific error handling procedures to react on these conditions.

When an error occures the PostScript interpreter saves the current state (i.e. operand stack, execution stack, error condition name and the name of the procedure being executed) into a dictionary called $error which is a subdictionary of the errordict dictonary. Then the stop operator is executed.

The job server starts the handleerror procedure (which is located at the errordict dictionary) which in turn sends an error message back to the host computer according to the information saved in $error. These messages have to be handled by the software driver running on the host system. Finally the input stream is flushed until the end of the job.

The handleerror procedure as well as the error condition specific error handling procedures can be redefined by the user (Adobe Systems Inc. 1988c).

3. Applications and Performance Problems

Many applications today both in the areas of text and document processing as well as in the area of computer graphics generate PDL files, mostly using PostScript. The availability of a PostScript driver for a certain application is almost a quality criteria.

Integration of the output of multiple PostScript generating applications however is very difficult, sometimes almost impossible.

The performance of PostScript printing systems however is still a point of disappointment. Device independent output via a PostScript device often takes many times longer than via devices using specific device codes.

The main reasons for these performance problems are hidden in two special facilities available in modern PDLs: thick transformed lines and clipping to arbitrary curved paths.

One example that shows the problems very clearly is the Fig. 14 given below (in reduced size); printing of the A4 original takes on the Apple Laserwriter about 40 minutes; the Apple Laserwriter II is still eight minutes busy with it. This is the time with 300 dots per inch resolution; this kind of print time goes up with the square of the resolution; to produce a similar image on a 3000 dots per inch laser typesetter leads to a factor of 100 in the execution time. This is unacceptable high. New ways have to be walked in implementation that reduce these excessive print times to a reasonable size. This can be done by using more intelligent algorithms and faster and possibly specialized hardware.

Fig. 14: Picture producing some performance problems.

4. Standardization of PDLs

PostScript is currently a de facto industry standard. However PDLs are also under formal standardization. Important in this respect is also the purpose of a PDL and its relation to the computer graphis standards, especially its relation to CGM.

4.1 The Standard Page Description Language SPDL

Within ISO/IEC (ISO 1989)there exists a project called Standard Page Description Language, SPDL. This project tries to standardize a PDL that fits in the reference model of document application. The key players in this project are Adobe and Xerox, the suppliers of PostScript and Interpress. At the beginning progress was reasonably fast, as long as features were dealt with that were common in both languages. Later the process slowed down significantly; however just recently there has come hope again that we finally will end up with SPDL becoming an International Standard.

The market success of SPDL will depend on many imponderabilities, but mainly on good implementations and on the time, it will take, until todays users of PostScript will switch to the new standard.

4.2 Relation to the Computer Graphics Metafile Standard CGM

One interesting question with regard to SPDL is ist relationship with CGM (ISO 1987). SPDL is intended to be final form generated by a document formatting process. This implies that no further editing will take place at this stage, but editing has to occur on revisible document form.

CGM is such a processable form for computer graphics, however some functionality is missing from the CGM to satisfy all the quality and control requirements of document processing. Here extensions are under development to include such attributes as line cap or line join, and additional primitives for curves, a requirement not only coming from the document area, but from the CAD area as well.

It can be expected that CGM will provide a reasonable basis for picture exchange and picture import in integrated document systems. The extensions however have to become available in a reasonable time frame. A very important feature to be included is the inherent extensibility like the one given by modern PDLs.

5. Conformity Testing

One important criteria for buyers of both printing equipment and document processing software is whether a certain product conforms to the specifications of a certain PDL. One pre-requisite before one can try to answer such questions is a specification that allows deduction of tests; this seems to be a rather trivial remark; however trivial it may be, it is by no means trivial to find such specifications, and neither PostScript nor Interpress does fulfill this requirement.

5.1 Conformity of PDL Interpreter Implementations

Conformity testing of PDL interpreter implementation requires a large set of test files producing reports on the conformance of the interpreter. One problem for automatic testing is the absence of pixel readback capabilities in PDL interpreters. So to some degree visual testing needs to be included in the testing process. One requirement for such testing to be feasible is the availability of a clean and formal specification of the capabilities of a specific PDL. Such a functional specification is currently for no PDL available.

5.2 Conformity of PDL Files

To test the conformity of PDL files generated by some application suffers under the same lack of formal specification of PDLs as the testing of interpreters. Reference implementations could be used to verify the validity of a specific PDL file; this however gives no guarantee that all PDL files generated by that particular application will be conforming, if one file is conforming. One other property that could be checked is whether structuring conventions were followed. Statistic information about the PDL file, e.g. use frequency of certain commands, or flagging of commands, that hinder integration, can be very useful.

6. Internal Structures of a PostScript Interpreter

The following is a non exhaustive list of important internal data structures of a PostScript interpreter.

```
Input Token Stream
Operand Stack
Execution Stack
Graphics State Stack
Graphics State
   - Current Page
   - Current Path
   - Current Point
   - Clip Path
   - Current Font
   - Current Transformation Matrix
Dictionary Stack
   - systemdict
   - userdict
   - currentdict
   - errordict
PostScript State
```

The following picture gives an overview of a PostScript implementation:

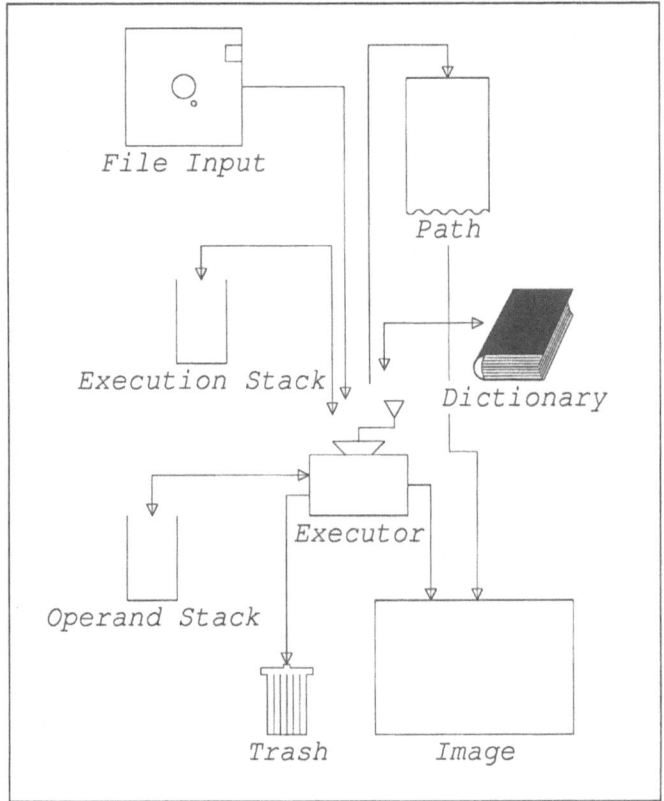

Fig. 15: PostScript data flow.

7. Conclusions

Page description languages are an important means for generation of quality output in a device independent way. The presence of PostScript interpreters not only from Adobe and the growth of the clone market shows a certain move towards more and better products.

The development of PDLs has already had a large impact on the development of interactive systems; the Network extensible Window System NeWS (Geschke 1988, Roberts 1988) and Display PostScript (Thompson 1988) are milestones on the impact of new concepts in this area. These systems show very obviously the trend to extensible systems and protocols. Standardization in this area will also have influence on computer graphics standards. Besides that high quality fonts and intelligent font scaling are a must in computer graphics too; poor text quality using the wide spread Hershey fonts are no longer sufficient.

For page description languages also standardization can be expected in a reasonable time frame; the market success of SPDL will depent largely on how fast is

178

can take over the market from PostScript, and whether Adobe will make easy upgrades from PostScript to SPDL possible.

PDLs already have imposed a significant impact on the requirements for computer graphics standards and this will continue to be so for a while. Computer graphics standards will be measured according to the capabilites of PDLs and will only keep a significant market share, if they are competitive.

Trademarks

Interpress is a trademark of Xerox Corporation.
Laserwriter is a trademark of Apple Computer, Inc.
PostScript is a trademark of Adobe Systems, Inc.

Bibliography

Adobe Systems Inc. (1985a, 4th printing 1986) PostScript Language Tutorial and Cookbook

Adobe Systems Inc. (1985b, 3rd printing 1986) PostScript Language Reference Manual

Adobe Systems Inc. (1988a) Color Extensions for PostScript Printer Description FIles

Adobe Systems Inc. (1988b) PostScript Language Color Operator Definitions

Adobe Systems Inc. (1988c) PostScript Language Program Design

Appelt, W.(1987) Existing systems for integrating text and graphics. In: Comput. Graph. (UK) 11 No. .4, pp. 369-75.

Barkes, K.G.(1987) The Ps & Qs of PDLs (page description languages). In: The DEC Professional 6 No. 10, pp. 44-50.

Bhatt, S.; Prestigiacomo, T. (1986) Page description languages. Computer Graphics World (USA) 9(Sept.) No. 9, pp. 79-80.

Bhushan, A., Plass, M. (1986) The Interpress page and document description language. In: IEEE Computer 19 No. 6, pp. 72-77.

Blumenfeld, M. (1987) Satzsprachen zur Wahl - Welche setzt sich durch? (Choice of page description language - which will win out?.) CHIP (Sept) 9 suppl. (CHIP PLUS). pp. 16-18.

Börner, W. (1988) PC publisher kit: DDL versus Postscript. Personal Computer (Feb.) No.2, pp. 100, 102.

Brown, H. (1986) Font information and device-independent output. In: Fundamental Algorithms for Computer Graphics. Proceedings of the NATO Advanced Study Institute (Ilkley, Yorks., England, 30 March-12 April 1985) / Earnshaw, R.A. (Ed.). Berlin: Springer, pp. 397-407.

Buckley, R. (1986) Interpress Standard for Color Printers and Workstations In: Lasers in Graphics - Electronic Publishing in the 80's (Anaheim, CA Sep 22-25, 1986) / Shipman, Tom (Ed.). Vista CA: Dunn Technology Inc., vol. II, pp.24-28.

Burns, D. (1986) Application of PostScript in a Graphic Design Environment. In: Lasers in Graphics - Electronic Publishing in the 80's (Anaheim, CA Sep 22-25, 1986) / Shipman, Tom (Ed.). Vista CA: Dunn Technology Inc., vol. II, pp.20-23.

Clarke, M. (1987) Back to Basics. Simple but high-quality text pagination systems In: Workstations and publication systems / Earnshaw, Rae A. (Ed.). Berlin: Springer, pp. 203-211.

Cohn, M. (1986) DDL - State of the art for a true document description language In: Lasers in Graphics - Electronic Publishing in the 80's (Anaheim, CA Sep 22-25, 1986) / Shipman, Tom (Ed.). Vista CA: Dunn Technology Inc., vol. II, pp.34-39.

Geschke, C.M.(1986) PostScript - A Page Description Language Informationstechnik it, 28 No.6, pp. 370-376.

Geschke, C.M. (1987) Describing pages (page description languages). In: Syst. Int. (GB) 15(June) No.6, pp. 65.

Geschke, C.M. (Chair) (1988) Screen PostScript. In: SIGGRAPH '88. Panels Proceedings (Aug 1-5), pp. 1-43.

Goswell, C.A.A. (1987a) Experiences in implementing Postscript In: Eurographics, G. Marechal (ed.), North-Holland, pp.25-38.

Goswell, C.A.A. (1987b) Experiences in implementing PostScript. In: Workstations and Publication Systems / Earnshaw, Rae A. (Hrsg.). Berlin: Springer, pp. 40-53.

Goswell, C.A.A. (1988) PostScript in the Real World Conference Proceedings: Interactive Documents - Today and Tomorrow. 26.10.88, Chilton, Didcot (UK): British Computer Society, Displays Group.

Hall, N.S., Laflin, S., Dodd, W.P. (1987) Integration of Graphics with Text in an Electronic Journal. In: Workstations and publication systems / Earnshaw, Rae A. (Ed.). Berlin: Springer, pp. 54-64.

Harrington, S.J., Buckley R.R. (1988) Interpress, The Source Book

Harris, D.J.(1986) An approach to the design of a page description language. In: Text Processing and Document Manipulation. Proceedings of the International Conference (Nottingham, England, 14-16 April 1986) / Van Vliet, J.C. (Ed.). Cambridge, England: Cambridge, pp. 58-64.

Harris, J. (1988) Demand Printing Today and Tomorrow Conference Proceedings: Interactive Documents - Today and Tomorrow. 26.10.88, Chilton, Didcot (UK): British Computer Society, Displays Group.

Hersch, R.D. (1982) Generating and Printing of High Quality Documents in a Distributed Office Automation Network Environment In: Eurographics '82 / Greenaway, D.S., Warman, E.A. (Eds.). North-Holland, pp. 169-180.

Hersch, R.D. (1987) Character Generation under Grid Constraints. In: Computer Graphics 21 4/July, pp. 243-251.

Holzgang, D.A. (1987) Understanding PostScript Programming

Hürbin, B. (1989) Die Seitenbeschreibungssprache PostScript und ihre Bedeutung für die Satzherstellung. Teil 1: Was ist PostScript überhaupt? Welche Vorteile bietet diese Seitenbeschreibungssprache? In: Deutscher Drucker, No. 11, pp. w1-w2.

International Organization for Standardization (1987), ISO 8632-1/2/3/4, Information processing systems - Computer graphics - Metafile for the storage and transfer of picture description information - Part 1: Functional specification, Part 2: Character encoding, Part 3: Binary encoding, Part 4: Clear text encoding.

International Organization for Standardization (1989), ISO/IEC JTC1/SC18/WG8 N789, Information processing systems - Text and office systems - Standard Page Description Language (SPDL), Fifth Working Draft.

Kleper, M.L. (1987) Interpress: Generating Pages in Binary Form In: The illustrated handbook of Desktop Publishing and Typesetting, Pittsford, NY: Graphic Dimensions, pp. 261-266.

MacDonald, S. (1986) PostScript in Commercial Printing. In: Lasers in Graphics - Electronic Publishing in the 80's (Anaheim, CA Sep 22-25, 1986) / Shipman, Tom (Ed.). Vista CA: Dunn Technology Inc., vol. II, pp.15-19

Marovac, N. (1987) Page description languages. Concepts and implementations. In: Workstations and publication systems / Earnshaw, Rae A. (Ed.). Berlin: Springer, pp. 14-26.

Mendelson, J. (1985) A Comparison of Interpress and PostScript. Palo Alto Calif: Xerox Corp., Apr..

Nanard, J., Nanard, M., Cottin, G. (1987) Pleiade, a system for interactive manipulation of structured documents. In: Workstations and publication systems / Earnshaw, Rae A. (Ed.). Berlin: Springer, pp. 73-86.

Oakley, A.L., Norris, A.C. (1988) Page description languages: development, implementation and standardization. In: Publishing: Origination, Dissemination and Design 1(Sept.) No.2, pp. 79-96.

Pelli, D.G. (1987) Programming in PostScript In: Byte 12, 5. pp.185-202.

Perry, T.S. (1988) 'PostScript' prints anything: a case history. In: IEEE Spectrum 25(May) No.5, pp. 42-6.

Querel, S., Borghi, B., de Rauglaudre, D. (1987) Smscript: an interpretor for the PostScript language under UNIX. In: Workstations and publication systems / Earnshaw, Rae A. (Ed.). Berlin: Springer, pp. 27-39.

Reid, B.K. (1986) Procedural Page Description Languages Text processing and document manipulation: Proceedings of th international conference, Nottingham, April 1986 / Vliet, J.C.van (Ed.). Cambridge (GB): University Press, pp. 214-223.

Reid, B.K. (1987) PostScript and Interpress Documentation Graphics - ACM Siggraph Course Notes, No.2, pp.47-62.

Roberts, W., Slater, M., Drake, K., Simmins, A., Davison, A., Williams, P. (1988) First Impressions of NeWS Computer Graphics Forum, 7, No.1, pp. 39-57.

Rubinstein, R. (1988) Page-Description Languages. In: Digital Typography. Addison-Wesley, pp.227-233.

Simpson, D. (1988) Color brightens desktop publishing. In: Mini-Micro Syst. (USA) 21(Feb) No.2, pp. 43-5, 47-8.

Thompson, T., Baran, N. (1988) Display PostScript. In: Byte November, pp. 170-171.

Chapter 7

Standards for Computer Graphics and Product Model Data Exchange

Michael Mittelstaedt, Anne M. Mumford

1. Introduction

Integration is a key issue for people writing or purchasing software or hardware, or indeed appointing new staff who need to be quickly assimilated into the new environment. New software and hardware need to be linked in with existing systems. Implementation of existing software and hardware need to be as easy and cost-effective as possible. Existing files of data, including graphical and product data, may need to be accessed and exchanged. It is the need to integrate products and people in a cost-effective way, that makes standards a desirable requirement in any computing environment.

This tutorial concentrates on standards in the areas of computer graphics and product model data and argues that the adoption of these standards is a useful progression in the quest for integration in many environments.

The first part of the tutorial aims to give an overview of the current standards for computer graphics, namely GKS, CGM, CGI, and PHIGS. The concentration of the information is towards those standards which are complete. It also addresses standards which are being developed and takes a look at the likely future directions of standards in this field. Furthermore it describes the need for, and the development of, graphics standards. The standards are described and their relationships outlined. The position of other emerging de facto standards is also addressed.

The second part of the tutorial which is an abbreviated but revised version of the EG'87 contribution, concentrates on the exchange of product model data among Cxx-systems and the corresponding international activities in the area of product data exchange. It covers a description of classical interface concepts and standards, namely IGES, VDAFS, and SET. Furthermore it includes a state of the art report about the international standardisation efforts toward STEP. Results of STEP based processor development and data exchange among commercial CAD systems will be presented.

The major aim of the tutorial is to give an introduction to the graphics and product data exchange standards. This should lead to an ability to see the value of these standards in the computing environment and to be able to compare and discuss the standards in this field.

2.   Computer Graphics Standards

2.1   Introduction

This section of the tutorial concentrates on the standards which have been developed within the computer graphics area. It is difficult sometimes to see what we define as computer graphics as many areas have not been standardised which might be considered to be in the area of computer graphics. Also many areas have been the concern of committees other than the ISO committee whose defined area is that of computer graphics. However with this problem accepted this section will attempt to explain what is the remit of the standardisation efforts in computer graphics; where these standards interface with related standards; and what work we can expect to see in the future.

These notes suggest that by using standards where appropriate we can move towards integrated solutions for computer graphics environments. We will see that portability of software, hardware and people is made possible. The notes suggest that there should be a positive approach to standards rather than the negative one which is all too often quoted.

Figure 2.1 shows typical graphics packages which are designed to be portable across machines and across graphics devices. They have a simple device interface to allow as many devices as possible to be connected. The software written for the application assumes as little as possible about the device. It may only assume that the device can draw single lines and that there may be the possibility of colour. The result of this is that the majority of the work is carried out in the application. There are no assumptions made that the device can do high quality text, that the device can store information, or that the device can manipulate graphical data.

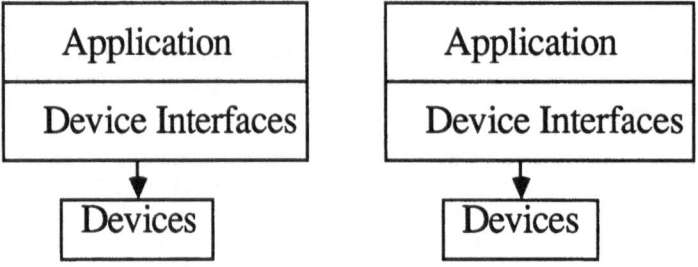

Figure 2.1:   A model of conventional portable graphics packages

Figure 2.2, in contrast, shows a simple model of the layers which are often present in graphical systems. The user interfaces with the application layer. The application layer may be divided into the application specific layer and an underlying general graphics layer which gives access to a device independent layer. This device independent layer allows the graphical output and input to be manipulated   We may, for example, wish to take several pictures which have been drawn using different coordinate systems and merge them to one picture for output. It is at the device independent layer that these coordinates can be transformed into a common coordinate system. Lower still is the device dependent layer where device independent information is made specific. For example a pen number may be mapped to colour on a colour device and to a dashed line on a monochrome device. The recoginition of these layers by an application software developer can free development time for work into the application which is of real interest both for research and commercial reasons.

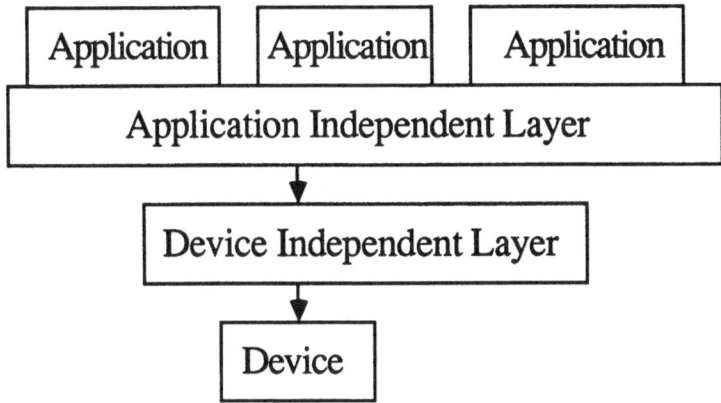

Figure 2.2:   A layered model of a graphics system

The distinction between these layers has been important in the development of standards for computer graphics. The computer graphics standards have been concerned with offering the application programmer a standard interface into the device independent layer. They have moved on to the standardisation of the interface between the device independent and device dependent layers. Storage is also important, and a standard for the storage of data at the device independent layer has been developed. The need for storage of data at the application layer within Computer Aided Engineering applications is discussed in section 3 of these notes.

It is often felt that the use of standards has to be a restriction for suppliers of hardware and software. There may be a feeling that this will result in loss of custom as purchasers will not be tied to a proprietary product. This is a very typical but negative viewpoint. Graphics standards should be seen as being an opportunity and not a restriction. The software supplier has a much wider base on which to build software. The underlying tools can be assumed to be at a higher level than has been the case. The exchange of graphical information between packages can also be seen as a positive move enabling software to be applicable in environments which have so far been restricted to proprietary products.

Graphics standards offer advantages of portability. Programs can be exchanged between sites and can have a strong and high level underlying assumption about the capability of the graphics system. The need for portability of code is often underplayed at the start of a project and the difficulty of translation between proprietary graphics systems can be a problem if this need is not appreciated. The portability of graphics standards extends beyond code though to the portability of ideas and jargon. Staff are more easily accommodated in different environments if the underlying graphics system is a standard one.

These notes will consider the following areas:

- the graphical interface for the application programmer
- the interface to the device layer
- device independent storage
- using standards - some real considerations and problems
- relating to other standards
- future work

The tutorial will suggest that graphics standards do offer an opportunity for freeing development time to consider other areas of graphics software. The use of standards can be cost effective for many people. We will see the suggestion that both suppliers and end users can benefit in the long term by adopting graphics standards and that such a move can have considerable strategic benefits.

2.2 Application Interfaces - Some Basic Concepts

2.2.1 Introduction

Computer graphics standards have often come in for a lot of criticism in many places. We hear tales that "GKS is slow"; that graphics standards do not allow people to draw graphs or pie charts. As with most things choosing to adopt graphics standards is all about using the right tool for the right job.

The users and the software suppliers viewpoints are inevitably different. Suppliers may see the graphics standards as forming a threat to their software which may have similar capabilities at the lowest level. Sometimes graphics standards will not be the answer and as with all things it is important to make the right judgements to ensure cost-effective working.

The graphics standards offer an application interface for both 2D and 3D graphics. These areas are now standardised within the International Standards Organisation (ISO) and have been adopted by many countries as national standards. This section shows that the basic concepts are common to all the graphics standards with extensions for the relevant standard being adopted where needed (for example viewing for the 3D standards). There is often much discussion about the standards competing with one another for the market place. This should not be the case. There is a role for the various standards and the appropriate standard depends upon the requirements of the application.

2.2.2 Workstations

There are many different graphics devices on the market today, with a wide range of designs and capabilities. It is vital that the standard application graphical interface should be usable in a wide range of different environmemts, and also that the application programmer does not have to be aware of the different device capabilities in order to write graphics programs. For these reasons, the graphics standards have the concept of a workstation which is an idealised abstract graphics device which allows different graphics devices to be treated within the application in the same way.

The application interacts with workstations to perform graphical input and output operations. The work of driving a real graphics device to perform these actions is handled by the implementation of the graphics standard. In this way, the user is shielded from the idiosyncracies of particular devices and can easily transfer applications to different implementation of the graphics standard.

2.2.3 Primitives

The standards work to the same basic set of primitives. These are shown in Figure 2.3 which shows that the primitives are all at a very low level. This is a feature of the application interface for graphics standards. The primitives give the application developer the required tools but are a means to an end and not an end in themselves. The standards work does not aim to provide applications for business graphics or engineering although they should provide the building blocks for applications to be developed on a broad interface to the device independent layer below.

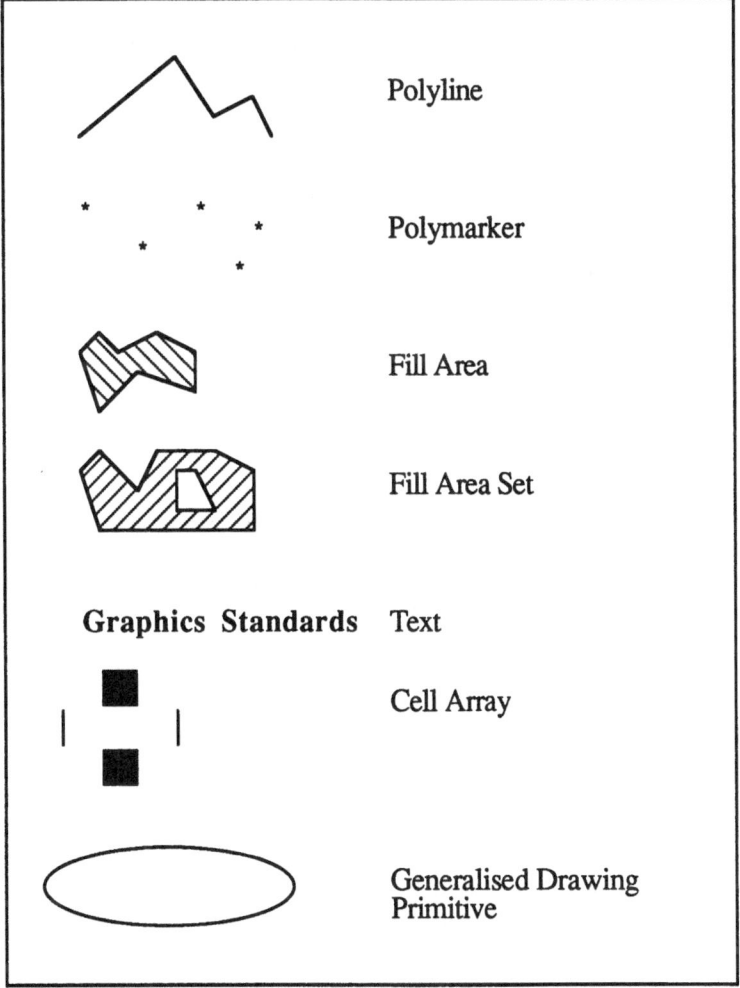

Figure 2.3: The primitives available in the application interface standards

2.2.4 Attributes

The appearance of the primitives can be controlled by attributes. We may wish to control the colour, line style, text orientation and so on. The graphics standards allow two ways of controlling the appearance of primitives. One of these is a conventional way which, for example, allows the application to set the colour of a line to red. The other is a more flexible and device independent way and one which can be recommended to writers of application software which is to be portable between a variety of devices of different types.

This second method is that of *bundled* attributes. The application indicates for example that a particular polyline is to be drawn with the polyline type number one and that a second polyline is to have polyline type two so that it can be distinguished from the first. The implementation of the standard then has associated with it a description of each of the polyline types for each workstation that is being used for drawing. For example on a colour workstation polyline type one might be a red line but the same picture when drawn on a monochrome workstation might show polyline one as a dotted line and polyline two as a dashed line. The same program can be used for both workstation with the result being the best possible for each. The types are thus associated with a bundle of attributes, hence the name.

The other, more conventional, form of attribute setting involves associating an *individual* attribute with a primitive. For example text colour might be set, or polymarker type. This setting means that the workstation selected may not do the best job that it can. Programming using the graphics standards can be improved by taking advantage of the freedom from individual settings and device control. More portable applications can be written with the application not having to be concerned with the nature of the end device.

2.2.5 Structuring Pictures

The need often arises in interactive computer graphics applications to store pictures or parts of pictures as they are developed, for later use in the execution of the program. The graphics application interface standards offer two methods of storing graphical data. The first is a relatively simple division of a picture into logical components. These components are known as *segments* and are a single level of division of the pictures. The only relationship that the segments have with one another is a priority for display and picking for input. A segment has a name and has associated attributes such as visibility, highlighting and transformation. These segments cannot be nested or edited but they do form a useful basic capability for interactive applications.

For more complex applications there is a recognition that hierarchical structure is a useful feature to allow for in a graphics application. Many graphical entities reveal some structure. Simple examples include a car which has four wheels and a number of doors. All are basically the same design and can be drawn by taking the basic graphical data and applying transformations. These entities are known as *structures* and these can be edited and manipulated within the application.

2.2.6   Input

The production of graphical output is vital, but it is only part of the story. The graphics standards are intended for interactive computer graphics programming and therefore graphical input is an important aspect of the standards. A typical interaction cycle might be:

- display picture
- operator reacts to picture by inputting some information
- picture modified according to operator's reaction

The model for input introduced for the graphics standards offers considerably more input capabilities in a standard way than many suppliers offered previously in their proprietary products. Even today there are not many applications which make good use of the full input capabilities offered by many implementations of the graphics standards.

Many graphics displays have some associated input devices. The most common imput device is the keyboard. Many displays will also have a device for inputting positional information, such as a mouse. There is a wide variety of input hardware supplying input data in many different forms. To isolate the physical characteristics of the different input devices from the application, the standards introduce six types of logical input device, classified according to the kind of data they return:

- *locator* returns a position for example a tablet might return the x and y co-ordinates of a point selcted with a stylus
- *pick* identifies an object in the display, for example with a mouse
- *choice* provides a selection from a set of alternatives, for example a menu
- *valuator* returns a numerical value, for example a dial
- *string* returns a sequence of characters, for example a keyboard
- *stroke* returns a sequence of positions, for example a digitizer

Each implementation of the standards determines how the available physical devices are mapped onto the logical devices.

The standards define three different styles in which input data can be entered. These specify whether it is the operator or the application program which has the initiative in an interaction. In *request* mode the application program and the operator work synchronously. The application program requests input and then waits until the operator supplies the required value. In *sample* mode the application samples the current state of an input device when input is required. There is no need to wait for the operator to do anything, the program picks up the latest value of the device. In *event* mode the operator and application program work asynchronously. The operator can generate input at any time, and this is stored in a queue. the application interrogates the queue when it requires some input.

Many different styles of user interface may be programmed using a combination of different input modes.

2.2.7 Inquiries

The graphics standards have been written to be flexible and fairly sophisticated tools for the application programmer. They are not tools for the beginner and should not be conceived as such. One major facility which the application programmer has access to is a wide range of funtions for inquiry. The application can inquire settings of workstation and device settings which can be used at run-time to enhance the interaction and performance of the application.

2.2.8 Functionality Distinct from the Language Binding

The graphics standards are intended to be used in a wide range of programming environments and therefore they are defined in abstract terms, independently of programming languages and are known as *functional descriptions*. Details such as the format of file names or the mechanisms for passing parameters to procedures have no bearing on a functional description. In order to integrate the graphics standards into a programming language, an interface known as the *language binding* is defined. The language binding associates the abstract functionality of the graphics standard with the syntax and semantics of a particular programming language.

For example, a list of data points can be represented graphically by joining the points with a set of straight lines as a polyline. In the definition of standards, an abstract data type is used to represent the data points, and this is a list of floating point (x,y) positions. In the Pascal language binding to standards, a data point is realised as a record containing two real values, x and y, and a list of data points is an array of point records. The function which connects a list of points with a sequence of straight lines in 2D is called "polyline" in the functional description. It has one argument: the list of points to be connected. In the Pascal language binding, this function is realised as a procedure called "GPolyline" which has two parameters: the number of points, and an array containing them. In the Fortran binding, the "polyline" function is a subroutine called GPL, and the list of points is represented by two REAL arrays, one for the x coordinates and one for the y coordinates of the points:

There are many ways in which a language binding could be defined, and therefore language bindings themselves must also be standardised. There are international standard bindings for GKS Fortran, Pascal and Ada. The C language is still being processed by the standards bodies and therefore language bindings for the graphics standards are awaiting its completion.

2.3 Application Interfaces - the Individual Standards

2.3.1 Introduction

In the last section we looked at the core of concepts which are common to the application interface standards developed for computer graphics. There are some variations as some of the standards offer 2D or 3D functionality and others more comprehensive functionality. This section will review the three application interface standards: GKS (the Graphical Kernel System [12]); GKS-3D (the 3D extension of GKS [15]); and PHIGS (the Programmer's Hierarchical Interactive Graphics System [16]). These are all international standards and have been adopted as national standards by many nations. This section will review how the core concepts are 'glued' together by the standards and any variations which occur.

A summary of the ways that these standards fit together is shown in Figure 2.4 which can be used in conjunction with the discussions below.

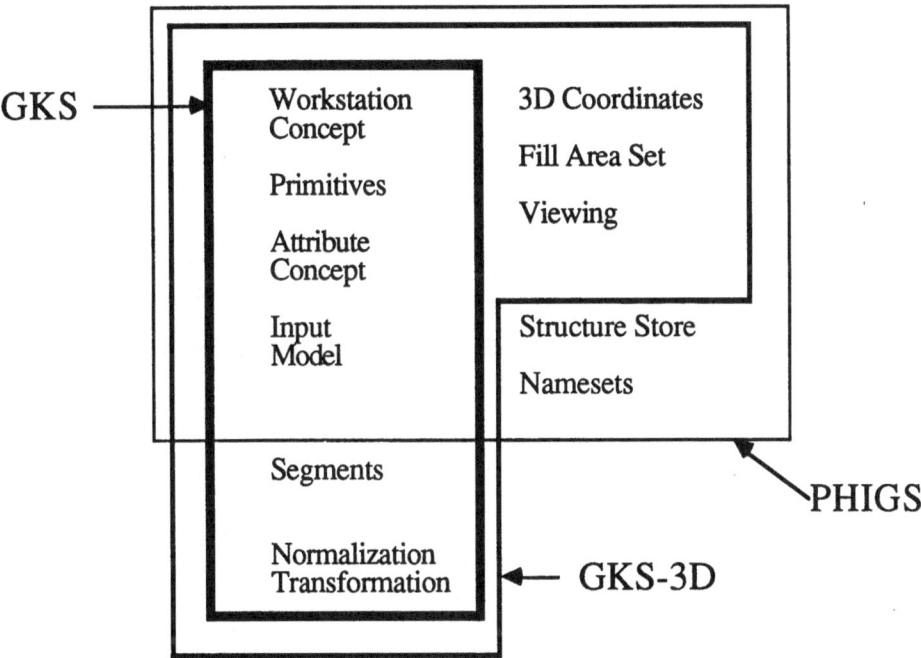

Figure 2.4: The content of the Graphics Standards for the Application Interface

2.3.2 GKS

The Graphical Kernel System (GKS) was standardised in 1985. It offers a 2D interface for the applications programmer and has been extended to 3D in GKS-3D which is also a standard.

GKS is a standard for two-dimensional computer graphics programming. It provides a set of functions for the specification and manipulation of pictures in an installation independent and hardware independent manner. It should be emphasised that GKS is not a commercial product or a particular implementation. It is a specification upon which implementations are based.

The core concepts descibed above were developed for GKS. The only primitive which is not included is Fill Area Set which was added for GKS-3D. Any future revision of GKS will have this primitive in. GKS has simple single level segments as its method of structure. The transformations used in GKS are described below.

GKS is intended to be used in many different applications. Each application should be able to define its graphics in a relevant coordinate system. For example, a molecular chemist might use nanometres, whereas light years would be more appropriate for the astronomer. The coordinate system specified for the device by

GKS-3D has three-dimensional versions of the GKS normalization, segment and workstation transformations. As well as these, GKS-3D output primitives also undergo two viewing transformations for the purpose of constructing a view of the 3D scene. These are known as the view orientation and view mapping transformations and performed after the segment transformation, and before the workstation transformation.

Each Primitive in GKS-3D has a view index attribute associated with it. This defines the viewing transformations to be applied to the primitive on a particular workstation. In this way different views can be used for different primitives on a workstation, allowing for example, annotation to be viewed from the front, and a 3D object to be viewed from some other angle.

The viewing transformations are specified as 4 x 4 transformation matrices by the application programmer. To help the application specify these matrices, GKS-3D provides utility routines based on the camera model. Here, a view is specified by defining the direction and position of the camera in space, together with a view plane onto which the picture is projected. Both parallel and perspective projections are permitted.

As well as the view index, GKS-3D primitives have another attribute, the HLHSR identifier. This provides a way in which the application can specify how hidden-line or hidden-surface removal (HLHSR) should be applied to a particular primitive. The interpretation of the HLHSR identifier is both workstation and implementation dependent. In addition, there is a workstation setting that can be used to control the behaviour of HLHSR on a given workstation. Once again, the interpretation of this is dependent on both the implementation and the workstation. In this way, GKS-3D provides 'hooks' for the provision of HLHSR, and the implementation of HLHSR facilities is not mandatory.

2.3.4 PHIGS

Many applications such as computer aided design (CAD), weather forecasting and flight simulation use computer graphics as a tool for modelling. Often, the most effective representation of the state of a model is achieved with graphics. GKS and GKS-3D are not designed to address modelling; instead they provide basic graphics operations which allow models to be displayed and put the burden on application programmers to provide modelling operations themselves.

There are many commercial packages for modelling, and many are tailored to particular applications such as CAD. But until now, there has not been a general standardised system for modelling with computer graphics. This need is addressed by PHIGS - the Programmer's Hierarchical Interactive Graphics System. While GKS is aimed at the standardisation of computer graphics techniques, PHIGS combines this with the standardisation of modelling techniques. Like GKS, PHIGS provides a set of functions for computer graphics programming.

GKS-3D is a minimal extension to GKS to allow for 3D graphics programming. PHIGS is also an extension of GKS but it builds on GKS-3D to provide modelling functionality integrated with the graphics. PHIGS incorporates the core concepts of GKS and GKS-3D as illustrated in Figure 2.4. The major difference between PHIGS and GKS is that the creation and display of a picture are two distinct operations in PHIGS. Whereas output in GKS is routed directly to all active workstations, output in PHIGS is stored in a centralized structure store, and nothing is displayed until a PHIGS structure (similar to a GKS segment, but more flexible) is explicitly posted to a workstation.

the manufacturer is likely to be different again, and different devices have different specifications; one device might have 1024 pixels in x and y, another 640, and so on. Somehow there has to be a mapping between the units used by the application and the physical requirements of display devices.

To unify these two variable, GKS introduces an abstract coordinate system called *normalized device coordinates* (NDC) in which the coordinate ranges for both x and y is [0,1]. The mismatch between application and device coordinate systems is resolved by dividing the mapping between application and device coordinates into two steps.

1. Map from the application's coordinate system (called world coordinates) to NDC. This is a window to viewport mapping known as the *normalization transformation*. It is often useful to compose a picture from several different scenes, and so GKS allows the application to define a number of different normalization transformations. A particular normalization transformation can be used for selected primitives. This allows pictures which have different world coordinate systems to be mapped into the NDC space without the application having to carry out the transformations.

2. Map from NDC to the physical device coordinate system. This is another window to viewport mapping, and is called the *workstation transformation*. Unlike the normalization transformation, this transformation maintains the aspect ratio of the picture being mapped. There is only one workstation transformation allowed for each workstation.

It is often the case that output primitives will extend beyond the window in which they are defined. In some cases the user will wish these to be clipped at the boundary of the window. GKS allows two possibilities; in one mode, drawing is allowed outside the window, and, in the other, drawing is clipped at the boundary of the viewport, so that only those parts of the output primitives inside the viewport are actually drawn.

2.3.3   GKS-3D

Many applications for which the GKS standard is otherwise suitable require the ability to define three-dimensional (3D) pictures. GKS-3D is a standard being developed for such applications; it is a 3D system which is upwards-compatible with GKS.

The principal features which GKS-3D has added to GKS are:

*   three-dimensional output primitives (i.e. points are specified by x, y and z coordinates)
*   additional transformations to support viewing operation
*   three-dimensional input
*   'hooks' for providing hidden-line and hidden-surface removal

The 2D functions provided in GKS are also retained in GKS-3D. This ensures GKS application programs can run unmodified in a GKS-3D system. The functions also provide a convenient shorthand for GKS-3D applications wishing to generate primitives in the $z = 0$ plane.

The basic unit of data in PHIGS is the *structure element*. There are several different kinds of structure element. Some define graphics information; there is a structure element for each output primitive (polyline, polymarker, etc.), and there are also structure elements for setting attributes (polyline index, view index, character up vector, etc.). Structure elements do not exist in isolation - they are collected together into structures which are stored in a single centralized location, called the centralized structure store, or CSS. This structuring mechanism in PHIGS replaces the GKS segmentation facility. The centralized structure store in PHIGS has the following additional functionality:

- hierarchy - structures can call, or invoke, other structures. In this way, the natural hierarchy which occurs in many models can be modelled using PHIGS structure networks.
- editing - once a structure has been created, it can be edited by deleting, replacing or inserting structure elements.

Both of the above features of the PHIGS structure store are provided by special structure elements. Structure instancing is achieved with an *execute* structure element. Label structure elements assist in the editing of structures by establishing navigation points within a structure.

There are also non-graphical structure elements which can hold information specific to an application. This allows the application data associated with the graphical model to be held in the same database.

Structure elements are inserted into the open structure by calling the PHIGS function of the same name. For example, the function "set polyline index" inserts a "set polyline index" structure element into the currently open structure.

An attribute called nameset has been added to the list of functions for PHIGS. Namesets allow the grouping of structure elements for visibility, highlighting and picking. Each primitive structure element can be added to or removed from the lists which are affected by these attributes. In GKS these attributes are associated with a segment.

Many pictures exhibit a natural hierarchy. For example, in both molecular modelling and electronic CAD, the picture to be displayed contains many repeated parts, such as the integrated circuits in a printed circuit board or the atoms in a molecule.

In PHIGS, the same structure may be called from a number of different structures (or even from a number of different places within the same structure), so that it has a number of parents. Thus to represent a car, only one wheel structure is needed, and this is instanced four times. Similarly, for molecular modelling, a single description of an atom would be held in a structure and instanced a number of times, at different positions, to make up the molecule.

As in GKS, PHIGS allows the user to define separate parts of the picture in a convenient coordinate system. In PHIGS this is known as the modelling coordinate system. Modelling transformations are then used to combine the parts of the picture together, into a single "world coordinate system". In the case of the car, a different modelling transformation is required for each instance of the wheel, to position it at the four corners of the car.

Structures are displayed when they are *posted* to a workstation. Posting causes the structure to be *traversed*, or interpreted, generating output for display on the workstation. The traversal process examines each element in a structure network until the end of the specified structure is reached. When a polyline element is processed, for example, the polyline will be drawn on the workstation to which the structure is posted, and similarly for polymarker, fill area and text elements. The traversal process is conceptually continuous, so that if any changes are made to the structure definitions the displayed picture is immediately updated to show the changes.

As in GKS, PHIGS provides functions for creating, deleting and renaming structures. There is also a function to delete a structure network, which deletes a structure and all its descendants.

In GKS, the contents of segments cannot be changed once the segment is created. If a change must be made, GKS has no alternative but to recreate the segment from scratch. In contrast, a PHIGS structure may be edited. An *element pointer* may be positioned at any structure element; new structure elements can be inserted after the element pointer; the structure element at the element pointer may be replaced with a different structure element; or it may be deleted.

2.4   The Interface with the Device

A standard which is concerned with the device independent/device dependent interface has been under discussion within ISO for some time. The standard is known as the Computer Graphics Interface (CGI [17]) and it is still being reviewed and modified by international experts in this area. It is anticipated that the CGI will be adopted by many graphics terminal suppliers as an option for driving their devices. The GKS device driver will interface with this standard interface which will mean that it will not have to interface with the codes of individual suppliers. This will increase efficiency of implementations of the standards. The terminals will also be able to be driven in a way which is consistent with the philosophy of the graphics standards.

The CGI is a complex standard because of the nature of the subject. This is despite the fact that it only addresses graphics in two dimensions. The standard has to address the interaction between the many activities that may be being carried out in the graphics environment both for input and output. It has to address the codes which will be used to communicate between the application and the device. As with the application interfaces the functional specification of the standard is independent of the coding used. It is anticipated that there will be alternatives available for coding and that there will also be programming language interfaces to access the CGI. The access to the CGI via coding techniques and programming languages is currently less important for development effort than the functional specification. Once this is stable there are well established procedures for developing the encoding and programming language bindings.

The CGI standard will offer a 2D interface for the application interface standards. The work has been built on the work carried out in the application interface standards. As with the addition of Fill Area Set in GKS-3D there have inevitably been some additions to the functionality beyond that defined in GKS. This 'leapfrogging' of standards is inevitable as experience is gained of the use and value of standards in the market place and their interaction with related standards. The standard is divided into six parts which are:

1.   *CGI Overview* which looks at the overall models for the interactions between the graphical data and the ways that the graphical data can be stored and refined within the CGI.

2.   *Control, Negotiation and Error Handling.* The creation of a picture is carried out in an abstract coordinate space. The CGI can position the picture according to viewporting and clipping information. This section also describes the setting up and termination of the graphics session. Negotiation as to the capabilities of the device and current settings is described as is the error log which can be accessed by the application.

3.   *Output and Attributes* are extended beyond those described for GKS. There is the addition of primitives for curves and a compound primitive as well as the extension of attributes to cover edge control.

4.   *Segments* are described in Part 4 of the CGI standard and the functions provided allow for a mapping from the GKS segments which are a single level and cannot be structured as in PHIGS.

5.   *Input* is descibed in Part 5 and considerable work has gone into this part to ensure that the features which could be activated occur in the correct order relative to other graphical activities which may be happening.

6.   *Raster* capabilities are supported in the CGI via the creation, storage, manipulation and display of images defined as a set of pixels known as a bitmap.

2.5   Graphical Data Storage

2.5.1   Introduction

There is a need to store graphical data at all levels of the graphical model shown in Figure 2.2. Storage at the application layer for an important example -CAE- is discussed in the next section of these notes. The computer graphics standards have concerned themselves with two standard forms of data capture: data capture at the device independent level in the Computer Graphics Metafile (CGM); and the storage of the PHIGS structures in the PHIGS archive file which is defined in the PHIGS standard. This section will review these standard formats.

2.5.2   The CGM

Most users of graphics applications packages will be concerned with viewing their output on a graphics screen. Often, once they are satisfied with the output, some form of hard copy is required, on a plotter for example. There are, however, many occasions when the output on to physical devices is not appropriate and some form of graphical storage of the picture is required. It may be necessary to:

* store a partly developed picture for later modification;
* store a picture for later viewing;
* queue the graphical image for spooled plotting;
* transfer the graphical data to another machine for display;
* include the graphical data in a document containing text and graphics.

In all these cases the picture will have to be stored in some way. The method chosen for storage must allow easy interpretation of the data so that the picture can be correctly displayed at a time in the future and/or on a different machine. The file in which graphical data is saved has become known as a *metafile*. The Computer Graphics Metafile (CGM [14]) offers a standard storage method for graphical data.

The CGM standard has two distinct roles. The first one is to define the functions which need to appear in the metafile and to lay down rules as to the structure of the metafile and the order and position of the various elements. This part of the metafile standard is defined in Part 1 of the standard. The second role is to define the way that these functions are recorded in the metafile. This is know as the encoding of the elements defined in the functional part. Parts 2, 3 and 4 of the CGM standard are concerned with the encoding of the elements whose abstract functionality is described in Part 1. The CGM also contains a formal grammar in an Annex to Part 1 which describes in detail the behaviour of the elements.

There are different requirements for data storage and transfer. This is not necessarily specific to the graphics community but will be addressed with reference to computer graphics here. These requirements include:

- minimal file size;
- ease of transfer across networks;
- the speed with which the data can be generated and interpreted;
- the readability of the stored files.

To address these different requirements the CGM defines 3 encodings. These three encodings being the character (for minimal file size and ease of transfer), binary (for ease of generation and interpretation) and clear text (for human readability) encodings contained in Parts 2 to 4 of the standard.

The CGM standard incorporates a range of elements which are on the same lines as those discussed thus far for primitives and attributes. The primitives are like those in the CGI and extend beyond the GKS primitives and attributes to include curves and edge control. There are also specifications as to how the data will be written, for example coordinates as integers or reals and to what level of precision. The CGM defines the structure for all the elements with a metafile containing a number of independent pictures with each picture having its own description as to the information stored.

2.5.3 The PHIGS Archive File

The PHIGS standard defines an archive file format in Part 2 of the standard and a clear text encoding in Part 3. No other encodings are currently defined. The archive file is a file format for storing the PHIGS structures and the details of the hierarchy. The elements in the PHIGS archive are precisely mapped to those in the PHIGS standard. The archive file format thus allows storage and exchange of the structure elements used in a PHIGS application.

2.5.4 Graphical Exchange in Practice

The National Computer Graphics Association (NCGA) event in March 1988 had a major demonstration known as INTEGRATE 88. The basis of this was the CGM.

At the INTEGRATE demonstration 33 vendors participated in sharing metafiles between their software and hardware. A wide range of software was demonstrated in engineering, finance, graphics art and printing and publishing modules. All the software could handle CGMs written in the binary encoding using an agreed subset of elements. The event was very impressive and proved the value of the standard as well as being a large advertisement for the use of the CGM. This has been followed by a similar demonstration at the Eurographics-UK conference at the University of Manchester in March 1989 which involved examples of all three encoding techniques. There are now a number of translation tools available on the market. The NCGA 1989 event ran a second integration demonstration. These events show that the CGM standard is useful and used.

2.6   Using Standards

2.6.1   Introduction

The theory of standards is a good one but out in the real world is where the problems are found. It is essential that the customer can have confidence in a product and testing is important. The standards are also being found to be complex and the reality of the situation is that many suppliers of software are limiting their implementations. This section reviews some of the issues involved.

2.6.2   Conformance and Testing

All standards have a section concerning conformance. The statements in this section concern the requirements of an implementation if it is to conform to the standard. In GKS, for example the standard was split into levels of increasing complexity of both input and output. An implementation can be said to conform to one of these levels. In the CGM the conformance requirements are of an individual metafile and not to the software which may generate or interpret it. It is vital to purchasers of implementations that they can have confidence that the product they are buying does conform to the standard. To this end there have been various initiatives towards setting up testing services for graphics standards. There is now a GKS testing service for Fortran implementations and purchasers should ensure that the product they are buying has been certified as conforming to the standard. Work is in progress to develop PHIGS testing tools and there has been work on extending the GKS tests to 3D. There are a number of CGM testing tools around which have been proving their value at the various CGM demonstrations and it is possible that a test service may be provided or that these tools receive the approval of the testing centres.

2.6.3   Application Profiles

There is much concern in the Open Systems Interconnection (OSI) standards to ensure inter-working between software and hardware. The standards tend to be very full and complex specifications offering many options. As a result there have been some initiatives via the groups known as the Manufacturing Automation Protocol (MAP [18]) and the Technical Office Protocol (TOP [27]). These initatives have been concerned to tie down any implementation dependencies in the standards and to select a sensible group of options for the companies involved to save on development work. These subsets are known as *application profiles*. The CGM is included in MAP and TOP (version 3.0). An Application Profile for the CGM has been developed. This Application Profile selects the most appropriate specification of the CGM for the MAP and TOP community. The profile uses the binary encoding. The document defines conformance requirements for the MAP and TOP community by choosing defaults which are a minimum requirement. The defaults chosen are mostly in line with those laid out in Parts 1 and 3 of the CGM standard. This has been a significant move and many suppliers only support this subset. This is a problem for interpreters which are limited if the pictures being sent to them come from a richer implementation of the CGM. It is to be hoped that implementations will improve to cater for a wide range of metafiles. It is early days for this standard.

2.7   The Relationship with Other Standards

Computer graphics cannot be seen as an isolated topic. Within ISO there are other areas of work which clearly impact upon the work of the computer graphics standards. These areas are notably:

- the need to include pictures together with text in documents. This area has been addressed in the Office Document Architecture standard [13] which defines its graphics content as a binary encoded CGM. There is also work to standardise the area of page description languages which have been seen to be important through the wide use of the Adobe System's PostScript [1,2]. PostScript is widely used in laser printers which can build up the image described. It is hoped that the standard will have the ability to incorporate a CGM within the standard. Future work to extend the CGM is likely to see an extension of the primitives and attributes available within the metafile which more closely maps with the higher level primitives and attributes currently found in PostScript. The CGM will always be more appropriate for file transfer of graphical images because of its compact form and the wide availability of interpreters within software which can incorporate CGMs into graphical packages. Incorporation of the picture in a page desciption in a standard way will however be a useful step forward.

- the need to adopt improved font descriptions in the computer graphics standards. The font descriptions in the graphics standards are at a fairly low level and there is need for information about font and glyph definitions. Work in this area is being carried out in ISO and this is likely to be adopted by the graphics standard community who are liaising with the font experts.

- the need to offer further support to applications. This work is particularly being pushed forward by liaising with the product data geometry group. It is important that future work in the graphics standards arena and product data geometry is carried out in liaison in areas where there is overlap. Integration is important as we move across the boundaries describe in Figure 2.2 of this paper.

- the need to include graphics programs in a windowing environment. The X Window system [29] has become a de-facto standard which has major implications for most users of computer systems in the future. It is possible that the work will come into the ISO arena and be standardised in the future. The graphics standards at the application programmer interface will run within a window. There have been various pieces of work to build the graphics standards on X. One example of this is the PEX [23] work which is a PHIGS implementation built on X.

In all these areas there is an increasing awareness of the need to cooperate between committees to ensure that the standards being produced will integrate in a straightforward way.

2.8 Future Work

Work is currently being carried out within ISO to extend the CGM for further 2D support and for 3D support. Other work which is being carried out is an extension to PHIGS for lighting, shading and the rendering of colour. The CGI has yet to be completed although there is hope that the document will be technically stable shortly. There is also work on extending the language bindings for the application interfaces.

The committee responsible for the development of computer graphics standards has recognised that the committee is close to the completion of what can be considered to be the first generation of graphics standards. These have had some success, particularly the CGM since its publications. The need for extension of the standards as they come up for review together with a consideration of recent technology is needed. The need for compatibility is recognised as being a strong motivator in future work. The work may take the form of a vertical cut across the standards work with groups considering areas of graphics standardisation such as attributes and input. The output of these groups can then be constructed into the required standards thus ensuring compatibility.

2.9 Bibliography

1. Adobe Systems Incorporated, PostScript Language Reference Manual, Addison-Wesley, 1986
2. Adobe Systems Incorporated, PostScript Language Tutorial and Cookbook, Addison-Wesley, 1986
3. Arnold, D.B., Bono, P.R., CGM and CGI, Springer-Verlag, 1988
4. Bono, P.R., Herman,I., GKS Theory and Parctice, Springer-Verlag, 1987
5. K.W. Brodlie, L.R. Henderson, A.M. Mumford, The CGM - A Metafile for GKS?, Computer Graphics Forum, Vol 6, No 2, 1987.
6. Computer Aided Design, Special Issue on Computer Graphics Standards, Vol 19, No 8, October 1987
7. Clifford, W.H., McConnell, J.I., Saltz, J.S., The Development of PEX, a 3D Graphics Extension to X11, Eurographics Conference Proceedings 1988, Springer Verlag
8. Enderle, G., Kansy, K., Pfaff, G., Computer Graphics Programming - GKS - The Graphics Standard, Springer-Verlag, 1987
9. Hopgood, F.R.A., Duce, D., Gallop, J. and Sutcliffe,D., Introduction to the Graphical Kernel System, Academic Press, 1986

10. IEEE Computer Graphics and Applications, Special Issue on Computer Graphics Standards, Vol 6, No 8, August 1986

11. ISO IS 7498 Information processing systems - Open Systems Interconnection - Basic Reference Model

12. ISO IS 7942 Information processing systems - Computer graphics - Graphical Kernel System (GKS) functional description

13. ISO IS 8613 Information processing systems - Text and office systems - Office Document Architecture (ODA) and Interchange Format - Part 8: Geometric Graphics Content Architectures (GGCA)

14. ISO IS 8632 Information processing systems - Computer graphics - Metafile for the storage and transfer of picture description information (CGM)

15. ISO IS 8805 Information processing systems - Computer graphics - Graphical Kernel System for three dimensions (GKS-3D) functional description

16. ISO IS 9592 Information Processing Systems - Computer Graphics - Programmer's Hierarchical Interactive Graphics System (PHIGS)

17. ISO DP 9636 Information processing systems - Computer graphics - Interfacing techniques for dialogues with graphical devices (CGI) - functional specification

18. Manufacturing Automation Protocol (MAP) Specification, Version 3.0 1988, Society of Manufacturing Engineers

19. Mumford, A.M., Application Profiles for Computer Graphics Standards - A Touch of Reality?, Eurographics Conference Proceedings, 1988, Springer-Verlag

20. Mumford, A.M., The CGM Today and Tomorrow, Computer Graphics Forum 1989 (forthcoming)

21. Mumford, A.M., Skall, M.W. (Eds), The CGM in the Real World, Springer-Verlag, 1988

22. Mumford, A.M., Wyrwas, K.M., Computer Graphics Standards - Myth and Reality, Eurographics-UK Tutorial, 1988

23. PEX Protocol Specification, Version 3.0, MIT, 1987

24. PHIGS+ Functional Description, revision 3.0, report by the ad-hoc PHIGS+ committee, 1988

25. Scheifler, R., Gettys,J., The X Window System, John Wiley, 1989

26. Singleton, K.M., An Implementation of the GKS-3D/PHIGS Viewing Pipeline, Eurographics Conference Proceedings 1986, Springer Verlag

27. Technical Office Protocol (TOP) Specification, Version 3.0 1988, Boeing Computer Services, Seattle, WA, USA

28. Verbeck,C., Michener,J., van Dam,A., Laidlaw,D., Extending PHIGS for Lighting and Shading - PHIGS+, Siggraph '87 Conference Proceedings.

29. X Window System Protocol, Vers 11, Project Athena, Mass Inst of Tech, '87

2.9 Acknowledgements

The notes presented in this section are based on a Eurographics UK tutorial given by myself and Karen Wyrwas who was at that time at the University of Manchester Computer Graphics Unit. I would like to thank Karen and the University of Manchester for allowing me to use the notes and to Bob Hopgood and Alasdair Liddell for assistance.

3. Product Data Exchange Standards

3.1 Basic Considerations on CAD-Interfaces

Since CAD has been introduced to industry in the mid-seventies, the CAD systems have gradually evolved from originally graphically oriented drafting systems to high efficiency design systems, i.e. the generation and provision of complex 2D and 3D product model data for the most diverse applications. In this context CAD should be understood as a module which has to be integrated in a company wide computer assisted overall concept.

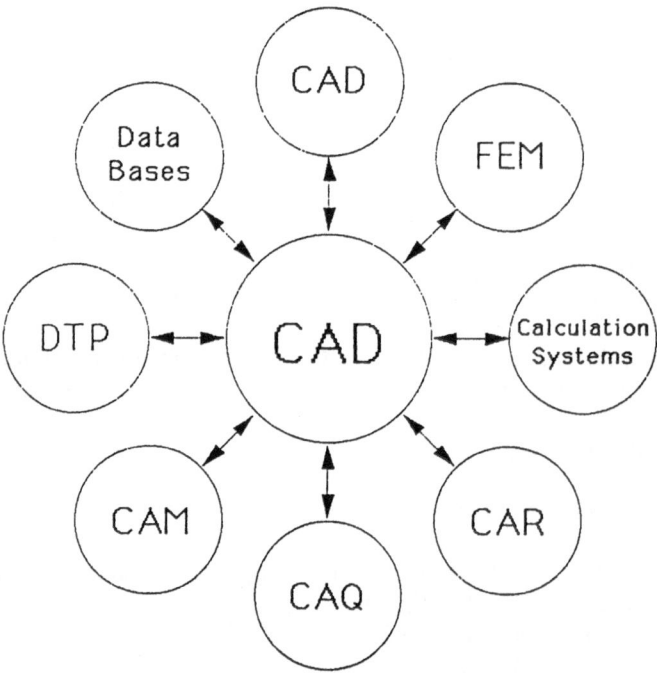

Figure 1. CAD-data for different applications and systems.

Computer Aided Design (CAD) means a computer aided tool for the use in all functional areas within the design process, it can be characterised as follows:

- a processor that generates, manipulates and interprets a product model;

- the corresponding internal models represent a product, a part, or an assembly;

- the representation is stored in a database, and

- the model serves as a basis for any further evaluation and documentation of the object.

At present [30], approximately 14000 CAD workstations are being used in the Federal Republic of Germany. About 80% of big industry, 40% of medium sized and 15% of small business enterprises are profiting from this technology. A total demand of 200000 CAD workstations are anticipated for the coming decade. On the other hand, more than 200 different CAD systems and a much greater number of different CAx systems (FEM-, NC-applications) are offered on the market.

Despite apparently identical program solutions and similar user interfaces there are not even two CAD systems so compatible that geometry or product model data can be exchanged completely. This is the backround for understanding how important, uniform and efficient, CAD interfaces are, with a view to integrating CAD systems into a developing CIM environment (Figure 1 on page 3), both within and outside an enterprise.

The following goals are to be attained by a CAD interface:

- Coupling different CAD systems, within and outside a business firm.

- Data exchange and integration of separate processes between CAD systems and different applications (e.g. FEM, CAM), preceeding and suceeding the corresponding CAD system.

- Utilisation of neutral data formats for system independent archiving.

The above mentioned term **product model** means a logical but not necessarily physically homogeneous ensemble of all data representing the structure of a product. It includes data describing the shape, function and technology as well as data relating to the fabrication and administration sectors.

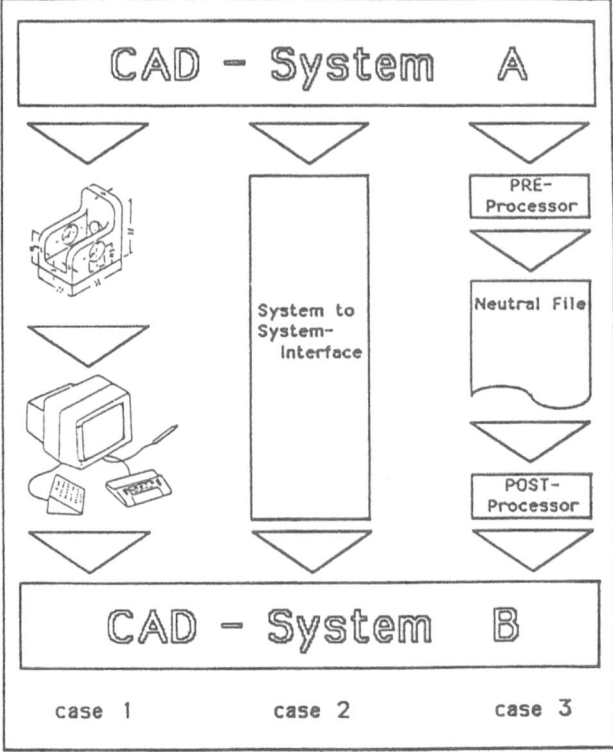

Figure 2. Possible CAD interfaces.

For exchange of model data between different CAD systems three fundamentally differing possibilities are presently known [41]. As shown in Figure 2 the data media used in the first case are the drawing and e.g. the parts list. This data media has to be read into the target system by extensive manual work and/or by means of computer aided scanning. For the paperless exchange of information two computer assisted interfaces are the direct system-to-system data transfer (case 2) and the system neutral interface (case 3). Besides, a combination is possible of the exchange concepts already described. In this context, the combination of data exchange via neutral data interfaces (case 3) and conventional data media (case 1) is applied in cases where information (e.g. technological information) cannot be transferred via available CAD interfaces. Direct system-to-system data transfer calls for Nx(N-1) translators for coupling N CAD systems and is being applied above all in cases where standardised exchange formats are missing. In practice, the data exchange goes via a joint neutral format so that - compared with the direct interface - the number of processors is [41] reduced by its multiple. The processors fulfil the function of the translator. Usually, processors are devided into two groups: (1) preprocessors, (2) postprocessors. First the data to be transferred is converted into a joint neutral data format via a preprocessor and translated from the neutral data format into a CAD-system dependent data format with the help of a postprocessor connected in series, refer to case 3 in Figure 2 on page 4.

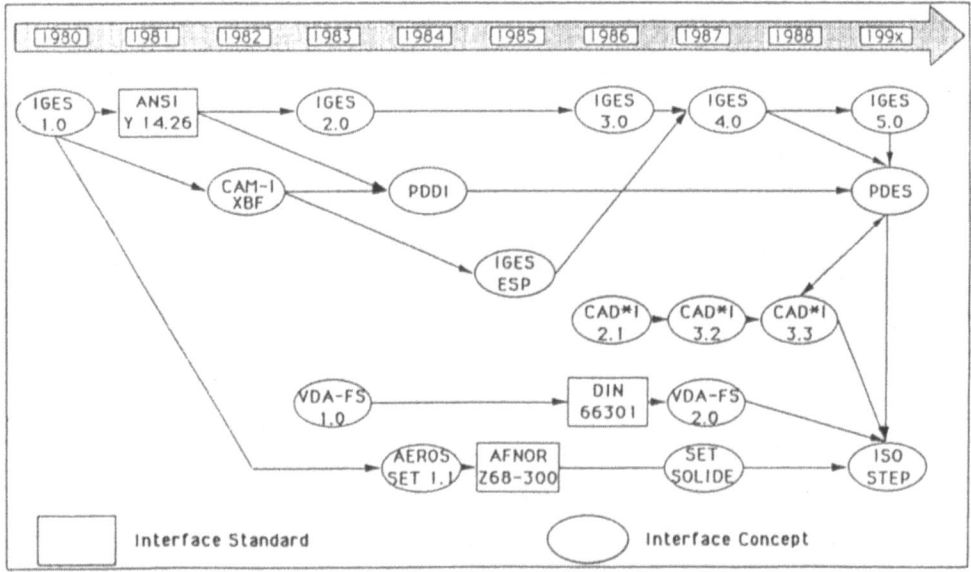

Figure 3. Known CAD-Interface proposals and standards.

3.2 CAD-Interface Standards

As appears from Figure 3 there are a number of different CAD data exchange specifications. They can be classified (from the standardisation point of view) as follows:

- draft or proposed standard,

- de facto standard, and/or

- national standard.

Besides a multitude of drafts and/or proposals, only three national standards for CAD interfaces are known worldwide, namely ANSI Y14.26M is IGES 1.0 [34] (IGES 3.0 has been ratified), DIN 66301 is VDA-FS 1.0 [37], and Z68-300 is SET 1.1 [32].

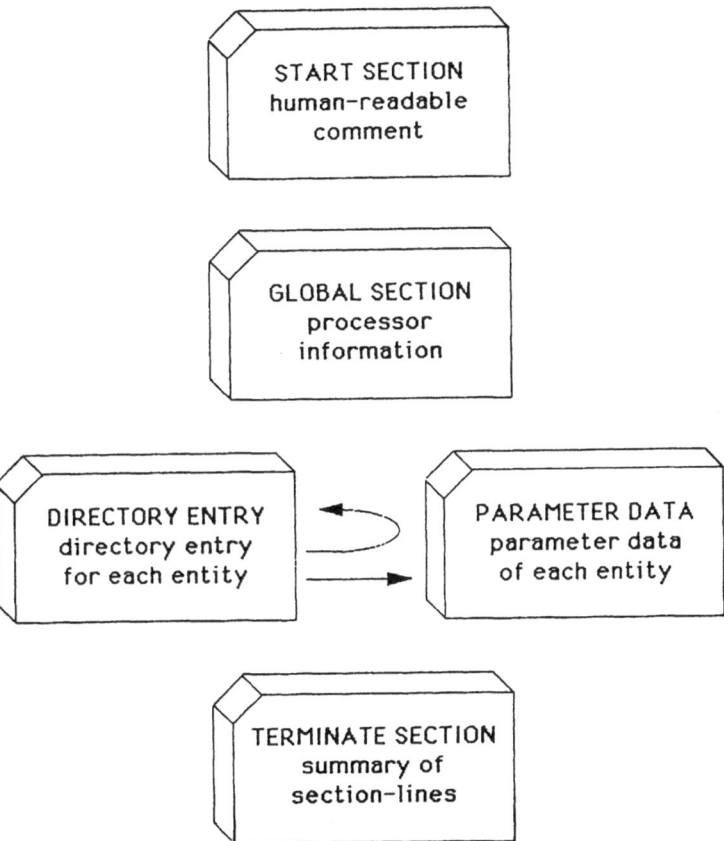

Figure 4. IGES file structure

3.2.1 The Initial Graphics Exchange Specification (IGES)

Today there are four different IGES versions - up to IGES 4.0 [43] - available. First steps were made in 1979 to develop a common CAD data exchange format for the data transfer of drawing data among different CAD systems. These activities were initiated by the American Department of Defence and by the National Bureau of Standards (NBS) and led to the first standardised interface IGES 1.0 (ANSI standard: Y14.26M) in 1981 [34]. All IGES versions are mainly concerned with the data exchange of technical drawings which are of importance in mechanical design and construction. All available IGES-entities and -elements can be classified as follows:

- geometry entities,

- annotation entities, and

- structure entities.

Each IGES file consists of five or six different sections (Figure 4), each section in a specific format [43]:

- *FLAG* in the case of the binary or compressed ASCII form;

- *START SECTION* with a user-readable text, e.g. comments;

- *GLOBAL SECTION* carries postprocessor directed information, e.g. length of real numbers;

- *DIRECTORY ENTRY SECTION* consists of two records for each entity to be transferred, e.g. entity attributes and references;

- *PARAMETER DATA SECTION* carries all entity specific parameter values;

- *TERMINATE SECTION* summarises the number of records of each section available on the neutral file.

The current version of IGES is V4.0 after V2.0 in 1983, and V3.0 published in April, 1986. Each IGES version is upwards compatible with the previously defined IGES versions. The main differences between IGES V1.0 and V4.0 are the extended range of technical entities, an additional number of applications (e.g. piping and electronic schematics), as well as many changes to improve the syntax, clarity, and consistency of the element description (by text and figures) in the specification. IGES 4.0 is mainly the result of the implementation experiences with previous IGES and ESP versions. The current Version 4.0 of IGES provides the following capabilities and functionality for the data exchange of CAD-data [43]:

- *Geometry*: 2D/3D curve-, surface-elements, and solid geometry (i.e. CSG);

- *Presentation*: Drafting entities for the data exchange of technical drawings, including annotations and some of the geometry entities are the same as in Version 3.0;

- *Application dependent elements*: Piping and Electronic Schematics, AEC elements;

- *Finite Element Modelling*: A number of application dependent elements for the data exchange among FEM systems.

As a result of the discussion between the IGES group and CAM-I the Experimental Solids Proposal (ESP) was developed, with a view to handle B-Rep models as well as as CSG models. After several industrial data transfer tests the CSG part of ESP was incorporated into IGES 4.0. The IGES development will be completed with the future version of IGES, Version 5.0.

Data exchange via the IGES interface at present makes up the largest part of the total volume of CAD data exchange. IGES is today the most important CAD interface for practical data exchange, but acceptance of the IGES qualities is generally low. These are the main reasons: inadequate interface specification and insufficient quality of the available processors. Some of the processors first available had not been capable - cycle test - of reprocessing (postprocessor) without error the IGES data generated by the corresponding preprocessor. Meanwhile, the processors have been improved to such extent that data exchange with selected CAD systems is possible. For this to be feasible, the models to be transmitted have to be specially conditioned (e.g. transmitting of subsets) for the receiving system and adapted upon arrival there.

```
 BEISPIEL. FUFR IGES-FILE                                                          S        1
..50HA1                                                          ,6HA1.IGS.33HMATRG         1
A-DATAVISION EUCLID-DTV80-4.2.16HEUCLID-IGES V2.0.32.8,24,8,56,50HA1           G         2
                                            .1.0.2.4HMM  ,1300,13.0,            G         3
13H870421.144219,0.030E-01.300.0.5HMACHE.12HCADCAM-LABOR;                       G         4
      212          1      1      1      1      0       0        0 0 0 1 1D          1
      212          0      0      1      0      0       OTEXT             1D          2
      110          2      1      1      0      0       0        0 0 1 0 1D          3
      110          0      0      1      0      0       OLINE             1D          4
      124          3      1      1      0      0       0        0 0 0 0 1D          5
      124          0      1      1      0      0       UMATRIX           1D          6
      100          4      1      1      0      0       5        0 0 1 0 1D          7
      100          0      0      1      0      0       OCIRCLE           1D          8
      110          5      1      1      0      0       0        0 0 1 0 1D          9
      110          0      0      1      0      0       OLINE             2D         10
      102          6      1      1      0      0       0        0 0 0 0 1D         11
      102          0      1      1      0      0       OLINI             1D         12
212,1,6,12.180,3.50.1.1.5708,0..0,0,26.375.21.482,0..6HKUNTUR;                1P          1
110,-10.0,-20.0,0..5.4415,26.325,0.;                                         3P          2
124,-1.0,0.,0..24.415,0..1.0,0..20.0,0..,0..-1.0,0.;                         5P          3
100,0..0.,0..18.974.6.3246,0..20.0;                                          7P          4
110,24.415,40.0,0..40.0,40.0,0.;                                             9P          5
102,3,3,7,9;                                                                11P          6
 S      1G      4D      12P      0                                              T          1
```

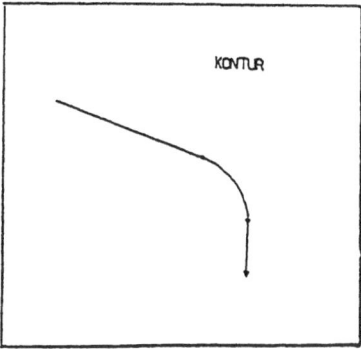

KONTUR

Figure 5. Example of an IGES file [42]

Because of missing IGES subset definitions system vendors only take those entities into consideration which have a counterpart in their system. Consequently entities which have not been implemented are disregarded by processors available on different CAD systems. In order to solve the mentioned processor problems, within the German Car Association (VDA) IGES processor implementation guidelines and subset definitions were specified. The corresponding VDA-IGES Subset (VDA-IS) supports the following geometry subset classes [41] :

- G1 basic geometry 2D,

- G2 basic geometry 2D/3D, and

- G3 basic geometry 2D/3D with quadric or ruled surfaces and free-form surfaces up to degree 3.

The corresponding annotation subset classes [41] are:

- B1 dimensioning, and

- B2 dimensioning and drawing-layout.

These well defined IGES subsets facilitates the development of IGES processors working on a minimum implementation level.

3.2.2 The Standard d'Échange et de Transfer (SET)

As an alternative to IGES the SET interface was initiated and developed by Aerospatiale in France, 1983. A so-called SET task force has been formed by Aerospatiale premises and a number of companies interested in product data exchange. The main tasks are the extension of the SET application field, development of a common interface software (e.g. XSET), validation of SET interfaces, and contributing to international standardisation efforts (ISO TC184/SC4). At present, it is used in particular by:

- the aeronautical industry (AIRBUS, HERMES),

- the automotive industry (Renault, PSA-group), and

- the French defence industries.

SET is a very pragmatic CAD-interface solution meeting the industrial-needs and -demands in the area of 2D/3D-product data-exchange and -archiving. It provides at least the same functionality as IGES, but with a different file format and a more efficient data set storage. The SET interface, which became the french standard AFNOR Z68300 in 1985 [32], concentrates on data-exchange and -archiving of:

- 2D/3D wireframe geometry (points, lines, vectors, circular arcs, polynomial curves, etc.);

- analytical- and freeform-surface geometry (planes, surfaces of revolution, polynomial surfaces, etc.);

- drawing and presentational data (texts, dimensioning, line fonts, colors, etc.).

In addition to the existing AFNOR document 'Z68300' the SET language specification has been extended to cover further application fields. These are the specifications for:

- the exchange and transfer of solid models (CSG models and exact/facetted boundary models), published in 1987 [31];

- the Finite Element calculation data transfer (FEM as well as loads and boundary conditions);

- the exchange of scientific data (e.g. units, matrices or tensor lists, etc.).

A SET file consists of a series of blocks or records of variable length. Each block begins with a block delimiter character and a block header. The number at the beginning of the block header defines the block type, as specified by the corresponding SET specification. The following items are the sequence number and a number of parameters followed by one or more so-called sub-blocks. The sub-blocks contain the actual data, as defined by the SET specification. The SET file is a sequence of ASCII- characters.

```
@9900  #9900,  'Z63-300.85.08' , 'l', 'CAO', '69','AEROSPATIALE','SU',
'DCT/KS', 'STIL'
 #9901, 1985, 8, l

@9901,l,'ENSI'#9930,0,1,2,4  #9930,2,1 #9920,:57,3,:51,0
# 9905, 3,1., 1, 0.001, 0, -10.,10., -10., 10., -10., 10.
@215,2,7,:9, 'ISO2'#310,1,-11.3,11.3
@1,3 #1,2.,3.,5.

@10,4,2,, 6.2 #10,:3,2, 2. ,0., 360., 5., 6.1 #252,:53,2,0,6,12


@9998,5

@9999,7
```

Figure 6. **Example of a SET file** [32]:   The file consists of seven blocks describing a simple 2D wireframe geometry.

3.2.3   The VDA-Surface Interface (VDA-FS)

VDAFS stands for Association of German Car Industry (VDA) Surface Interface (FS). It is the intention of the German car manufactures to provide with VDAFS a CAD interface for the transfer of free-form curve- and surface-geometry up to the degree three. VDAFS Version 1.0 and Version 2.0 meet the demands and requirements of surface modelling systems used by the car industry and their suppliers. Version 1.0 became the German standard DIN 66301 in 1986 [37].

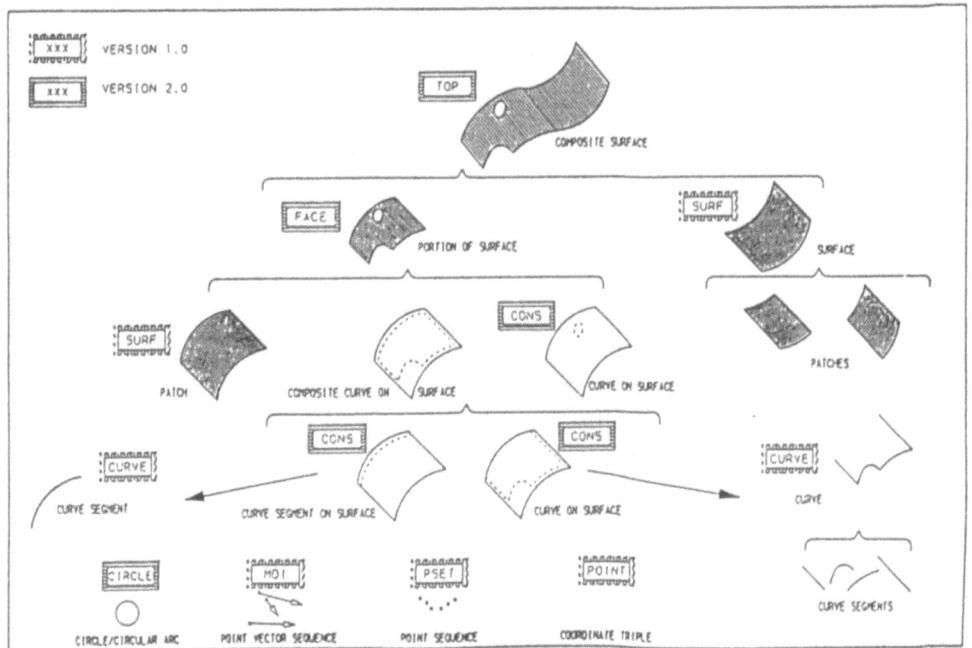

Figure 7.   VDAFS Version 1.0 and Version 2.0 entity types

The current VDAFS Version 2.0 [52] which comprises the VDAFS-V1.0 entities as a subset, allows the data transfer of the following entities (refer also to Figure 7):

- *GEOMETRY*: Point, Point Set, Circles, Point vector sequences (MDI), polynomial curves (CURVE), polynomial surface patches (SURF), curves on surfaces (CONS), and connected portions of SURF and CONS elements.

- *STRUCTURE and ORGANISATION*: element grouping mechanism (GROUP), transformation matrices (TMAT), and transformation lists (TLST).

As shown in Figure 7 on page 10 VDAFS V1.0 and V2.0 have a limited number of entities. This is one reason for the rapid progress in processor development. Today VDAFS is a very popular and well accepted interface standard for data exchange of freeform-curve and -surface geometry in the European (mainly in Germany) automotive industry and their suppliers.

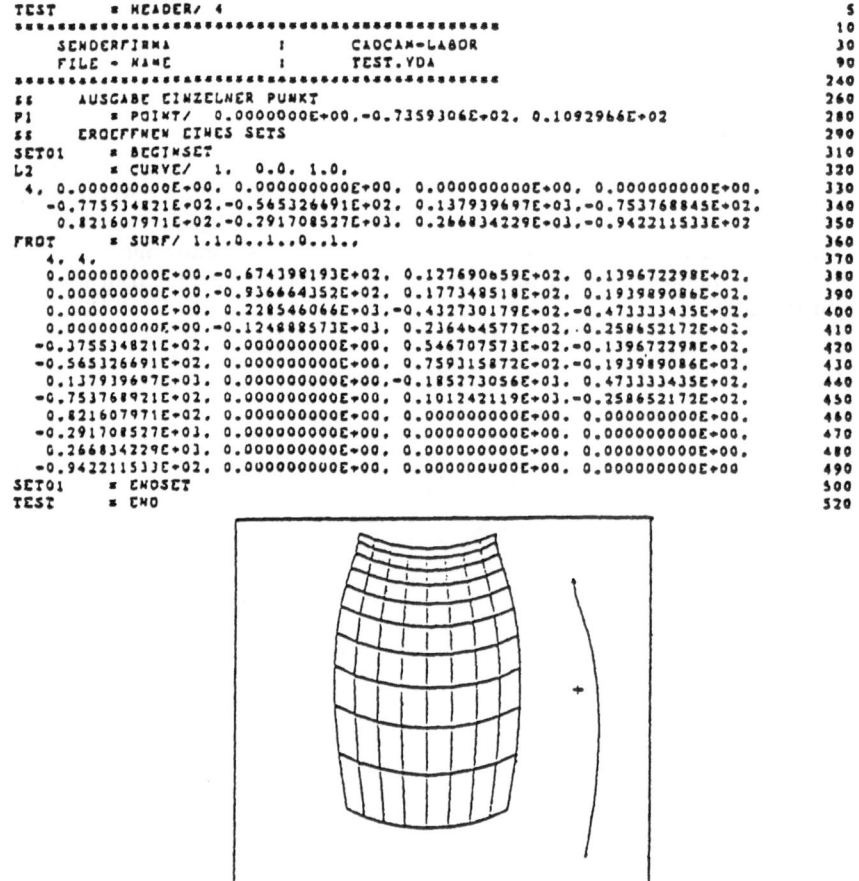

Figure 8.   Example of a VDAFS-Version 1.0 file.

Difficulties are encountered when the mathematical basis between the transmitting and receiving systems are not consistent. An example is the transmission of surface data between a multi-patch oriented system, mostly with a low polynomial degree (usually degree 3) and a single-patch oriented system with a high polynomial degree. In this case, dissection of the patches might prevent a meaningful subsequent processing. There are basically problems in data transfer among CAD systems of different polynomial degrees. In addition to the processor programs proper, special conversion programs are required which reduce or increase (depending on the requirements) the polynomial degree.

3.3 Towards STEP

3.3.1 Introduction

The Standard for the Exchange of Product Model Data (unofficial acronym: STEP) is a project begun in mid-1984 by the TC184/SC4 committee of the International Standards Organisation (ISO) to develop a mechanism for the exchange of complete product model data [46]. The ISO group ISO-TC184/SC4/WG1 (Figure 9 on page 12) breaks down into:

- the Technical Committee 184 responsible for "Industrial Automation Systems",

- Subcommittee 4 responsible for "External Representation of Product Definition Data", and

- Working Group 1 established to work out a STEP Draft Proposal.

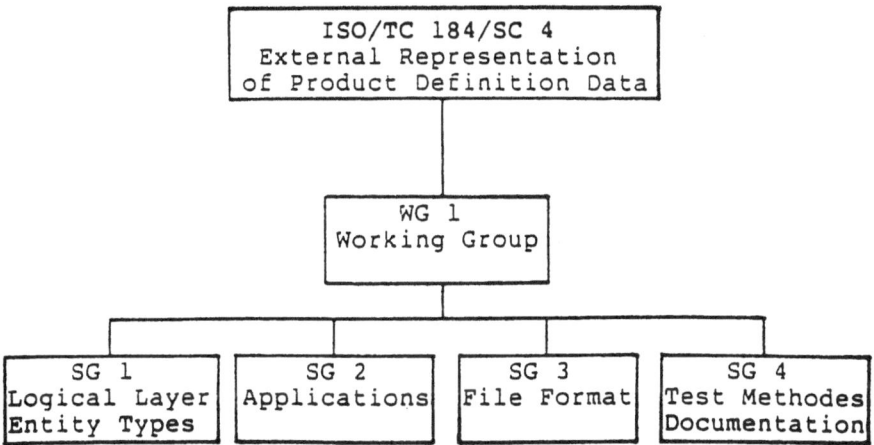

Figure 9. The ISO/TC184/SC4 and its WG1

As a result of the work performed by the TC184/Subcommittee 4 and its Working Group 1 the STEP specification was registered as an ISO-Draft Proposal (ISO-DP) at their meeting in Tokyo, November 1988. The future timetable of STEP development provides both for future stabilisation of the topical models and for the elaboration of important follow-on versions involving other partial models.

3.3.2 Deficiencies of present CAD interfaces

The CAD interfaces presented before may be assigned to the first generation of neutral file based CAD data exchange interfaces. Experience accumulated with these interfaces in respect of specification, pre- and post-processors, testing, and practical data transfer have provided the basis for a new generation of CAD interfaces which are tailored to the demands and oriented towards the future. The requirements to be imposed on future CAD interfaces can be derived from the following deficiencies of currently used CAD interfaces [41]:

- no orientation or incomplete orientation with regard to presently known CAD model philosophies;

- redundant and equivocal element description;

- limited number of supported elements and no mechanism or insufficient mechanism for element subsets;

- specified scope of elements (e.g. geometry elements) doesn't correspond to the scope of elements supported by the CAD systems;

- lack of or insufficient structure- and semantic-definitions and no clear element classification;

- no compact exchange format;

- limited capabilities to extend the specification in view of future developments;

- verbal description of the specification content;

- no recommended practices for uniform processor implementation;

- no recommendations for process control while running interface-processors (e.g. processor status output).

3.3.3 STEP Objectives

The STEP interface is being developed within the framework of the International Standard Organisation (ISO) with a view to exchanging:

- product definition data,

- product life cycle data, and

- application specific data.

The main target [45] of the STEP development consists in developing, harmonising and standardising a specification of product model data. The ultimate goal of STEP is the exchange and archiving of product defining data, i.e. all data pertaining to the life cycle of a product. The requirement is that data is transmitted without loss of information, i.e. not only data but also function oriented transmission. Data belonging to the life cycle of a product relate to design, calculation, fabrication, assembly, quality assurance and include information about maintenance and product operation [46]. This means that besides the geometry also tolerances, material properties, surface quality as well as function and structural component related properties have to be transmitted. This product describing information can provide the basis for work scheduling, fabrication, quality assurance, etc. Another requirement is that STEP is capable of extension without the inventories of information resulting from earlier implementations becoming invalid. The STEP data format is to be compact, efficient and compatible with other standards. Redundancies in structure and element definitions are to be avoided because they might result in erroneous interpretations and implementations. To ensure freedom of errors of STEP information inventories a certificate must be supplied together with pre- and post-processors which takes into account specified STEP test methods and test cases.

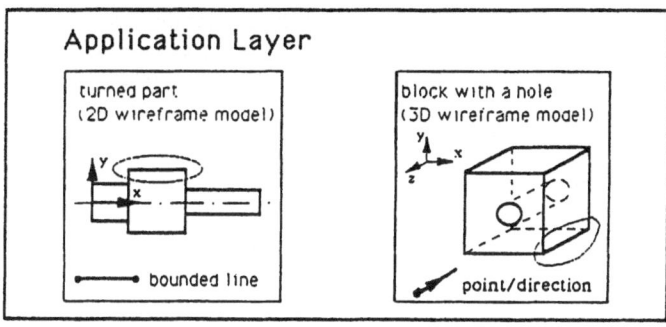

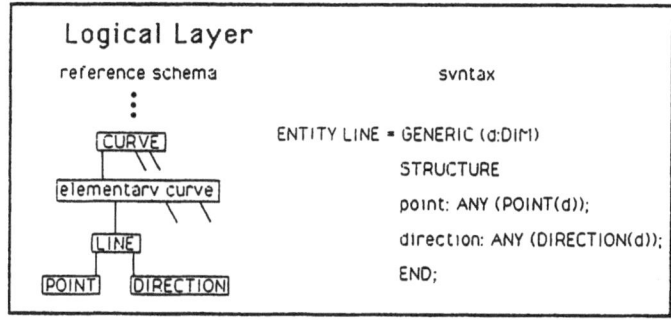

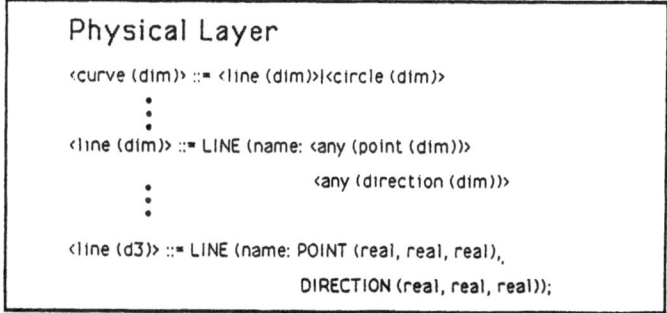

Figure 10. The three layer architecture: CAD*I terms are used on the logical and physical layer

3.3.4 The STEP methodology

STEP has been devised on the basis of knowledge derived from information technology, especially data base technology. The methodological approaches and principles are:

- **The Reference Model:** Reference model for consistent model specification and model extension. The reference model of the STEP specification provides for a topical information model concept. The topical information model is a model scheme for well defined sets of information which are interconnected by associations. The topical information model concept of STEP provides for resource and application model classes. Resource models (such as geometry and topology) of general are topical information models applicability to which several user independent models refer. Unlike the resource models the application models (AEC, FEM, etc.) have been defined under specified application oriented aspects.

- **The Three Layer Architecture**: The three layer architecture for stepwise information mapping has been derived from the ANSI/X3/SPARC three scheme architecture which allows to define and implement data bases. The corresponding interface design process has been subdivided into three well defined and separate parts based on the level of abstraction of the corresponding data. The three layers are:

  - the application or user layer,

  - the logical or conceptual layer, and

  - the physical layer.

  Thus, the application dependent information will be separated from the logical entity definition which will be separated from the physical definition as shown in Figure 10 on page 14. Each such partition will be called a layer.

- **The Formal Languages**: Use of formal languages on the logical and physical layer (e.g. 'EXPRESS' on the logical or conceptual layer) for the exact and processable description of the various layers of the standard. As one major part of the STEP Draft Proposal the Integrated Product Information Model (IPIM) is defined using the above mentioned EXPRESS language.

3.3.5 Contributions by CAD*I and PDES

The future international standard STEP is mainly influenced by the IGES-, PDES-, SET-, and CAD*I-group. Two of them, namely CAD*I and PDES will be dealt with here because they will satisfy best the future requirements made on CAD interfaces.

CAD*I: The ESPRIT 322 project "CAD*Interfaces" runs for five years from 1984 to 1989. Project work is being performed by twelve partners of five different countries of the European Community [48]. Project work concentrates on the following three main interfaces [36]:

- CAD data exchange interfaces for the transmission of wire frame models, surface models and solid models;

- internal interfaces, i.e. the CAD data base interface and the CAD user interface;

- interfaces of FEM analysis programs for the description and optimisation of models as well as for the experimental analysis.

The central topics of the CAD*I project, are the development of a language for the description of geometry models as well as the design and implementation of the involved pre- and postprocessors, on the basis of commercially available CAD, FEM, and Data Base systems as shown in Figure 11 on page 16. Of practical importance is the CAD*I [49] based data exchange between CAD- and CAR-systems (robot-simulation and -display) of application-dependant data like robot- and workcell-components [40].

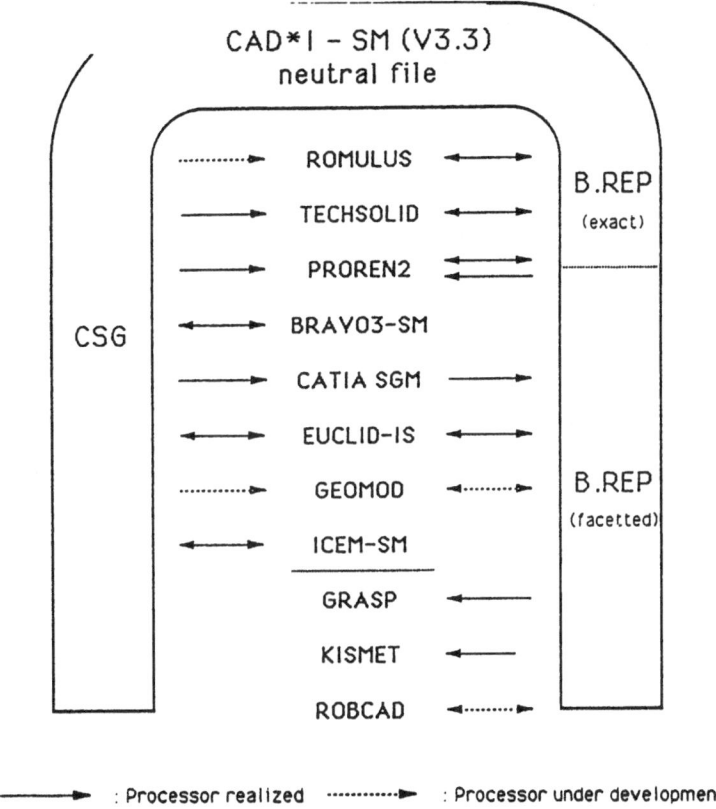

CAD*I – SM (V3.3)
neutral file

ROMULUS

TECHSOLID

PROREN2

BRAVO3-SM

CSG

CATIA SGM

EUCLID-IS

GEOMOD

ICEM-SM

GRASP

KISMET

ROBCAD

B.REP (exact)

B.REP (facetted)

——————▶ : Processor realized   ·············▶ : Processor under development

Figure 11. CAD*I Processor development for different solid modelling systems.:   The processor development is based on CAD*I-V3.3.

The CAD*I project does not strive to develop an interface standard of its own but tries to make important contributions to the development of the future international STEP standard (ISO/TC 184/SC4). The structure of the CAD*I neutral data file has been decribed in detail in [49].

Based on the CAD*I-results and -experiences a second ESPRIT project called CADEX (CAD Geometry Data Exchange) is underway. It is a three year project beginning in 1989 with the general goal to develop STEP pre- and postprocessors. The participants are industrial partners (interface users), and software firms (e.g. CAD suppliers) of five different European countries. The project objectives are:

- development of STEP based prototype processors using appropriate 3D data subsets,

- solve the expected problems in CAD geometry data exchange based on STEP,

- maintain and support the excellent position of European CAD- and CIM-activities,

- strengthen the European influence on international standardisation efforts.

PDES: On the basis of PDDI and IGES, development work has been carried out since 1984 on the CAD-interface project Product Definition Exchange Specification (PDES), promoted and financed by NBS. PDES will at least provide the functionality and capabilities of IGES, but with differences in data- and storage-formats [54]. PDES will be a non-upward compatible version form IGES. Based on the experiences made with IGES the PDES project aims to develop a high quality information exchange specification. The main objective of PDES is to be capable of completely representing product data, namely:

- product definition data,

- product life cycle data,

- application specific data, and

- administration and control data.

PDES Version 1.0 will provide entity capability for mechanical piece parts, mechanical assemblies, electrical printed wiring board products including both schematic and physical designs, AEC models, FEM models and drafting applications. Supporting technical areas will also be provided in PDES for manufacturing (Form Features, Tolerances), solids modeling, curve and surface modeling and presentation data [38]. One central activity of the PDES project has been the development of a suited solid model data transfer concept for CSG, Sweeps and exact/facetted Boundary Representation.

It can be assumed that PDES and STEP will be identical.

To speed up the development of PDES (STEP) the establishment of a company was intiated by the US Department of Defence (DoD) and formed by industrial interest groups [44]. The work is being carried out by PDES Inc, which is backed by at least ten of the world's major defense contractors and Cxx system suppliers. There are three classes of membership, each contributing a certain amount of money and one or two full-time technical people. PDES Inc aims:

- to speed up the product data exchange development (one major requirement by the defence industry),

- to contibute to international standardisation activities,

- to influence the content of the future data exchange standard PDES/STEP,

- to produce a practical implementation (pre- and post-processors) of the PDES/STEP standard as quickly as possible,

3.3.6 The STEP Draft Proposal

The TC184/SC4 approved the registration of STEP as an ISO Draft Proposal (DP) at the last ISO meeting in Tokyo, December 1988. The Draft Proposal will be circulated for review and balloting. It comprises the following documents:

- Introduction, Scope, and Definitions;

- The Integrated Product Information Model (IPIM);

- Definition of the formal language EXPRESS;

- The Physical File Structure;

- Mapping from the logical layer (EXPRESS) to the Physical File;

- Test Methods.

In total, the documentation comprises more than two thousand pages of technical material. One document, the Integrated Product Information Model (IPIM) - originally designated as the Initial Testing Draft - forms one major component in STEP [46]. The content of the IPIM represents best the current STEP scope. The IPIM covers both, a number of applications and topical information models, it is formally specified by the formal language EXPRESS. Briefly, the IPIM defines those aspects of product data which will be possible to transfer. The IPIM covers roughly 700 entities. Three major sections can be recognized [46]:

- **resources:**

  - geometry,

  - topology,

  - shape (design shape, features, etc.),

  - tolerances,

  - material, and

  - presentation.

- **life cycle**

- **applications:**

  - product manifestation (drafting),

  - mechanical product (e.g. configuration management),

  - architecture, engineering and construction,

  - electrical (e.g. electrical functional),

  - analysis (FEM), and

  - data transfer.

An editing committee has been formed to complete the DP (with ballot responses and technical upgrading) for submission as a so-called Draft International Proposal.

New topical models have been proposed, for example in the areas of kinematics and robotics as well as the development of models for assembly and disassembly operations.

3.3.7 Issues still under consideration

The available STEP-Draft Proposal doesn't mean that all requirements made on future CAD interfaces are taken into consideration by the corresponding TC184/SC4 organisation. There are still some open issues regarding the future standard STEP. Some of them are listed below:

- more intensive and active participation of European industry in STEP development;

- forming groups with common interests and joining efforts of STEP users and CAx system suppliers;

- determination and specification of additional applications;

- specification of suitable model subsets to be transferred, i.e. in order to support different levels of CAD system capabilities;

- working out guidelines for implementation of processors;

- early development of STEP processors (prototype processors) and tools (e.g. test aux-iliaries) in order to get an early feedback from processor development into the STEP specification;

- definition and specification of software-tools and -modules in support of processor development;

- arrangements regarding interface software and utilities to be developed jointly (e.g. Parser, Syntax checker, library of routines for writing and reading functions, etc.);

- development of guidelines and rules for conformance testing services for STEP based data exchange interfaces;

- Use of processor only with certificates, i.e. STEP will not replace existing CAD data transfer systems until validated processors of comparable or better functionality and performance become available;

- development of migration tools to convert existing neutral files (based on IGES) into STEP based format.

3.4 Conclusion

With the IGES 1.0 interface format the first neutral CAD data format was published at the end of the 1970s. While the first CAD interface developments (e.g. IGES) basically provide the possibility of exchanging drawing data, some new developed interface concepts strive to enable the exchange of complete product models. Above all, this is very important with respect to the presently much discussed computer integrated manufacturing (CIM). The basic components of an overall CIM architecture are neutral data interfaces which enable the exchange of information between the individual CIM components (CAD, PPS, CAQ, etc.). The currently available draft proposal (DP) of STEP is one major step towards inte-grated product model data transfer. STEP will not become an international standard before 1990/1991 [46]. The meeting of SC4 in Tokyo at the end of 1988 made any more accurate prediction difficult and even 1991 may be an optimistic figure. However the present STEP-IPIM offers a first opportunity for implementation and demonstration purposes and the practical usage of the STEP ideas [46]. Further national and international (e.g. PDES and CAD*I) activities and contributions are necessary to extend the already existing capabilities and functionality of STEP.

4. Abbreviations

AEC	Architecture, Engineering and Construction
AFNOR	Association Francaise de Normalisation (France)
ANSI	American National Standards Institute
B-Rep	Boundary - Representation
BSI	British Standards Institute
CAD	Computer Aided Design
CADEX	Computer Aided Design - Geometry Data Exchange
CAD*I	Computer Aided Design*Interfaces
CAM	Computer Aided Manufacturing
CAR	Computer Aided Robotics
CAx	Computer Aided Techniques (e.g. CAD, CAM, CAQ ,etc.)
CGI	Computer Graphics Interface
CGM	Computer Graphics Metafile
CIM	Computer Integrated Manufacturing
CSG	Constructive Solid Geometry
CSS	Centralized Structure Store
DIN	German Institute for Standardization
DoD	US Department of Defense
DTP	Desk Top Publishing
ESP	Experimental Solids Proposal
ESPRIT	European Strategic Program of Research and Development in Information Technology
FEM	Finite Element Methods
GKS	Graphical Kernel System
GKS-3D	3D-Extension of GKS
IPIM	Integrated Product Information Model (STEP)
IGES	Initial Graphics Exchange Specification
ISO	International Standardisation Organisation
ISO/TC184	ISO/Industrial Automation Systems
KfK	Kernforschungszentrum Karlsruhe, West Germany

KISMET	Kinematic Simulation, Monotoring, Off-Line Programming Environment for Tele Robotics
MAP	Manufacturing Automation Protocol
NBS	National Bureau of Standards (USA), now NIST
NC	Numerical Control
NDC	Normalized Device Coordinates
NF	Neutral File
NIST	National Institute for Standards and Technology, formerly NBS
PDDI	Product Definition Data Interface
PDES	Product Definition Exchange Specification
PHIGS	Programmer's Hierarchical Interactive Graphics System
SET	System d'Exchange et de Transfer
SM	Solid Modeller
STEP	Standard for Exchange of Product Model Data (ISO)
TOP	Technical Office Protocol
VDA	Verband der deutschen Automobilindustrie
VDA-IS	Verband der deutschen Automobilindustrie - IGES Subset
VDA-FS	Verband der deutschen Automobilindustrie - Flächenschnittstelle
XBF	Experimental Boundary File

5. References

[1]   Adobe Systems Inc: "PostScript Language Reference Manual", Addison-Wesley, 1986

[2]   Adobe Systems Inc: "PostScript Language Tutorial and Cookbook", Addison-Wesley, 1986

[3]   Arnold,D.B.; Bono,P.R.: "CGM and CGI", Springer-Verlag, 1988

[4]   Bono,P.R.; Herman,I.: "GKS Theory and Practice", Springer-Verlag, 1987

[5]   Brodlie,K.W.; Henderson,L.R.; Mumford,A.M.: "The CGM - A Metafile for GKS?", Computer Graphics Forum, Vol 6, No 2, 1987

[6]   Computer Aided Design: Special Issue on Computer Graphics Standards, Vol 19, No 8, October 1987

[7]   Clifford,W.H., McConnell,J.I., Saltz,J.S.: "The Development of PEX, a 3D Graphics Extension to X11", Eurographics Conference Proceedings 1988, Springer-Verlag 1988

[8]   Enderle,G.; Kansy,K.; Pfaff,G.: "Computer Graphics Programming - GKS - The Graphics Standard", Springer-Verlag, 1987

[9]   Hopgood,F.R.A.; Duce,D.; Gallop,J.; Sutcliffe,D.: "Introduction to the Graphical Kernel System", Academic Press, 1986

[10]   IEEE CG + A: Special Issue on Computer Graphics Standards, Vol 6, No 8, August 1986

[11]   ISO IS 7498: Information processing systems - Open Systems Interconnection - Basic Reference Model

[12]   ISO IS 7942: Information processing systems - Computer graphics - Graphical Kernel System (GKS) functional description

[13]   ISO IS 8613: Information processing systems - Text and office systems - Office Document Architecture (ODA) and Interchange Format - Part 8: Geometric Graphics Content Architectures (GGCA)

[14]   ISO IS 8632: Information processing systems - Computer graphics - Metafile for the storage and transfer of picture description information (CGM)

[15]   ISO IS 8805: Information processing systems - Computer graphics - Graphical Kernel System for three dimensions (GKS-3D) functional

[16]   ISO IS 9592: Information processing systems - Computer graphics - Programmer's Hierarchical Interactive Graphics Systems (PHIGS)

[17]   ISO DP 9636: Information processing systems - Computer graphics - Interfacing techniques for dialogues with graphical devices (CGI) - functional specification

[18]   MAP: "Manufacturing Automation Protocol (MAP) Specification", Version 3.0, Society of Manufacturing Engineers, 1988

[19]   Mumford,A.M.: "Application Profiles for Computer Graphics Standards - A Touch of Reality?", Eurographics Conference Proceedings, Springer-Verlag, 1988

[20]   Mumford,A.M.: "The CGM Today and Tomorrow", Computer Graphics Forum (forthcoming), 1989

[21] Mumford,A.M.; Skall,M.W. (Eds): "The CGM in the Real World", Springer-Verlag, 1988

[22] Mumford,A.M.; Wyrwas,K.M.: "Computer Graphics Standards - Myth and Reality", Eurographics-UK Tutorial, 1988

[23] PEX: "PEX Protocol Specification", Version 3.0, MIT, 1987

[24] PHIGS+: "PHIGS+ Functional Description", Revision 3.0, Report by the ad-hoc PHIGS+ committee, 1988

[25] Scheifler,R.; Gettys,J.: "The X Window System", John Wiley, 1989

[26] Singleton,K.M.: "An Implementation of the GKS-3D/PHIGS Viewing Pipeline", Eurographics Conference Proceedings, Springer-Verlag, 1986

[27] TOP: "Technical Office Protocol (TOP) Specification", Version 2.0, Boeing Computer Services, 1988, Seattle, WA, USA

[28] Verbeck,C.; Michener,J.; van Dam,A.; Laidlaw,D.: "Extending PHIGS for Lighting and Shading - PHIGS+", Siggraph '87 Conference Proceedings

[29] X-Window: "X-Window System Protocol", Version 11, Project Athena, MIT, 1987

[30] Abeln, O.: "Referenzmodelle für CAD-Systeme", Informatik-Spektrum (1989) 12: 43-46

[31] AEROSPATIALE: "SET-SOLIDE", Groupe Operationnel S.E.T., Aerospatiale, Suresnes-France, April 1987

[32] AFNOR: "Automatisation industrielle, Représentation externe des données de définition de produits. Specification du standard d'échange et de transfert (SET), version 85-08" Z68-300, AFNOR 85181, 1985.

[33] Bey, I; Leuridan, J; (Ed.): "ESPRIT Project 322: CAD*I CAD Interfaces Status Report 4", PFT report 1392, Kernforschungszentrum Karlsruhe GmbH, 430 pp., March 1988.

[34] BNS: "Digital Representation for Communication of Product Definition Data", ANSI standard Y 14.26 M, September 1981.

[35] Braendli, N: "The application of compiler-generators for the generation of post-/preprocessors in the ESPRIT-project CAD*I", VDI-Berichte No. 610.5, 1986

[36] Braendli, N.; Mittelstaedt, M.: "Exchange of solid models: current state and future trends", computer-aided-design, volume 21, number 2, march 1989

[37] DIN: "VDA - Flächenschnittstelle (VDAFS) Version 1.0, DIN 66301" Beuth Verlag, 1986.

[38] IGES/PDES: "Welcome to IGES and PDES", Newcomer Material, July 1988

[39] ISO: "External Representation of Product Definition Data", document number 4, version Tokyo, ISO TC184/SC4/WG1, October 1988

[40] Mittelstaedt, M.: "The CATIA-KISMET link at JET - Concept, Realization, and Operation", JET, Culham/GB, JET-Report, December 1988

[41] Mittelstaedt, M.; Trippner, D.: "CAD Data Exchange", In: de Ruiter,M. (ed), Advances in Computer Graphics III, Springer-Verlag, pp. 241-292, 1988

[42] NBS: "IGES 1.0", NBS, US. Department of Commerce, Washington DC 20234, January 1980

[43] NBS: "IGES 4.0", NBS, US. Department of Commerce, Washington DC 20234, June 1988

[44] N.N.: "Defense Rules", CADCAM International, October 1988

[45] N.N.: "Entwicklungsstand des internationalen Standards STEP", Tutorial Notes, CADCAM-Labor, April 1989

[46] Owen,J.; Schlechtendahl,E.; Shaw,N.; Smith,B.: "SEMINAR: Exchange of Product Model Data - Present and Future-1", Seminar Notes, Tokyo, 6th December 1988

[47] Requicha, A.A.G; Voelker, H.B: "Solid Modeling: A Historical Summary and Contemporary Assessment", IEEE, CG&A, Vol. 2, No. 2, pp. 9-24, March 1982.

[48] Schlechtendahl, E.G.; Gengenbach, U. : "CAD data transfer: The goals and achievements of Project 322, CAD Interfaces (CAD*I)", ESPRIT '87, pp. 1547-1569, North Holland, 1987.

[49] Schlechtendahl, E.G. (ed.): "Specification of a CAD*I Neutral File for CAD Geometry, Wireframes, Surfaces, Solids", Version 3.2, Second, Revised and Enlarged Edition, ESPRIT Research Reports, Vol.1, CAD*I, Springer Verlag, Heidelberg, 1987.

[50] Schuster, R.: Progress in the Development of CAD/CAM-Interfaces for Transfer of Product Definition Data", In: Encarnacao,J. et. al. (ed.), Product Data Interfaces in CAD/CAM Applications, Springer-Verlag, 1986

[51] Van Maanen, J; Thomas, D. (ed.): "Specification for exchange of Product Analysis Data", PFT report 131, Kernforschungszentrum Karlsruhe GmbH, March 1987.

[52] VDA/VDMA: "VDA-Flächenschnittstelle (VDAFS) Version2.0", N96.4/21-87

[53] Wilson, P.R.; et.al.: "Interfaces for Data Transfer Between Solid Modeling Systems", IEEE, CG&A, pp. 41-51, Jan. 1985.

[54] Wilson P. R.: "A Short History of CAD Data Transfer Standards", IEEE, Computer Graphics and Applications,   Vol. 7, Nr. 6, pp. 64-67, June 1987.

Addresses of Authors

Edwin H. Blake
Centre for Mathematics and Computer Science (CWI)
Kruislaan 413, 1098 SJ Amsterdam, Netherlands

Mikael Jern
V.P. Technology, UNIRAS A/S
376, Gladsaxevej, 2860 Soborg, Denmark

Martti Mäntylä
Laboratory of Information Processing Science
Helsinki University of Technology
Otakaari 1 A, 02150 Espoo 15, Finland

Michael Mittelstaedt
Kernforschungszentrum Karlsruhe (KfK)
P.O.Box 3640, 7500 Karlsruhe 1, FR Germany

Anne M. Mumford
Computer Centre, University of Technology
Loughborough, Leicestershire, LE11 3TU, Great Britain

Gerald M. Murch
Tektronix Laboratories
Tektronix Industrial Park, P.O.Box 500, Beaverton, Or 97077, USA

Mark Overmars
Department of Computer Science
University of Utrecht
Padualaan 14, P.O.Box 80.089, 3508 TB Utrecht, Netherlands

Jürgen Schönhut
Fraunhofer Arbeitsgruppe Graphische Datenverarbeitung
Wilhelminenstraße 7, 6100 Darmstadt, FR Germany

Joann Taylor
Tektronix Laboratories
Tektronix Industrial Park, P.O.Box 500, Beaverton, Or 97077, USA

Peter Wisskirchen
German National Research Center for Computer Science
Schloss Birlinghoven, 5205 St. Augustin 1, FR Germany